But I Digress...

Collected Articles, Speeches, and Scripts

James Tracy Tresner II, 33°, Grand Cross

But I Digress . . .

Collected Articles, Speeches, and Scripts

© A∴D∴ 2012 by James Tracy Tresner II A∴L∴ 6012

All Rights Reserved. No part of this book may be reproduced or transmitted in any form or by any means, electronic or mechanical, including photocopying, recording, or by any information storage and retrieval system, without permission in writing from the author.

First Edition in Paperback Published in 2012

ISBN-13: 978-0615657004
ISBN-10: 0615657001

Published by Starr Publishing, LLC
Colorado Springs, CO 80917

Dedication

This book is dedicated to my family, my extended family, and my greater family, including:
Bill, Bob, Bob,
Cameron, Chuck, Chuck, Clay, Cliff, Clint,
Damon, Dana, Dane, Dennis, Dennis, Derek, Dick,
Glen, Greg, Greg, Gregg,
Jack, James, Jim, Jimmy, John, John, Jon, Josh
Kevin, Kyle,
Larry,
Mark, Matt, Max, Michael, Mike (Will), Mike,
Pook,
Randy, Richard, Rick, Robert, Ryan,
Sam, Sam, Steve
Tim, Tim, Tom,
and Z

and especially to the two Brothers and Editors who helped me find my "voice" as a writer, whether I wanted to or not.
Dr. John Boettcher 33°, Grand Cross
Former Editor of the Scottish Rite Journal
and
Richard Fletcher, 33°, P∴G∴M∴ of Vermont
Past Executive Director of the Masonic Service Association
and Editor of the Short Talk Bulletin

Table of Contents

Foreword. 1

Introduction. 4

Articles
    The Fabulous Beast. 7
    Brotherhood: Do We Really Mean It?. 9
    Compasses Above: The Spiritual Aspect of Masonry. 13
    Mirror, Mirror on the Wall. 18
    Desk Lamps and Candles.. 24
    Believers and Belongers. 29
    The Morning After.. 33
    The Starry Canopy. 38
    A Large Compassion. 47
    The Temple Shook With Hate. 51
    When is a Symbol an Emblem?. 56
    On Third Thought. 59
    A Short Ramble Through Freemasonry And
        Communication Theory or Stop Me Before I
        Introduce Again. 62
    Multiplex Masonry. 72
    Great Aunt Effie and Moses. 77
    The Old Dog Barks Backward.. 80
    Family. 83
    A Little Sand in The Gears. 87
    "Fan My Brow And Call Me Moses!". 91
    Prepared. 94
    Sex as Symbol. 97
    Pigeons in the Rocket. 102
    Our Really Rather Radical Brother, Albert Pike. . . . 108

Ritual: Who Needs It?. 111
The Tragedy of the Third Degree.. 116
Using Masonry. 121
Faded Plastic Flowers.. 127
I Had It Good. 130
Abe Lincoln's Axe. 135
Before the Flood.. 138
The Imposition of Ashes. 141
Masonic Symbols Don't Mean. 145

Speeches
The Symbolism of the Fellow Craft Degree.. 191
Privacy, Peace, & Harmony. 210
Obstacles and Outside Influences: Willie Wonka
    and the Lodge. 215
Pedal Vulneration.. 225
A Work in Progress. 233
The 23 Lives of Albert Pike. 240
"The Greatest Work of Alchemy" Albert Pike
    and the Question of Race. 245
Fundamentalism is not Faith. 265
The Annoying Prospect of Living. 270
Something Fishy in the Lodge. 289
Rebirth. 293

Scripts
Myth: The Footpath Within. 299
    Truth ≠ Fact. 299
    Tender Feet and Green Thumbs. 303
    Goldilocks.. 307
    The Boy Who Was Left Behind. 316
    Apollo & Dionysus. 319
    Myth and Masonry. 322
    The Mythic Quest of the Scottish Rite. 326

The Most Radical Era: 19th Century Values. 327
    Overview.. 329

Progress: Every Day in Every Way. 330
Duty: "Stern Daughter of the Voice of God". . . . 335
Honor: "Without it, all is dross". 339
Sentiment: Emotion+Intellect. 340
Idealism: "We live, Mr. Worthing, in an
    Age of Ideals". 344
Law and the Individual:
    "The law, sir, is an ass.". 346
Spirituality: "He hath within him a
    spiritual nature". 349
Rationality: "But sir, is it reasonable?". 351
Social Consciousness: "Let each find some
    good work to do". 353
Reform: "To set free the Captives of power". . . 355
Nature: "My heart leaps up". 358
Eloquence: "Word strung to word like a
    strand of richest pearls. 361
Breeding: "With men or horses, sir,
    bloodline will tell". 364
Cultural Chauvinism:
    "The White Man's Burden". 366
Summary: Mr. Ingersoll's Oration. 369

The Guild Lodge of St. Canice: A Reconstruction
of a Meeting Of a Scots Operative Lodge
in the early 1600's. 373

Birdseed.. 415

Index. 426

About the Author

Foreword
W∴ G. Cliff Porter, 32° K∴C∴C∴H∴

I am less traveled than some, and my life experiences are not more than any other's; but in my years of bouncing here and there I have noticed a thing or two that seem to ring true throughout the world. I am not claiming qualification to be a commentator on humanity, but it has become my task to comment to some degree because I was honored with the humbling experience of being asked to write a forward for this book. Before *But I Digress,* I was discussing a particular thing, a thing observed, a trend maybe.

It appears to me that there are many people with intellect. (Mind you, I don't always believe this to be true: the morning commute, anytime of day on the Interstate, or my decade and a half working in law enforcement have tested this principle on more than one occasion.) Nevertheless, with many a person, man, woman, and child, I've been struck by their intellect, be it honed or raw. They simply had a knack to grasp the ungraspable. My friend Brad, as an example, had a miniature wind tunnel in his basement that he used to study the dissipation of vortices and, when not studying the dissipation of vortices, he built or drafted different kinds of Sterling engines as a means of fun and passing the time. Brad is, by any stretch of imagine and every current academic standard, extremely bright.

But few, I have perceived, possess both intellect and the necessary skill to communicate, and those who do seem to lack the ability to do so to a wide and diverse audience. They may be able to get their message across, but only to a small dynamic or subgroup.

Brother Jim Tresner is one of those rare men that possess both intellect and wisdom, and can communicate with a wide variety of people in a way that each person can take from his lessons what they need.

Freemasonry is the perfect art for such a Master. It could be argued that Brother Jim is a product of Masonry, but I don't believe this to be the case. I believe that Masonry lived in his heart and found purchase in his soul because he was already a special kind of man.

I have witnessed Brother Jim in a crowd of men made of up of Brothers as diverse and divergent as the topics being discussed—each man sharing the title of Freemason, but having within their own personal approach to Masonry with widely varying perspectives of the same Craft. I've seen their eyes wide, hearts open, (and some with mouths slightly agape) as Jim works his magic and spins his tapestry of understanding and unity. The esoteric men in the crowd find in his words deeply meaningful proverbs of ancient insight expertly woven in an allegory of fatherly type wisdom. The simply loving men who consider themselves more "fraternal" or "social" Masons find solace in the same words as they take them as stories of literal decency and applied Masonry in the life of any man trying to do good to "ever walk and act" as a Mason.

In a world where people seldom listen to a story long enough to hear the end—in a world where people are sitting slightly forward, even a little out of their seats, waiting for their turn to talk, having missed most of the speaker before them in their anxiousness to share their wisdom, not really caring if anyone hears it so long as they talked—in world where wealth and recognition are more important than how it was won, there is Brother Jim, sitting on a porch, a bench, around a fountain, wherever; sharing a bit of wisdom, sharing from his heart, and doing it in such a way that there is a quiet silence of admiration, respect, and smiles abound.

I will shift gears only a moment, and then close. Brother Jim is in the habit of giving lavish praise to those he loves even when they are not deserving of such accolades. At the same time he quickly turns aside and compliment which it coming toward him. This just might be the only chance I have in life to pay a man and Brother whom I love the highest praise words can attribute, and which, in the end, will still be woefully inadequate, without Brother Jim silencing me and firing of volley of high praise back so as to cause me to turn bright red and silent. So here it goes.

Brother Jim Tresner is one of the best men I know. He has touched many lives, mine included, with his wisdom and the subtle and loving way in which he delivers it. This is every Brother's chance to share in those wonderful moments his friends all cherish, and have a little "porch time" with a man whose intellect and knowledge of Masonry is extraordinary, and who can share it in a way we can all hear, see, and feel it.

Introduction

It was a pleasure when Cliff Porter, one of the most important rising stars of contemporary Masonic writing agreed to pen the foreword. Now all I had to do was try to organize all this scattered material into some cohesive form.

I failed.

The material represents writing over a considerable period of time, with more than one article or speech on some topics. When I managed to pull all those together which dealt with Masonic ethical values (for example), I quickly discovered the wisdom behind the show business/political dictum "Never follow a banjo act with another banjo act." In addition, many of the articles, speeches and scripts covered more than one topic. I do tend to digress. So, in the end, I decided to divide the material by type—article, speech, or script—and let an index organize the ideas.

I truly hope you find some fun in this book. Masonry has been many things for me: a source of inspiration, a shared experience with my family members, the fertile ground of many friendships, a continuing challenge to my mind, a direct path to the beauty of the world—but most of all it has been fun.

A few words about consistency:

"Do I contradict myself? Very well, then, I contradict myself." Walt Whitman

"A foolish consistency is the hobgoblin of little minds, adored by little statesmen and philosophers and divines. With consistency a great soul has simply nothing to do."
Ralph Waldo Emerson

Of course, it can also be the result of wavering rather than being a great soul. In some of what follows, I may seem to take one position at one time and a differing one at another. That's probably exactly the case. These were written over a span of time, and thoughts change. And, frankly, there are some topics on which I simply remain conflicted. Class conferrals of Blue Lodge Degrees is a case in point. Unlike many states, in Oklahoma the tradition is that only one candidate can receive a Degree at a time. In spite of that, we have had classes in which several hundred received the Degrees at once. Good thing? Bad thing? I don't know. I have helped with those conferrals, and would do so again, and yet I think the traditional joining process is very important. I know many Brethren, very active in their Lodges, who have told me they would never have joined the Fraternity without the classes. And yet, those same Brethren have told me that they wish they had taken the Degrees in the traditional manner, even though they admit they would never have done so. History will have to judge that one.

A word about the "scripts" section. In order to provide more Masonic education. for members, the Guthrie Scottish Rite Valley, under the leadership of the General Secretary, Robert G. Davis, 33° Grand Cross, developed the College of the Consistory. It is a directed self-study program which now has hundreds of participants both across the United States and in foreign climes. The first two scripts are audio CD scripts prepared for those students. The last script—The Guild Lodge of St. Canice—is a play set in the transition from operative to speculative Masonry. I did not reprint costume notes, prop construction notes, etc. here to save space and because they would be of interest only if one planned on staging the play.

Is there any underlying theme to all this material? I think so. I think that it all, in one way or another, says that Freemasonry is one of the most amazing institution the world has ever seen. It is a group of men, joined together not for power, or protection, nor to exploit something or someone, nor for self-aggrandizement, nor to force ideas or opinions or dogmas on others, but rather for support in becoming more as human beings. It is a quest to become more ethical, more honorable, more sensitive, more aware, more compassionate, more forgiving, less ego-driven, less intolerant, less bigoted, and less given to anger. That is astonishing. What is even more astonishing is that it works—not perfectly—but by and large, it works.

Jim Tresner

Articles

The Fabulous Beast

In a very kind letter I received a few days ago, a Brother referred to me as an "expert in Masonry." In a significantly less kind conversation a few weeks ago, I am told that an Oklahoma Brother referred to me as that @!*+~\ know-it-all in Guthrie.

Both Brethren are in error. It is said that the dragon is a fabulous beast (meaning a beast which exists in fable, but not in reality). The expert in Masonry is a fabulous beast as well.

There are Brothers who are experts in Masonic ritual—Robert G. Davis, 33° and Art deHoyos, 33° spring immediately to mind. There are experts in Masonic Jurisprudence; Roscoe Pound is an outstanding example. There are experts in Masonic history, symbolism, origin theories, the deeper esoterica, etc. But an expert in Masonry?

According to one published estimate, between 75,000 and 100,000 different books have been written about Freemasonry and its various branches. My own Masonic library has about 900 books, and I have read perhaps 100 more. That's a grand total of one percent of the information available. A Masonic expert? you bet, both me and the dragon.

Actually, dragons have been my personal totem animals for as long as I can remember. The painter Will

Hurd and I have been best friends for decades, and for most of that time, I have been trying to get him to paint my portrait, garbed as Merlin, riding a stormy sky aback a great golden dragon, lightning flashing from my upraised hand as I fight the forces of darkness, the powers of ancient wisdom surrounding me with a numinous glow.

He tells me a psychiatrist has advised him to stick to landscapes.

But the point of all this is that Masonry is a vast ocean, not only wide but deep. No one has a hope of knowing it all, or even a significant portion of it. There is no such thing as an expert in Masonry. Well, to be accurate, there is one.

It is you.

It is part of the genius of the Craft that no person speaks officially for Masonry. The fundamental reason is that no one can. Masonry is an intensely personal experience--a largely internal experience. As the late Masonic scholar Jerry Marsengill was wont to remark, a man could read every Masonic ritual there is, and discover all the "secret work," but he still would not be a Mason; because being a Mason is something that happens in your heart and mind when you take the Degrees.

All the history, all the symbolism, all the relationship to human psychology and the history of human thought which is a part of Masonry is fascinating, and provides many hours of joy for many Masons, but, the bottom line is this: Masonry is what happens in a man when he takes the Degrees and practices their lessons. That is individual, unique, and personal to each man. So no Mason should ever be intimidated, or feel that he is somehow less a Mason than a Brother who has had the opportunity to read more or study further. No one ever needs to feel that he is a second-class Mason.

Whatever wisdom dragons are said to possess, you are the only expert on what Masonry means to you; and you are real, not fabulous.

"The Fabulous Beast" appeared in *The Scottish Rite Journal* for September, 2002

Brotherhood: Do We Really Mean It?

Sometimes the strangest things trigger memories. I was having my hair cut. I have to go to a beauty shop which also cuts men's hair, because it's about the only place in town where you can make an appointment and my schedule usually makes that necessary. Many men get their hair cut there, so that part doesn't feel strange, but there is always a smell of ammonia and the arcane potions used in permanent waves. The sound of hair dryers lulled in the background, and I probably dozed a bit. But when I opened my eyes and looked up into the mirror, for just a second, I saw not the young lady who was cutting my hair, but Brother Claude Fox. And I blessed his memory, and wished I could go back.

Fox's Barber Shop in Enid was a real barber shop, something few of our younger Brethren have ever experienced. You took half a flight of stairs down from the sidewalk, and opened the door, where a little, spring-mounted bell rang, and it was another world. The wooden floor had long since lost its varnish, but it was polished to a patina by the leather soles of shoes and the constant sweeping of hair.

The barber's chairs were things of wonder, made of white porcelain and steel and red leather, and you knew you were a man on the day when Claude no longer had to put a board across the arms of the chair for you to sit on. There were the smells, strange, mysterious smells from tobacco and leather and bay rum and rose water and the dozens of bottles, all made of clear glass with long necks and black stoppers with little holes through which the barber could shake the mysterious liquids into his palm before rubbing them into your hair. They contained liquids which glittered like jewels, like rubies or emeralds or amethysts or topaz. And there was the smell of lather, and the particular smell of a leather razor strop. The lather was whipped up in a mug with a brush. Claude bought a small black lather machine one day (you had to keep up with the times) but all his customers were glad when he went back to the mug and brush. In those days, even when you were a kid, the barber shaved the space between the top of your ears and the hairline.

And kids came in with their fathers, but you were expected to be a man while you were in the barber shop. For this was a man's country. Women simply didn't enter. It would have surprised me less to see an elephant walking down Independence Street than to see a woman walk into Fox's Barber Shop.

And I looked up, and saw myself in a mirror in the beauty shop, sixty years later, and my heart cried out for Brother Claude.

Because, and this is the point, there was brotherhood in that barber shop. It was as much a part of the background as the smells and the squeaking of the black cast iron ceiling fan, or the gurgle of the water fountain or the soft clatter of the black tin wire-handled dustpan into which the barbers swept the clippings after each haircut. Claude Fox had two other barbers working in the shop with him, and all of them were Masons. And so were many of the customers. Sometimes my Father and Grandfather and I would all go in for haircuts together. Grandad and Claude were both on the Garfield County Scottish Rite Rose Croix funeral team, And they would "run language" while Grandad got his hair cut. Conversation was almost always about the Lodge, and what it was doing or planning. And I learned early how to tell when a Reunion was coming up, because one or two days before, almost all the men I knew were in Claude's shop, getting trimmed to be ready. Two of the Degrees were staged by teams from Enid, and several men were on other teams as well. I took the Scottish Rite Degrees in that shop long and long before I took them in the Temple.

There was peace in that barber shop, and companionship, and perfect Brotherhood. These men trusted each other completely. It was many, many years afterward when I began to learn how much they had relied on each other, helped each other out, attended weddings together, celebrated births together, and bore the pall together. But I knew, even then, that it was special and real, and when these men called each other

"Brother Jack," or "Brother Claude," or "Brother J.T.," in a half-teasing, half-sacred tone, they meant it.

There are few places of Brotherhood today; few worlds which are reserved for men alone. I'm told that some athletic clubs are like that: for those of us who get our exercise bearing the pall for our friends who are health freaks, they might as well be on the moon.

But Masonry is such a refuge.

I don't mean that women aren't allowed in the Temple. Many ladies attend the Reunion at Guthrie. We're glad to see them and we have special programs to encourage them. But they are not and cannot be part of the Brotherhood, any more than we can be part of the sisterhood of P.E.O.

We teach Brotherhood. But I sometimes wonder if we teach it to our younger members in such a way that they understand we really mean it. And, in some cases, I wonder *if* we really mean it.

I heard a Mason, the other day, dismiss the plight of another Mason by saying, "I didn't take him to raise." Oh yes, you did! We all did. We all took each other to raise. And if we lose that, we have lost everything. We must find a way to communicate to the new Mason, and to remind ourselves, that we must and will be there, no matter what. No matter how stupid a situation may be, no matter how childish we may think some reaction may be, no matter how angry we may become, no matter how tired of trying to help we may become, no matter how frustrated, or involved in our own affairs, or just simply weary we may be, we have promised to God and our Brethren that we will be there. If we lose sight of the reality that our job is to help each other, then all the promises of Brotherhood are simply a sham. If we are

Brothers only when it is convenient, we are not Brothers. If we are willing to be Brothers when our Brother has some neat and clean problem, but ready to shun him if he should develop a problem with drugs or alcohol or the law, we have no claim to fraternalism. Any strangers from the street could do that.

But when it is real, Brotherhood is one of the most powerful, creative, healing and redemptive forces in the universe. It's up to us to make it real.

It's up to us to mean it.

A version of this article appeared in *The Scottish Rite Journal* for January, 2001

Compasses Above: The Spiritual Aspect of Masonry

We seem to be becoming fearful of our heritage. Perhaps it is because we have encountered so many religious fanatics who try to insist that Masonry is a religion; perhaps it is because the cynicism of our age has begun to affect the fraternity; perhaps it is because some feel that spirituality is hard to discuss, or even somehow less than manly to contemplate. But, whatever the reason, many Masons seem uncomfortable when confronted with the spiritual aspects of the Craft.

But spirituality and spiritual growth are an essential part of our heritage and our purpose. To deny them would be like a doctor asserting that his task was to cure disease and denying preventative medicine.

This spiritual aspect of Masonry is indicated most clearly in the Blue Lodge by the movement of the Compasses during the three Degrees. In the Scottish Rite, the use of the Compasses as symbols of spirituality is strongly reenforced.

The Compasses are a ... symbol of the Heavens, and of all celestial things and celestial natures.[1]

For the Master, the Compasses of Faith are above *the Square of Reason; but* both *rest upon the Holy Scriptures and combine to form the Blazing Star of Truth.*[2]

The Compasses, therefore, as the Symbol of the Heavens, represents the spiritual, intellectual, and moral portion of the double nature of Humanity; and the Square, as the Symbol of the Earth, its material, sensual, and baser portion.[3]

The Compasses are ancient symbols of spirituality and spiritual creativity. Hundreds of drawings and manuscript illuminations from the Middle Ages, as well as more modern illustrations, show God creating the Universe with Com-passes.

William Blake, the great mystic poet of the late 1700's, used the image to describe the Creation, and John Milton uses the image in "Paradise Lost," in this beautiful passage:

... and in His hand
He took the golden Compasses, prepared
in God's eternal store, to circumscribe
This Universe, and all created things:
One foot He centered, and the other turned

*Round through the vast profundity obscure,
And said, "thus far extend, thus far thy bounds,
This be thy just Circumference, O World."
Thus God the Heaven created, thus the Earth,
Matter unformed and void: ...*[4]

The movement from the Square to the Compasses is so central in Masonic imagery that we simply cannot deny the importance of spiritual development as a goal of the individual Mason.

But what do we mean by "spiritual?" It is a surprisingly hard word to pin down.

One meaning, obvious from the contexts in Masonry, is "concern for values and ideals rather than things." It is obvious that material things can be put to spiritual uses. Wealth is material but the use of wealth in charity is a spiritual act, because charity is motivated by love and compassion. But, with many people, the more wealth they accumulate, the more material and less spiritual and charitable they become. The thing becomes more important that the ideal. Masons are reminded that the spiritual must always come first.

Another related meaning of "spiritual" is "focused away from ourselves and our desires." Lust is not spiritual, love is. Selfishness is not spiritual, selflessness and self-sacrifice are. The desire to dominate is not spiritual, the desire to emancipate is.

Yet another meaning of spiritual is "a desire to experience the beauty and suffering of the world." It may seem strange to add suffering to beauty, but the great spiritual teachers seem always to have been aware of both. The shortest, and many feel most poignant verse in the Bible is, "Jesus wept." Mother Theresa is honored by millions, including those not of her faith, because she embraced the suffering of those around her, while keeping her eyes fixed ever on the beauty she saw in them. As part of the spiritual journey of the Scottish Rite, we are reminded in Degree after Degree of the suffering of others and of the importance of participating in their suffering, just as we are reminded of the beauty, seen and unseen, of the world.

Finally, spiritual can mean "concerned with the great forces of the universe which operate at a non-physical level." Pike, along with many other thinkers, believed that there were such forces--that Love and Sympathy and Compassion and Will and Intellect and Expectation were among them. They were forces which, like the wind, were invisible and detectable only by their effects on persons and things. That may seem strange, at first, and yet most of us have experienced those forces, Certainly it has been shown that when a teacher has high expectations of her students, when she genuinely cares about them, they do far better than average.

Most of us would rather have the good wishes than the ill will of the people around us. Many of the most successful programs for working with youth who have drug or discipline problems begin with the determination of those running the program to love the young people.

There are many perfectly practical explanations of how such things may happen (the teacher with high expectations may teach to a higher standard, for example), but the point is that the spiritual orientation makes a difference.

We have all heard stories of people, injured and told they will never walk again, who have made the spiritual determination (the act of will) to walk, and who have astonished the doctors by remarkable recoveries.

It is a man's spirit, not his body, which limits his potential.

Again, it is the position of the Compasses which indicate spiritual growth and progress. It is the task of every Mason to undertake a journey of spiritual growth and development. In one of the most beautiful passages in *Morals and Dogma,* Pike puts it this way:

Freemasonry is the subjugation of the Human that is in man by the Divine; the Conquest of the Appetites and Passions by the Moral Sense and the Reason; a continual effort, struggle, and warfare of the Spiritual against the Material and Sensual. That victory, when it has been achieved and secured, and the conqueror may rest upon his shield and wear the well-earned laurels, is the true Holy Empire.[5]

---

[1]*Morals and Dogma*, p. 850
[2]*Ibid.*, p. 841
[3]*Ibid.*, p. 851
[4]John Milton, *Paradise Lost*, Book VII
[5]*Morals and Dogma*, pp. 854-855

"Compasses Above" first appeared in *The Scottish Rite Journal,* July, 1997

Mirror, Mirror on the Wall

The beautiful but evil queen in "Snow White" wasn't really asking a question, of course, when she asked her magic mirror who was the fairest one of all. She wasn't seeking information—she was seeking reassurance. "Thou art the fairest in the land," was the answer she fully expected to get. She was annoyed and angered when the mirror said that Snow White was more beautiful.

I have been thinking about the mirror recently, when I think about the future of Masonry. Are we asking the mirror for information, or are we asking it to tell us what we want to hear? For example:

In a state which shall remain unnamed, a Masonic organization (which shall remain unidentified) for both men and women recently held its annual meeting. The issues to be discussed centered around two topics: "How could the organization attract more young women to join?" And "Should we add an extra day to the annual meeting so there will be more time for introductions?" The irony was painful. I was talking about it to a friend.

"Tim," I said, "can't they see that young women aren't going to be interested in those endless introductions? If they want to attract young women, that's the worst possible way to do it!"

"You don't understand, Jim," he replied. "They don't want to attract young women; they want to attract old women in young bodies. They want women who like the same things they like, want to do the same things they want to do, love dressing up in chiffon and sequins—but are 40 years younger."

Mirror, mirror on the wall.

Same state, but an organization for men only. It is rapidly dying, and one reason seems to be because its leaders cannot agree on a long-term plan or strategy, and they have no interest in adapting to the world. As one of the leaders actually said to me, "As long as it stays the way it is for my lifetime, I don't care if it dies." It's going to be a close race; I'd guess he has about 10 years left.

I'm not picking on or attacking these two organizations. I have the same concern for all of Masonry. I wonder if we may all be guilty of doing the same thing. Are we seeking young men in the fraternity so we can benefit them by our teachings and experience, while benefitting ourselves from their energy, their new ideas, the restlessness of the young, the insights into their world which they can bring to us? Or are we simply wanting a blank slate on which we can chalk our opinions, our ways of doing things, our view of the world? What would the mirror tell us?

This hardening of the mental arteries can happen subtly, even when we think we are guarding against it. For most of my life, I have predictably been one of the youngest Masons in any Masonic gathering. One of my favorite soap box speeches is the importance of the old guard listening to the ideas from us young guys. I was holding forth on that with "the group" recently.

"Tres," said Greg, rather gently for him, "have you looked in a mirror recently?"

"Oh! Er—Ah! On the other hand, we must never forget the need for the experience, the calm judgement, the sense of perspective and even detachment which comes only with age and experience."

(Mirror, mirror on the wall.)

I suddenly realized I was old enough to have fathered any of the men I was talking with. I had long ago ceased to be a young turk, and was well on the way to becoming an old coot. And I am not alone in my cootage. We often ignore what is important to the younger men, even the way they live their lives and communicate. And we do that to our peril.

It is the mantra of the moss-backs that Masonry never changes—but that simply isn't true. We don't meet above taverns any more. We don't share the festive board nearly as often as our Masonic ancestors did (more's the pity). We know that the Master Mason Degree is new, coming into the system just before 1730. You need only read the old exposures to know that the Masonic ritual of today would be barely recognizable to such Brethren as George Washington or Benjamin Franklin. The ideas, the Truths, the teachings are still here, but they are garbed in language those Brethren would never have heard in Lodge.

That has been the great genius of Masonry over the generations. It *has* changed. It has kept its foundations while adapting to the world in which it finds itself. It has always been a meeting place for both old men and young men, not just old men in young bodies.

If we look, really look, into that mirror—if we ask about the younger men of today, we may not like some of the answers. And because they, too, are human, some of the answers are not consistent.

It is a fact that only 5% to 8% of the men who belong to Lodge are active, in the sense of attending regularly or taking an officer position in the Lodge. A survey by the Grand Lodge of Oklahoma of more than 400 members under the age of 40, suggested that a very small percentage of younger men liked memorizing things. We were told that the necessity of memorizing lengthy categorical lectures is a major deterrent to men petitioning the fraternity, or continuing past the Entered Apprentice Degree. Yet, actual experience tells us that many if not most *are* willing to memorize the ritual and take part in the work. Both the survey and experience tell us that most of them do not regard the memorization of the cat lectures as sufficient Masonic education. Lodges which have included Masonic education, even rigorous education, with the memorized categorical lectures have found that they not only have a more informed member, they have more members. Wisconsin is a case in point.

It is a fact that conferrals on more than one candidate at a time attract more men. They have to be done with thought, and without any intent of "running people through the system," but they work, and not just in the short run. Research done in the Grand Lodge of Oklahoma shows that the men who joined in the Chance to Advance conferrals of the Fellowcraft and Master Mason Degree are LESS likely to go suspended (roughly 20% less likely) and MORE likely to learn officer's parts and be active in their Lodges (11.5% as opposed to the traditional 5% to 8%). Yet the howls of protest continue from those who want old men in young bodies, not young men, to petition the Fraternity.

It is a fact that, while a majority don't want to memorize the words of the ritual, they do enjoy *hearing* it. The words are old—they were in an archaic style even when they were written—but the words and language pattern have a beauty to which the young respond. We've found that out in many interviews. But they want to hear it well done. They are not anti-ritual, but they want it to be meaningful. And they are patiently amused, not moved, when it is accompanied by music transferred from 78 rpm records to tape or CD, scratches and all, sounding like the background of a 1940's radio soap opera.

Most of all, perhaps, they want quality. This generation has grown up expecting the best, and, generally, they have received it. Whatever one may think of most of the shows on television (my cootage is showing again) they are expensively produced, with excellent production values and careful attention to detail. This generation expects the organizations they join to have quality, too. As to the things one finds in many (certainly not all) Blue Lodges—stained ceiling tiles, worn carpets, bathrooms not quite in repair and not quite clean, steep stairs on which you have to know which treads to step over because they are loose, chairs in need of refinishing, burned-out light bulbs—they are less forgiving than those of us to whom they are simply part of the background.

(Mirror, mirror on the wall; how do they see our Blue Lodge hall?)

They communicate by the Internet. It annoys them when a Lodge or Grand Lodge doesn't have a web site they can visit for information. They point out that if a mom and pop corner grocery store can be on the net, there's no reason their Lodge can't be. That's a difficult one for those of us in the coot tradition. Several of the young ones have been after me to start a web site, and have trouble believing me when I tell them I don't have the remotest idea what to do with one. But, like it or not, it is the way they communicate, and we had best learn.

We don't have to sell out. They don't want that. They are even willing to learn from us. But they will learn on their terms, not ours. They will respect the fact that Masonry teaches through symbols and allegories—it's a new way for most of them to learn, but most whom I know personally find it interesting and challenging. But it would be a good idea to develop a video game which contains some of the great lessons of Masonry as well.

For them, the mirror on the wall bears a striking resemblance to a computer monitor. I've seen a whole room full of them get excited when you point out that the Degrees and Star Wars are the same story. They will listen, they will join us, and they will get excited about the Scottish Rite.

If we're just smart enough to look in the mirror.

"Mirror, Mirror on the Wall" appeared in *The Scottish Rite Journal* for February, 2002

Desk Lamps and Candles

In the April/May 2002 issue of the Mensa Bulletin[1], Chairman Jean K. Becker has a column which reads, in part:

"As a member of the American Mensa Committee and International Board of Directors, I am often asked to approve changes. You might posit that being intelligent increases the chances that one will be an 'early adapter.'....However, just as we are talented in seeing many possible new ways of doing things, we are also quite skilled in generating reasons for not changing.

"It is also said that nobody likes change except a wet baby. My natural inclination is, 'If it ain't broke, don't fix it.' ...

"[But] these days, if you aren't moving, you can't even hold still. We must develop and change. Talking about returning Mensa to 'the good old days' is neither reasonable nor desirable in today's world."

Obviously, Mensa is in the same boat as so many Masonic organizations. It's a crowded boat.

---

[1] Mensa is an international organization, whose only membership requirement is that the person be in the top 2% of their nation in intelligence as measured on a standardized IQ

Generally, when it comes to change, I enjoy it about as much as my cat does. But, like all critters, we have a general ambivalence. Most of us enjoy the change of the seasons. We like watching Spring arrive and the subtle shifting of Summer into Fall. Most of us approve of the changes in medical technology, even if we are uncomfortable about some of the ethical questions which arise. Most of us enjoy, or at least take advantage of, the changes in communications technology, albeit I would far rather read from a book in my hand than from the computer's screen. But I do that reading by aid of a halogen desk lamp, not by a candle.

Actually, that halogen desk lamp and candle may well represent both the perplex and an answer to the issue of change. It's important to find an answer, because the issues of change are causing real and genuine distress to many Brethren, including me. There is a good desk lamp on the table at which I do most of my reading. But there is a candle on that table as well. For reading, I turn on the lamp; but when I want to think about what I have read, or when I want to talk with friends in my study, I turn off the lamp, and light the candle. Both contemplation and conversation go better with the living light of the flame.

How to have both? that's the problem.

If I had my "druthers,"

We would confer the Degrees of the Masonry—Blue Lodge and Scottish Rite—on one candidate at a time; each focused on him as the center of attention. We could then make the Degrees more nearly the mind-altering soul-shifting experiences they are intended to be.

We would offer discussion groups before and after each Degree, to explore in depth the symbols, the issues, the ethical lessons and the moral assumptions of the

Degree, and show the candidate how to use that information in daily life.

We would never apologize to the world in thought, word, or deed, for what we are, what we do, or what we represent. We are the oldest, largest, most prestigious fraternity in the world, older and more honorable that almost any government on earth. We are an elite organization for men, teaching the lessons we consider important in the ways we consider effective, and, as the Ill∴ Rev. Forrest Haggard, 33°, Grand Cross, once said, speaking on the same topic, "If others don't like that, they can go to the devil."

But I don't have my "druthers," and, outside of the world I create for myself, I am not likely to have them.

So how do we use both the halogen desk lamp and the candle? How do we adapt without losing what we consider essential? (And for that matter, how on earth are any three Masons going to agree on what is essential?)

First as to multiple conferrals, Grand Master's classes, or what ever name you call them. Yes, I would rather do the Degrees of all the branches of Masonry one-on-one. But the reason is that I want the candidate to have the maximum impact from the experience. So which is more likely to provide that impact—being part of a class of a thousand candidates, watching a Degree well performed, by men who not only know the words but the MEANINGS of the words, with all the emotional impact which good staging, lighting and sound can add, with a solid 30 minutes to 1 hour of Masonic education before or after each Degree---or, as is true in some Lodges, a Degree performed by men who used to know the work, being constantly corrected during the Degree by shouted words from the sidelines, with the ritual delivered in a flat and toneless manner, and no education except for the teaching of the categorical lectures?

Which would I rather experience? Which would you?

And it is obvious that the classes work, if they are well done. I've hear the caviling and I am sure you have too. "They ain't REAL Masons!" "They won't learn the ritual and serve in offices or come to Lodge!" "They go suspended, they aren't really committed!" Or, and this is unforgivable in a fraternity, "By Harry I had to suffer through it and they should, too."

(I always want to ask those who raise that last objection if they want to go without anesthesia the next time they have surgery, just because it used to be done that way.) As to the other objections, let me quote from the research reported by Past Grand Master of Oklahoma M∴W∴ Robert T. Shipe in his Grand Master's Address to the Grand Lodge.

"In my study of the listing of the Masons who joined in the '97 and '99 classes, I found some surprising facts! Of the 2,863 men 91 percent (2,609) were still active as of August 2001. 174 or six percent went SNPD, two percent (67) had died, 12 withdrew, and 1 had been suspended for unmasonic conduct. Of the 2,609 remaining 298 were Lodge officers (11.4 percent). We had 12 past masters, 20 Worshipful Masters, 32 Senior Wardens, 41 Junior Wardens, 6 Secretaries, and 13 Treasurers for a total of 124 elected officers. And there were 174 appointed officers with 29 Senior Deacons, 51 Junior Deacons, 23 Senior Stewards, 40 Junior Stewards, 20 Tylers, and 11 Chaplains. 140 Lodges (54%) were benefitting

from the participating of these brethren as officers."

In other words, the Brethren who joined in the classes had a lower suspension rate, a higher participation rate, and a better attendance record then the typical men who joined in the traditional manner.

When I am reading at my desk, the important material is that written in the book. The material is the same, whether I read it by the halogen lamp or the candle. I learn just as much one way as the other. But there is a difference in eye strain, a difference in how long I can read without becoming tired, and a difference in the pleasure/pain ratio. The choice isn't between "going modern and losing Masonry" and "being traditional and keeping Masonry." Masonry is kept when men care, really care, about the candidate and what he learns and experiences, whether that is one-on-one or in a class of a thousand. It is lost when the point of a Degree becomes the ego of those doing the ritual, whether one-on-one or in a class of a thousand.

We can have both the clarity of the halogen lamp and the warmth of the candle light. We just have to be smart enough to do it well.

It truly is the same in Masonry.

"Desk Lamps and Candles" appeared in *The Scottish Rite Journal* for November, 2002

Believers & Belongers

"The times, they are a-changing." "The more things change, the more they remain the same."

Both things seem true in our age. Perhaps they have always been true. But I think not. Our great-grandparents assumed that their children would live much the same lives as their own grandparents had. Historically, that had certainly been true. There had been minor changes, even some major ones, but no one, in generations past, doubted that the world of tomorrow would be essentially the same as that they had always known. Work would still be work, play would still be play. No one had anticipated the rate of change with which we live daily.

In her pre-teens, my Grandmother made a trip of several hundred miles in a horse-drawn wagon, helping to take the wheels off each night and grease the axles. She lived to see men walk on the moon. In the last few years, we have seen the word "work" redefined. It now consists largely of actions which people thirty years ago would not have recognized, let alone defined as work, with computers becoming not just part but the center of almost every job.

If possible, an even greater change is taking place in faith, in spirituality. And it may have even more profound implications than the changes in work. The characterizations which follow are both over-generalized and over-simplified, but they are essentially true.

The 1950's were, by and large, a time of comfortable spirituality. It was not, for most people, a matter of personal quest or even involvement. It was, as the poet Lampson had written a century earlier:

And many of them say their prayers
And go to church on Sunday;
And many are afraid of God--
And more of Mrs. Grundy.

The majority did go to church on Sunday, with a comfortable piety, and because they were a little afraid of comment from the neighbors if they did not. It was the proper thing to do, and people did it. It was not insincere—it was just that spirituality did not seem to require much thought.

The 1960's seem to bring an "external spirituality" with them. Spirituality and faith seemed less a matter of wrestling in the soul and more a matter of being easy and free, letting it all hang out and doing your own thing. Spirituality was something which would happen to you, if you just hung loose. The pace of change was beginning to accelerate, and the way to handle that change was just to drop out for a while.

The 1970's externalized that spirituality almost violently. Music turned hard and faith turned cruel. The evangelical movement had been growing for some time, but among some people evangelicalism, which is an essentially compassionate and caring faith, even if somewhat literalist, began to turn into fundamentalism. Fundamentalism is to faith what Nazism is to politics—an intolerant "believe my way or else" attitude which regards the subjugation of others "for their own good" as perfectly appropriate.

The 1980's tried to substitute career for faith and gain for spirituality.

But the 1990's saw a subtle shift. One by one, men and women discovered that they "have it all and it isn't enough." The decade was marked by an increasing search for spiritual values and truths on the part of many people. But in many cases, this search took place either outside of or partially outside of the churches.

So true is this that sociologists have been forced to add a new category to those they have traditionally used in analyzing surveys of American faith and spiritual practice—"Believers but not Belongers." The category describes men and women who believe in the existence of a soul and in life after death, but who are not members of any church. According to the most recent survey data, more than 30 million "baby-boomers" fall into that category. Some drift from guru to shaman, hoping to find an answer to that spiritual need within themselves. But more and more are discovering that one must wrestle with the angels on the quest. And, indeed, more and more are discovering that it *is* a quest.

That is, perhaps, where Masonry can help.

Masonry is not a religion, of course, and it cannot substitute for a religion. It does not and cannot offer salvation, or religious orthodoxy, or the many other things which a man or woman derives from faith. But it can and does help with spiritual growth.

The nature of the relationship between spirituality and faith has been debated by the wisest men of the church for centuries, and we cannot resolve the issue here. But few question that an awakening and strengthening spirituality often leads to a faith. That is the primary reason that so many wives and ministers have said and written that the men they know become far more active in their churches after they join Masonry.

For Masonry is essentially spiritual. It is the modern version of the great quest, echoed in initiations from the earliest times, in which the person encounters and discovers himself—confronts his strengths and his weaknesses, and in so doing achieves awakening or enlightenment. It is the *Odyssey*, the *Epic of Gilgamesh*, the Search of Galahad for the Grail. It is the theme of *Beowulf*, of *The Lord of the Rings*, and *2001*.

The genius of Masonry is that the quest is not reserved for a Greek king, an oriental despot, a British knight, a Saxon thane, a hobbit or an astronaut—Masonry makes it available to the common man, to you and me and people like us, if we simply decide to undertake the quest seriously.

That quest is what Masonry has to offer those 30 million people who are searching for a meaning. The growth in spirituality which arises from that quest will probably point most of them to a faith. We may well continue to be, as we have historically been, the greatest friend and asset organized religion has.

If we're just smart enough not to blow it.

Let us, as Masons, take pride in our *heritage* of developing spirituality (always remembering that taking pride in one's own spirituality is, perhaps, the ultimate act of spiritual suicide). Let us not be afraid to say to our non-Mason friends who are searching for meaning, "If you search here sincerely, you will find it, for Masonry gives what is earnestly sought." Let us share what we have with potential new Brothers.

They are already Believers. They may well become belongers.

"Believers and Belongers" first appeared in The Scottish Rite Journal of August, 1998

The Morning After

You really want to know? OK. I was scared—well, not really scared. No, that's not true; I was scared. I wasn't really afraid of the men in the Lodge. A couple of them are good friends; I was pretty sure they wouldn't set me up—unless maybe they thought it was funny. But they wouldn't set me up for anything bad.

"Besides, Grandad was a Mason.

"But I couldn't see anything. Yeah, I know, but I don't take many things on faith and trust in my life—I've been burned too often. The idea that there was a whole group of men you could trust, I mean really trust . . . I know they're brothers; but I know some of the things my older brother did to me when we were kids.

"No, I'll tell you the truth: I was a little afraid of what they might do to me, but I figured I could fight my way out if I had to. What I was really afraid of was that I'd do or say something wrong or stupid—I'd disappoint the friend who'd given me the petition.

"When did I relax? When they started with a prayer. I figured no one would start any horseplay by praying. I know they'd told me there wasn't any horseplay, that it was serious and beautiful—and they were sure right about that!—but still, it's a fraternity, and you hear stories about college fraternities.

"But one of the men was talking to me before it started, and he gave me some good advice. He said, 'Don't try to analyze it or figure out the meanings while you're taking the Degree. There's time for that later, and there's more information packed into this Degree than into a volume from an encyclopedia. But for right now, just experience and feel, go with the flow. Then you can start looking for answers and meanings.' He was right! You know, there were a couple of times I almost wanted to cry. I haven't done that in 20 years. I wouldn't have believed it, but you can actually feel it when a room-full of people are concentrating on you and wishing you well!

"Sure I have questions!

"Why did we walk around the room just after we got started?

"Why did people keep asking and answering the same questions?

"It was flattering, but what did they really mean when they said I was well-qualified, worthy, and duly truly prepared?

"Why did I have to walk up to the altar in a special way?

"What if I'd given the wrong answer to the first question the Worshipful Master asked me?

"Why is it called a 'cable tow?'

"What is a 'Lodge of Entered Apprentices?'

"Is the Degree the same everywhere?

"What does the Lodge really expect of me?"

Those comments and questions came for a real Entered Apprentice, the day after his initiation. Sometimes we can forget what a new member of the Craft thinks and feels and wonders. But we have a duty to him, to help him find information, be aware of his feelings, and "be as ready to give, as you will be ready to receive, instruction."

Some good books for the Lodge to own and lend to Entered Apprentices or members who want to know more about Masonry include:

The Complete Idiot's Guide to Freemasonry by Dr. S. Brent Morris
Masonic Questions & Answers by Paul M. Bessel
Masonic Trivia and Facts by Allen E. Roberts
Masonic Words and Phrases by Michael R. Poll
The Craft and Its Symbols by Allen E. Roberts
Alchemical Keys to Masonic Ritual by Timothy Hogan

The original article ended with the list of books above. When he was reading through the text for me, Brother Porter suggested (strongly) that I should answer the questions. I said I didn't really think that was necessary. He then threatened to let Biscuit, his English mastiff, lick me. I had already had my bath for the week. Remember, opinions and ideas are only that. There is nothing "official" in what follows.

"Why did we walk around the room just after we got started?" Because all initiation involves a journey. It may be into the past, or from the past to the future, or from the present to the future. It also involves a jounrey into yourself, which is the deeper symbolism.

"Why did people keep asking and answering the same questions?" As a practical matter, in the days prior to amplified sound, so that everyone in the room could hear. But it also reflects the hierarchy of the Lodge and the passing of information. If you think about it, the rite of passing information happens at many points in the ritual.

"It was flattering, but what did they really mean when they said I was well-qualified, worthy, and duly truly prepared?" It means that you have met the qualifications for membership, not just those of age, but those of moral stature and intellect. And it means that you are prepared—that you have cast aside everything which is not essentially you; necessary if you are to discover who you truly are.

"Why did I have to walk up to the altar in a special way?" You are approaching a sacred location. In both religion and mythology, such an approach is not made directly or without preperation. The symbolism here is not something to be discussed in print.

"What if I'd given the wrong answer to the first question the Worshipful Master asked me?" It happens. Sometimes the candidate will give the name of the friend who signed his petition. If that happens, the Worshipful Master will say something to give you a clue as to the sort of answer needed.

"Why is it called a 'cable tow?'" Largely because of Masonic tradition. In early rituals it is also called a "rope tow," a "rope line," and a "cable line." It has many meanings, but one of the most powerful is that of a visible sign of a pledge or vow given.

"What is a 'Lodge of Entered Apprentices?'" There is a Lodge of each of the three Degrees. When the Entered Apprentice Degree is to be performed, the Worshipful Master opens a Lodge of Entered Apprentices. Technically, in some jurisdictions, a Lodge composed almost entirely of Entered Apprentices can open and work, as long as there is one Master Mason among them.

"Is the Degree the same everywhere?" With fairly minor exceptions in language, it is the same in most jurisdictions in the United States. There is more variation as one goes to outside jurisdictions.

"What does the Lodge really expect of me?" That you will work at becoming a better man; more dedicated to honor and integrity, more compassionate, more honest—that you will try to improve and to show that improvement in your life and actions.

Originally published as the Newsletter of the Masonic Lodge Education Committee of the Grand Lodge of Oklahoma, March, 2007

The Starry Canopy

The drawing shows the ceiling of a Lodge room as described by Albert Pike. He appears to have developed the layout from old French Masonic sources. While the American and English rituals describe the ceiling of the Lodge as the "starry canopy of Heaven," there is no description of the stars and their positions. That information may simply have been given to candidates or left as a matter of study. Obviously, until buildings were purposely built as Lodges, it would have been impractical to paint the ceilings.

Astrological phenomena play a larger part in the symbolism of Freemasonry than is sometimes realized. The Entered Apprentice Degree contains the reference to the starry canopy the Fellowcraft Degree includes the celestial globe with the comments made about it, and also lists Astronomy as the highest of the liberal arts and sciences. It should be understood that it means what we today would call astrology. The field had not divided into astronomy and astrology when the ritual was written. In the Master Mason Degree, the 12 Fellowcrafts are generally considered to represent the 12 signs of the zodiac as well as the 12 tribes of Israel. Death and burial take place at the solar opposites of high twelve and low twelve, etc.

The Four Royal Stars

Four stars have been especially significant throughout recorded history. The Persians, who in Babylon, seem to have first systematized the field of astrology, so named them, and they have been important to almost every culture since, including Christendom, which associated the stars with archangels, and the modern times, when the same four stars are among the most important in navigation. The Royal stars were believed to watch over and govern all other celestial bodies. At one time, these four stars marked the two solstices and the two equinox, As you will see, the Four Royal Stars appear on the ceiling of the Lodge.

Regulus - "Watcher of the North" The healing archangel, Raphael

Regulus is located in the constellation Leo (the Lion). The name means "ruler" or "little king." It is known as the " heart of the Lion."

Traditional Associations

A portent of glory, riches and power. *"They born under this star are thought to have a royal nativity."* It is thought to give high and lofty ideals, strength of spirit, and magnanimity. Regulus *"makes astrologers to kings, men of high position, and noble men, if but the heart be pure."* BUT it can also bring violence, misuse of power, fall from honor and imprisonment.
Note:

Masons may find it interesting that Regulus, in Leo, guards the door from the preparation room into

the Lodge. Thus a candidate entering the Lodge is "born" under Regulus in the sign of Leo.

Fomalhaut - "Watcher of the South" The archangel of the Annunciation and therefore the herald of great changes, Gabriel

Fomalhaut or Formalhaut (pronounced [**foh**-mah-low]) is in the constellation *Piscis Australes*, or Southern Fish. The name is from the Arabic for "fish mouth." The old maps showed the fish as drinking the water poured by Aquarius.

Traditional Associations

Immortality, the civilizing force, death and rebirth, change from material to spiritual forms of expression. BUT is can also be a powerful influence for evil.

Note:

Fomalhaut is located in the Southeast corner of the Lodge, the point from which the candidate begins his circumambulations (if we assume that the journey only truly beings after the first rap of the gavel). It can be said that he begins his Masonic journey under the influence of Fomalhaut.

Aldebaran - "Watcher of the East" The warrior archangel, Michael

Also known as "The Eye of the Bull," Aldebaran is located in the constellation Taurus. The names means "the follower" in Arabic because the star seems to follow the stars of the Pleiades in the sky.

Traditional Associations

Aldebaran was said to confer honor, intelligence, eloquence, public honor, wealth, BUT also ferocity, sedition, and sickness. But there are some special attributes of Aldebaran. *"As the star of illumination, Aldebaran irradiates the Way using the applied power of transformation. In seeking illumination, we can cultivate the ability to use the mind as a reflection of soul light."* Some 3,000 years ago, Aldebaran marked the Autumnal equinox and thus the beginning of the Babylonian New Year. The Hebrews of the time of Solomon called Aldebaran "God's Eye," It is also called the Eye of Revelation. *"Taurus is often associated with royalty and divine power. Throughout the ages, Aldebaran has been spiritually recognized for its alinement with divinity. There is a symbolic relation between Aldebaran, the Eye in the head of the Bull, the third eye or the light in the head, and the diamond. The alignment symbolizes 'As above, so below.'"*

It should also be noted that the bull was the sacred animal of Dionysus; bringing with it all the associations of Dionysian consciousness.

Note: *When the candidate is placed in the North East corner of the Lodge as the youngest Mason, he is placed under the constellation of Taurus and of Aldebaran. Consider the significance of the placement in terms of the attributes of the star.*

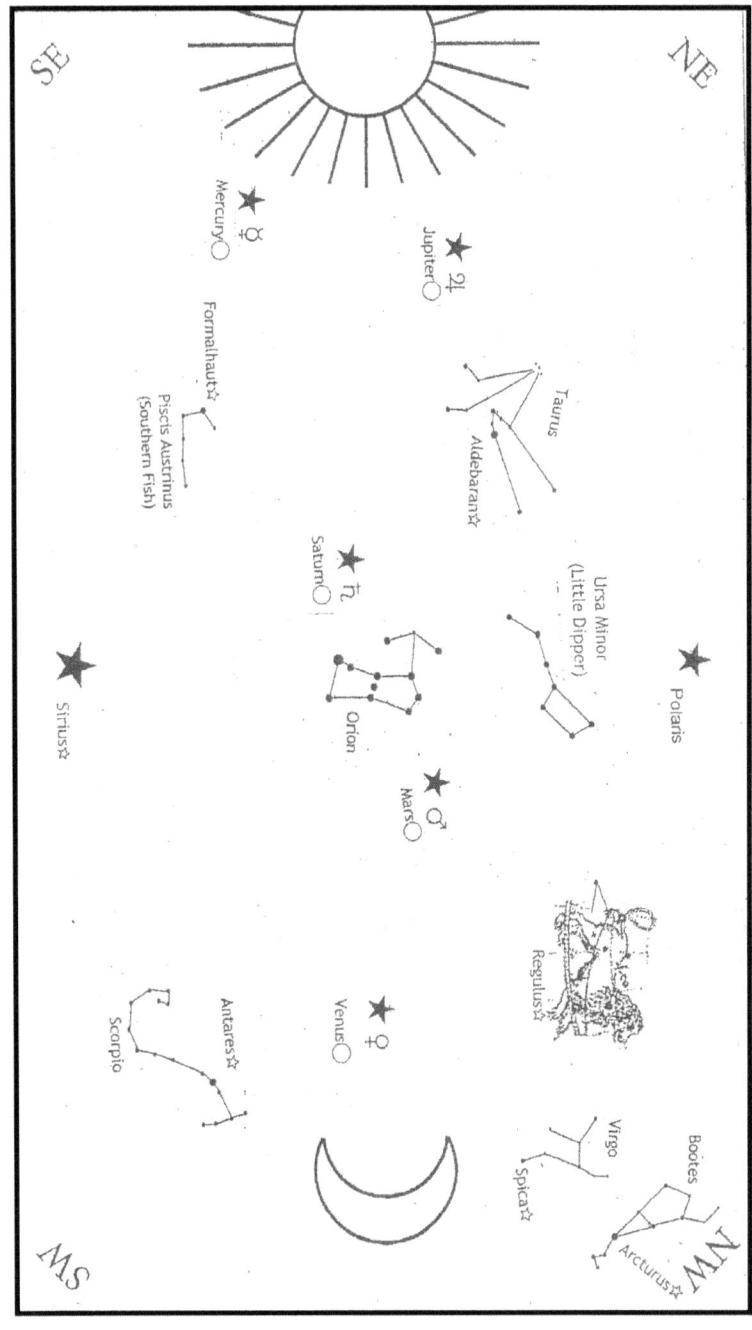

Antares - "Watcher of the West" The archangel of destiny, Oriel

Arcturus is in the constellation Scorpio and is also known as *Cor Scorpio* or Heart of the Scorpion.

Traditional Associations

Like the other Royal Stars, it is said to confer honor and glory. BUT it is also associated with rashness, stubbornness, destructiveness and violence. *"They have to conquer themselves first, before they can make a contribution to others."*

Note:

Scorpio and Antares guard the door to the Lodge room through which the Brethren normally enter. Consider what has been said about the attributes of Antares and then consider it as a reminder of "I come to learn, to control my passions, and to improve myself in Masonry."

Note on the Royal Stars

You will have noticed that each of the Royal Stars has both positive and negative attributes. The generally accepted lesson is that the person has within himself the possibility of greatness, but that greatness must be developed by overcoming the impulses to his lesser nature. He becomes who he chooses to become.

The Other Stars and Constellations
Orion

Pike places Orion in the center of the Lodge, above the altar. Orion was especially sacred to the Egyptians since they identified it as the home of Osiris. Orion was famous for his prowess, both as a hunter and as a lover.

He boasted that he would eventually rid the earth of all wild animals. That prompted the great Earth Mother to send a scorpion to kill him. In the night sky, when the stars of Orion sink beneath the western horizon, the stars of the scorpion are just rising in the east. The next night, Orion rises again, restored to full health by Ophiuchus, the ancient physician, whose constellation can be seen above Scorpio. Orion is one of the oldest known symbols of death and rebirth. The significance of the constellation above the altar, the place in the Lodge in which the person, by virtue of the obligation, becomes renewed and regenerated, is obvious. But there is also the symbolism of the hunt. *"It has two aspects. There is the slaying of the beast, which is the destruction of ignorance and the tendency to evil, and there is the search for the quarry and its tracking, which bear the sense of spiritual quest."*

Boötes

Boötes [boo-**oh**-tees], with its principal star, **Arcturus**, is directly over the preparation room door. Boötes represents a herdsman, shepherd, plowman, or hunter. He follows the two bears around the pole. It is the most ancient identified constellation, being mentioned by Homer in *The Odyssey*. Boötes is associated with grain agriculture. He is the Elder, *"the Wise Old Man, who is interested in principles and underlying causes, theories, ideologies, and how the past effects the future."*

Traditional Associations

Arcturus means "The bear guardian." It is a star of many associations. Esoterically, it represents Sacred Geometry, the way home through consciousness and mathematics. Arcturus encourages self-determination and independence, fondness for rural pursuits, and fame. Arcturus is known as a gateway through which souls pass on their way to and from earth. Arcturus is also associated with the tarot card "the hermit," *"The Hermit is the <u>master who works on the drawing board, where he casts the exact plan of the intended construction.</u> Before taking form everything pre-exists as an abstract concept, as an intention; he represents the mysterious artisan, the drawn-up plan. .. <u>He is the master capable of directing the work of others</u> and of discerning what is in the embryo in the sphere of human development."*

Virgo

A principal star in the constellation Virgo is **Spica** [**spee**-ka].It marks the sheaf of wheat in the hand of the virgin. The Hebrew name for Spica was *Shibboleth*, which means sheaf of grain or ear of corn. The Virgin is associated with Isis, Ceres, and the Mother Goddess tradition. She was celebrated in the mysteries of Eleusis. The constellation is also located by the door of the preparation room.

NOT TO BE OBVIOUS ABOUT IT, but the three stars located at the door of the preparation room have obvious reference to the three degrees:

Regulus: {Entered Apprentice} *"They born under this star are thought to have a royal nativity."* It is thought to give high and lofty ideals, strength of spirit, and magnanimity.
Spica: {Fellow Craft} The Hebrew name for Spica was *Shibboleth*, which means sheaf of grain or ear of corn.

Arcturus: {Master Mason} *"The Hermit is the master who works on the drawing board, where he casts the exact plan of the intended construction."*

Sirius

Sirius [serious] is the brightest star in the heavens as seen from earth. It is known as the dog star, and the days in summer when it is ascendent are known as the "dog days." Sirius has been an important symbol since antiquity.

Traditional Associations

Sirius is associated with the transformation stage--moving consciousness from one reality to another, changing levels of consciousness. It is also known as the "Spirit of Wisdom."

Note:

Sirius is above the station of the Junior Warden--the first barrier a candidate passes in each of the Degrees.

Polaris

Polaris, also known as the North Star, the Pole Star, and the Lode Star marks the north pole in the heavens. This is especially important because it is from it that we determine the cardinal directions North, South, East and West.

Traditional Associations

Because it does not rise and set like the other stars, Polaris is a symbol of trustworthiness, honor, constancy, dependability, stability, etc. In the Lodge room it appears at the center point on the northern edge of the ceiling.

Thinking through the symbolism involved with the stars and constellations can add considerable richness to the symbolism of Freemasonry and the impact of the Degrees. As always, such speculation is valid only for the individual doing the speculation, but it's nice to have some meaning for the "starry canopy."

This material was first prepared as a hand-out for class discussion at a Guthrie Scottish Rite Reunion.

A Large Compassion

Fireflies

With what a quaint extravagance of light
The inventive universe compounded these
From fire and flight.

Yet there was something of a large compassion
In so devising for this fickle planet
Stars after its own fashion.[1]

Bonaro Overstreet is one of my favorite 20th century American poets. She wrote of the small things in life: of fireflies and telescopes, and teachers grading papers. And in all these little things, she found evidence of a large compassion.

---

[1] Bonaro W. Overstreet, from *Hands Laid Upon the Wind*, 1955

If I were foolish enough to try to sum up, in one idea, why I think Freemasonry is vital to the world, it would be because it has, and teaches, a large compassion.

Most of the institutions in the world teach us to limit compassion, in one way or another, even if that is not the intent. Many churches take unto themselves the divine prerogative of separating the sheep from the goats, and are remarkably certain of the division. College graduates tend to divide the world into those who went to the same school and those who did not (observe two fans from different schools watching their teams play football). Labor is suspicious of management, which is suspicious of labor. The divisions created by political parties are so great that they would be comic if they were not destructive. In recent decades we have worked to divide the aged from the young, the professional from the craftsman, and the dying from everyone.

Of compassion--of feeling what another feels, and understanding that those feelings are valid; of being willing to understand that our own choice or view or opinion or need is no more important than those of others--there is very little.

Freemasonry stands virtually alone as champion of a "large compassion."

There are groups which work for ecumenicism between denominations, organizations which try to bridge the gap between rich and poor, institutions which try to assure that the drying do not die in lonely isolation, councils which strive to get labor and management to work together for common goals. Power be unto them all!

But where, except in Freemasonry, will you find an insistence on ALL those things, and much more in addition? I am always amazed when I think about it.

Freemasonry is an elite organization! Let us quit trying to pretend it isn't and quit acting as if we should be ashamed of the fact. It is an elite organization. We guard the doors of admission. We select. But it is an elitism based not on money, not on social rank, not on educational level, not on professional stature, not on descent from a fabled ancestor, not on ethnicity, nor on fashion, but based solely on this question: Is he a good man? The high school dropout minimum-wage ditch digger, who is a man of integrity and honor, caring for others, eager to help those with less and eager to learn and grow and develop as a person is welcome in the fraternity. The millionaire who is cold, uncaring, willing to exploit others, and who measures his integrity by his chances of getting caught, is not welcome. It's that simple.

And what does this elite organization do? Most such organizations spend their time teaching their members that they really do deserve special treatment, that it is "only right" they should receive preferred treatment because they are, after all, special. ("Oh Lord, I thank Thee that I am not like that man...")

Freemasonry does just the opposite. We teach our members that they have an obligation to everyone else in the world; that their task is to serve, not to be served. We teach that if a Mason starts to feel superior to his fellow man, he is setting himself up for a terrible fall.

"Had you been tempted like him, you might have fallen like him, and perhaps with less resistance." "Have you contributed to showy charities, but turned the poor away from your door?" "No man hath a right to sit in judgement upon others." "Who best can work and best agree." "To take pride in the fact that you never admit

fault is to take pride in your own damnation." "Some men take pride in the fact that they do not have to work-- neither do swine." "We are called upon to be God's almoners, not His tax collectors."

This large compassion is desperately needed by the world. The alternative is a society which fragments itself into smaller and smaller pieces. It was a large compassion which united people around the world in shock and sympathy when the planes crashed into the towers of the World Trade Center. It was fanaticism and contempt, exactly the lack of compassion, which drove those airplanes into the buildings. But there are tens of thousands of small acts of contempt in the world each day. A woman berates the girl at the supermarket check-out stand because the product she wanted wasn't on the shelf. A man drives carelessly close to construction workers on the highway. A person cuts into a line at the bank because his time is too valuable to spend standing in line. People savage the reputations of others by passing on gossip and adding to the story, without knowing or caring if what they say is true. There, and a thousand similar acts all carry the same message: "I matter, you don't."

Each of us adds daily to the sum of human joy or the sum of human pain in the world. The large compassion taught by the Craft helps us make sure that we are adding to the joy, not the pain. It is an "extravagance of light." It is also an extravagance of Light. But it brightens the path for everyone.

"A Large Compassion" first appeared in *The Scottish Rite Journal*

The Temple Shook With Hate

Bob Davis, 33° Grand Cross, General Secretary of the Guthrie Scottish Rite Bodies, Joe R. Manning, Jr., 33°, Manager of the Masonic Charity Foundation of Oklahoma and I were in Bob's office, making plans for the next Masonic Renewal program. It was just after 9am, the morning, of April 19th., 1995.

A sudden shudder went through the massive stone Temple—one of the largest Masonic buildings in the world. It takes a lot to shake that building. The stained glass windows rattled.

"That felt like a sonic boom," Joe said.

About a minute later one of the secretaries came in. "That sound we just heard—the Federal Building in Oklahoma City just blew up." The Temple is more than 35 miles from downtown Oklahoma City.

We went to another office, turned on the television set there. The news was already on the screen, with a picture shot from the top of a television station's broadcast antenna. "Dear God," Bob prayed, unconscious that he spoke aloud, "let it have been a gas leak!" I knew what he meant. Let it be a horrible accident, not a deliberate act of hatred. It was only minutes until it was reported to be a bomb.

Bob and I both looked in the direction of the small auditorium. Two weekends ago we had our Spring Reunion. Reunions at the Guthrie Temple are built around themes, and the theme for this one had been the International Year of Toleration, declared by the United Nations. Two Saturday evenings ago, as part of the Reunion, I had done a program in the large auditorium called "How to Hate." I had traced the bloody history of intolerance, using clips from the film "Intolerance" by Brother D.W. Griffith, and video clips of film from the Holocaust. I had ended my section of the program with the words of Albert Pike from *Morals and Dogma*:

"Is freedom yet universal? Have ignorance and prejudice disappeared from the earth? Are there no longer enmities [anger and hatred] *among men? . . . Do toleration and harmony prevail among religious and political sects? There are works yet left for Masonry to accomplish, greater than the twelve labors of Hercules; to advance ever resolutely and steadily; to enlighten the minds of the people, to reconstruct society, to reform the laws, and to improve the public morals. The eternity in front of it is as infinite as the one behind. And Masonry cannot cease to labor in the cause of social progress, without ceasing to be true to itself, without ceasing to be Masonry."*

We had set up display panels in the Atrium of the Temple--one showing political intolerance, one showing social intolerance, one religious intolerance, one economic intolerance. And there were panels of Masonic heroes—men who had made powerful statements of toleration in an intolerant world. There was Brother Abd-el-Kader, who, in 1860, placed himself in grave personal danger by saving many Christians from massacre by rioting Muslims in Damascus. Brother Simon Bolivar, known as the "George Washington" of South America. Brother Jean Dunant, winner of the first Nobel Peace Prize, who founded the Red Cross. And many others. We had moved the panels to the stage of the small auditorium to await disassembly, in order to clear the Temple for the annual Scottish Rite Easter Pageant last weekend. Two weekends in a row dedicated, in different ways, to the lessons of love opposed to hatred. Two weekends of warning of the power of hate in the world. And today, the Temple shook with that blast of hate.

Most of today is already a blur. There are a few moments I can remember with terrible clarity.

The people, lining up at the hospitals in Oklahoma City and the towns around here, sometimes lining up out the door, to give blood for those who would need it.

Lodge after Lodge calling me at the Temple. "Is the Fraternity getting ready to do anything to help? What can we do? Do we need to raise money? Do we need to organize blood drives?" And, behind every call, every query, the unspoken plea "Can you help me make any sense of this?"

A moment of wry humor—a call to the Temple from a newspaper in Aberdeen, Scotland, obviously the result of a computer search of area phone listings for any listing with the word "Scotland" or "Scottish." "Can you tell us anything about any Scots nationals who may have been injured?" I wish we could have helped.

About 2:00pm I wandered into the small auditorium. The shock of the explosion had tumbled the panels onto the floor. I think that's when it really hit me that all this was real.

A shot on television of the Episcopal Cathedral, a church I know and love well, with its beautiful windows shattered.

People, sitting at their desks, mechanically going through the actions of work, as if sanity could be grasped by routine, but with eyes never wandering far from the portable television set, whose flickering, fuzzy picture was somehow more real than the stained glass and marble paneling around us.

Seventeen children known dead, and the number sure to increase.

No one knows how many hundred people dead, yet. It may be days before we know.

President Clinton, saying we'd catch the evil cowards. God, help me to know—is it ever right to hate? Can't I hate the people who did this?! For the first time in my life I wish, for just a moment, that I were neither a Christian nor a Scottish Rite Mason. Both tell me the answer is "No," and I'm not sure I can stand that answer.

I don't know when this day will end. Most of the pictures on the television are repeats of earlier coverage. I leave it for a few minutes, but I keep drifting back.

8:30pm, fifteen minutes ago, a call from a friend of mine, a paramedic who works in downtown Oklahoma City. I've worried about her all day, but they asked people not to make unnecessary phone calls, and I know she's busy. She's on a short break, due back in ten minutes. She's been at the scene since it started. "Oh

God, Jim, I saw the children! There are bodies everywhere, we've hardly started to take them out. But the children, they're like broken toys. Oh God, help the children!" I wish I knew what to say to her.

And then I had to write. I had to come to the computer and try to make some sense of this, hoping that seeing the words form on the screen will give some order of my thinking, some structure to this day. We've been under a tornado watch most of the day, too. I can accept mindless destruction from nature, but how do I approach mindless destruction from man.

But I begin to see why Albert Pike wrote "labor and pray." I begin to understand why the Scottish Rite teaches over and over, pounding it into our heads against our wills, that we must insist on toleration, on love rather than hatred, on working to make the world better. I understand passages in the Degrees on a level I never understood before.

Another friend just called. He lives in Oklahoma City. We talked about the 30°. I think, perhaps, I understand it, now.

But I know that I know this: the Scottish Rite must survive, it must teach, it must convince men that every person has a right to their own faith, their own political destiny, their own dignity, and that no one, under any circumstances whatever, has the right to use force against others to gain their ends.

For there is no place we can run for refuge, when even the Temple shakes with hate.

The material was written the evening of April 19, 1995—the day of the bombing of the Alfred P. Murrah Building—and published in the next issue of *The Scottish Rite Journal*

When is a Symbol an Emblem?

We say that Freemasonry is taught by symbols. Generically, that is true enough. But while "symbol" may be a sort of catch-all term, we actually use many different kinds of images— including emblems, types, trophies, and much more. Here is a brief listing of the various types of images and their definitions.

attribute — a symbol used in art to identify a person, especially a saint, whose attribute is usually the means of their martyrdom —since no one knows what the people actually looked like. Thus a male figure with an attribute of an X-shaped cross (holding an X-shaped cross) is St. Andrew; a female figure with an attribute of a wheel is St. Cathryn, etc.

emblem—technically, an emblem is a image used to represent an idea, whereas a symbol is simply a substitution of a sign for a thing. In practice, the word symbol is generally used to mean both.

ensign — a flag or banner used to represent a nation, organization, or individual of power (king, president, pontiff, etc.)

icon — an image, traditionally flat as opposed to three-dimensional, used especially, but not exclusively, in reference to religious symbolism.

iconography — a collection of icons, symbols, signs, etc., which are associated with a given context. We can speak of the "iconography of the 4th of July," or of "Episcopal iconography," which is a division of "religious iconography," or of "Blue Lodge iconography," "Scottish Rite iconography," or "York Rite iconography," which are subsets of "Masonic iconography," etc.

insigne (plural, **insignia**) — a symbol or image used as a badge of identification.

logo (**logotype**) — originally, a cast metal slug, used in printing, which imprinted a design used to identify a business or store. Now the design itself.

MSA logo

Insigne

referent—the real-world object or idea represented by a symbol

semiotics/semiology — the study of signs (symbols, etc.) and how they convey meaning.

sign—an image, action, etc., which operates at a simple level and requires only limited knowledge to communicate (e.g. waving someone through an intersection). Compare with signal.

signal— a symbol operating at the most basic level, working by instinct and not requiring knowledge on the part of the observer (e.g. a deer signaling danger by flashing its white tail).

symbol — in the broadest sense, anything which triggers a meaning or makes us think of something else almost every time we encounter the symbol.

symbolism — the use of a sign or symbol to communicate a message

symbology—the study of symbols or signs in their various manifestations.

symptom— the image of a thing which accompanies a second thing and is regarded as evidence of the second thing's presence (e.g. a flashing red light accompanies dangerous situations and is considered a warning that a dangerous situation is present).

signet — a seal, usually carved into a ring and impressed into sealing wax, hence, by extension, a mark used for the identification of property, etc., (now sometimes seen in tattoos).

trophy—generally, any symbol or image which represents victory, either over an adversary or in some event of skill or ability. In religious iconography, an image which represents victory over death and the grave.

type—an image which is seen as representing the best or finest example of the thing symbolized

---

First published by the Masonic Lodge Education Committee of the Grand Lodge of Oklahoma, 2007

On Third Thought

"'Just the place for a Snark!' the Bellman cried,
As he landed his crew with care;
Supporting each man on the top of the tide
By a finger entwined in his hair.

"'Just the place for a Snark! I have said it twice;
That alone should encourage the crew.
Just the place for a Snark! I have said it thrice;
What I tell you three times is true.'"

It may be that some of you have not read "The Hunting of the Snark" by Lewis Carroll. If you have not, let me encourage it. You can down-load the entire poem from the Internet. It is less well known that his *Alice in Wonderland*, or *Through the Looking Glass*, (and if you have not read those recently, let me encourage that as well—the man had an amazing mind and was a superb example of the intellectual and cultural basis which gave Freemasonry its present form and ritual). It is non-sense, in a way, of course, but Carroll loved playing with symbols and he lets himself run riot in the poem, all the while making it appear little more than a child's entertainment. (Further side note: it is, we are told, perfectly safe to hunt Snarks, unless it turns out that the Snark you are hunting is a boojun. In that case, it is very dangerous and may kill you. This has led to a habit, among several of my friends, when some day or some project has proven remarkably difficult, of observing, "My Snark was a Boojun.")

But I regress.

I have long been fascinated by the ways in which the number three appears in culture. I don't need to recount its use in Masonry, of course, but it is worthwhile looking at some of its other manifestations.

Both three and nine (three times three) appear often in both folk expressions and literary expressions of magic. "Third time's the charm." "Bad (or good) things come in threes." Or Macbeth: "When shall we three meet again? In thunder, lightning, or in rain? [three elements] When the hurly-burly's done, when the battle's lost and won. That will be ere set of sun." [another three elements] "Thrice to mine, and thrice to thine, and thrice again to make up nine. Peace, the charm's wound up." "Thrice the brindled cat hath mewed."

It is a generally-agreed principle of logical thinking that one occurrence of something may be accident, two occurrences may be coincidence, but three occurrences is a pattern.

We are encouraged that "If at first you don't succeed, try, try again." Hansel and Gretel return from the first two attempts of their parents to lose them in the forest, the adventure begins on the third trip; the third little pig's house is proof against the wolf; the maiden has three chances to guess Rumpelstiltskin's name; Goldilocks encounters three bears; most full-length plays are divided into three acts; the three note chord is a basic component of western music; language is divided into the three primary tenses of past, present, and future.

In religion there are the three persons of the Christian trinity, and the three individual letters which form the tetragrammaton. Among the Norse there were Odin, Frea, and Thor. The Aryan trinity was composed of Agni, Indra, and Vishnu. In Hinduism we find the trinity of

Brahma, Vishnu, and Shiva, and in the religion taught by Zoroaster there are Ahura Mazda, Spenta Mainyu and Vohumano. There are many other examples.

In an allusion to Carroll's poem, Robert Heinlein's hero, Lazarus Long, when talking to his intelligent space ship, uses the coded phrase, "I tell you three times," to indicate that an order is valid. (On the other hand, Brother Porter, whose expertise as a criminal investigator gives credence to his words, tells me that when someone says something three times during an interrogation, they are almost always lying.)

It is true, of course, that one could pick almost any number and find literary references and folk references to it is well; but the number three seems to have a special resonance for us. A creative writing teacher told me many years ago that research had shown readers were less satisfied with adventure stories in which the hero triumphed after only one or two trials. Three seemed to be the best, with four leaving many readers feeling that the story was dragging. The great American mid-century poet John Ciardi, remarked that alliteration worked better in groups of three words than in any other number.

A witness swears to tell the truth, the whole truth, and nothing but the truth. (Albeit the cynic in me observes that most witnesses are not permitted to tell the whole truth, but only so much of it as the questioner wants to hear.)

Freud divides the psyche into the Id, the Ego, and the Super-ego, and Johann Fichte suggests that the development of thought takes place as thesis, antitheses and synthesis.

Perhaps it is merely true, as another of my professors remarked, that we simply "feel more comfortable" with three than with any other number. But I think that somehow, deeply in us, there is a sense that three is a completion. It truly does seen to represent some sort of equilibrium, some reestablishment of order and balance in our thinking. And, if nothing else, it is interesting to contemplate our thinking in threes.

Prepared as a handout for the Beyond the Ritual discussion group.

A Short Ramble Through Freemasonry And Communication Theory
or
Stop Me Before I Introduce Again
4 Basic Principles of Communication for Masonic Leaders

In some ways, Communication Theorists are not very good communicators. We tend to try to pack too much into too little space. It's efficient in its own way, but it does sometimes mean we have to explain the explanation.

Some of the principles below are like that, but their compact nature lets you apply them to several situations which a different phrasing would make difficult.

PRINCIPLE #1
Person "A" has status in the eyes of Person "B" to the extent that "B" perceives "A" to represent "B's" goals.

That mouthful says several things that are important for Masons communicating with non-Masons. I think of you as a status figure to the extent that I see you as being what I want to be, or having what I want to have.

A few examples.

PERCEPTION: I think you have a lot of money.
GOAL: I want a lot of money.
RESULT: You are a high status figure for me.

PERCEPTION: I think you have a lot of money.
GOAL: I don't really care that much about money.
RESULT: That fact will not make you a high status figure for me.

PERCEPTION: I see you as a leader of men.
GOAL: I want to be a leader (or I admire leadership).
RESULT: You are a status figure for me.

PERCEPTION: You are a great football player.
GOAL: I have no interest in football.
RESULT: You are not a status figure for me.
Obvious, isn't it?

Now consider this opening from a news release:
> **Most Worshipful Isa Blowhard, the Most Worshipful Grand Master of the Most Worshipful Grand Lodge of Ancient Free and Accepted Masons of the State of Confusion, will place a cornerstone with full Masonic Ritual at the new State Home for the Bewildered next Sunday.**

The obvious hope (and what a hope it is!) is that the non-Masonic public will be impressed with the grandeur and glory of the man and the Fraternity.

QUESTIONS:

- Does the non-Masonic public know what a Grand Master is?
- Does the non-Masonic public want to be a Grand Master?
- Is it likely that the non-Masonic public will think Brother Blowhard represents its goals?
- Is that public likely to draw a distinction between Most Worshipful Grand Master, Grand Dragon, and Lord High Pooh-bah?
- Is anyone surprised if the newspaper decides to run a filler on the rabbit problem in Australia instead of the cornerstone story?

ANOTHER EXAMPLE:

You are having a Friend's Night. Several non-Masons and their wives are there. The program, of course, starts with introductions.

Master of Ceremonies: *"There are a few people I would like to introduce before we get started.* {By the way, shouldn't it tell us something that we think of introductions as something to do "before we get started?"} *First of all, we are honored to have with us tonight M∴ W∴ Willy Guidewell, M∴ W∴ Grand Master of the M∴ W∴ Grand Lodge. Then there's M∴ W∴ — oh, no. I'm sorry, Right Worshipful, I should have said* **Right** *Worshipful Titus Canby, R∴ W∴ Grand Treasurer of the M∴ W∴ Grand Lodge...........and, of course, Illustrious Brother D. Eagles, Thirty-Third Degree, Sovereign Grand Inspector General..... Past Watchman* *of the Shepherds ....Past Grand Electa...*(that soft, background sound is the non-Masonic guests, catching a few winks)*......and Brother Earnest Goodfellow who once seriously considered running for a Grand Lodge office........now is there any Dignitary here I have not introduced?"*

SO HOW CAN YOU USE Principle 1?

To make Masonry relevant, to give it the proper status in the eyes of the non-Mason, decide what the goals of the non-Mason probably are, then show how Masonry represents or furthers those goals.

Let's list a few of those goals. Your own knowledge will show you how the various programs, charities, and activities of Masonry fit. **Then, structure your messages so that they show how Masonry dovetails with the goals of the audience.**

They probably want:
- Security
- To live in a good, caring community
- Recognition of their own worth as people
- To feel that they are accomplishing something
- To know that social problems are being addressed
- To help those less fortunate
- A better world for their children
- Security for their spouses
- To feel good about themselves and their own talents and abilities
- To associate with people of good standing in the community
- To be wanted and appreciated

PRINCIPLE #2
Meanings are in PEOPLE, not in WORDS.

That's another obvious one, and one we overlook. Words are symbols. The meaning of any symbol is in the mind of the symbol-user, not in the symbol itself. When we learn a meaning for a word, we develop a whole set of reactions and feelings as well as a "dictionary meaning" for a term.

That's important for this reason: **JUST BECAUSE A WORD IS CLEAR, SIMPLE, AND STRAIGHT-FORWARD *TO YOU* DOESN'T MEAN IT'S CLEAR, SIMPLE OR STRAIGHT-FORWARD TO YOUR READER OR LISTENER.**

If we're going to communicate clearly about Freemasonry, we must use the meanings our audience is most likely to have.

WORD	Masonic Audience Would Think	Non-Masons Might Think
Esoteric. . . .	not written down. . .	witchcraft? new age?
Monitorial. .	written in the Monitor.	something to do with the Civil War Battle-ship?
Profane.	not a Mason.	dirty, sacrilegious,
Worshipful. .	honored.	to be worshiped like a god.

EXERCISE: Translate the following sentence as a non-Mason might. ***The Worshipful Master says we should not talk about the esoteric work in the presence of the profane.***

PRINCIPLE #3
A communication includes *all* messages, verbal, non-verbal, visual and auditory sent at any one time, plus

all the thoughts, ideas, and associations aroused in the mind of the receiver

There really is no such thing as a simple message. All messages are extremely complex, because so much more than words are involved.

Communications contain thousands of clues, and each clue changes the meaning slightly.

Let's take a fairly straightforward example first.

"I believe you." Three simple words. You can say them in such a way that it is a reassurance to the listener. But you can also say them with sarcasm, making it clear that you don't believe the person at all. Or you can say them suggesting doubt and uncertainty, as if you were really saying, "I'd like to believe you, but I wish you'd convince me a little more."

If those words can be so changed just by a tone of voice, think what can modify the meaning of a longer, more complex message.

To communicate effectively, you have to consider as many of the "hidden" messages as possible.

SUPPOSE YOU ARE PREPARING A WRITTEN COMMUNICATION, a pamphlet or flyer about Masonry, for example. Here are some things you must take into account *in addition to the words you choose and their meanings.*

- ✔the quality of the paper and its "feel" in the hand
- ✔the look of the paper, whether it is glossy or matte in finish
- ✔the color of the paper
- ✔the color of the ink

✔the size and style of the type [research tells us that serif type (type with little lines added, like that on the bottom of the "P") is easier for persons over 50 to read than sans-serif type like this].
✔the contrast between paper color and type color
✔the margins
✔the illustrations, the size of blocks of type, the emotional content of pictures

SUPPOSE YOU ARE PREPARING A DVD. In addition to the words, you must consider:

✔the "image" of the narrator. Does he look as if he conforms to their values and would be a status figure for them?

✔his speech pattern. Is it likely to be offensive to your viewers?

✔the locations shown. Do they re-enforce the message or interfere with it?

✔Does it look professional, or like the loving hands of home?

✔is there "visual junk" in the way of the message?

One otherwise good Masonic video suffered from these problems:

    There were loose threads around the buttonhole of the speaker's suite

    Beside the Master, one could see half of a covered Eastern Star signet. A non-Masonic audience would be bound to wonder what it was

    A slightly crooked picture of Washington was on the wall.

These things draw audience attention away from the message.

SUPPOSE YOU ARE DOING A 'FRIENDS NIGHT' AND INVITING NON-MASONS INTO THE LODGE BUILDING

✔ What does the building say about Masonry?
- Is the building very, very clean?
- Are there stained ceiling tiles?
- Are the walls clean and well painted?
- Does the building smell?
- Does the plumbing work?
- Are there torn or worn places in the floor covering?
- If there is food, is it ample, tasty, hot?

(Those who do Friends Nights serving dried-out beef, watery mashed potatoes, canned gravy and salad of discouraged lettuce will receive exactly the amount of success they deserve.)

✔ Has someone been dispatched to see to it that Brother Alonso Grump (who treats non-Masons in the Temple as if they were carriers of some loathsome disease) is out fishing that night?

PRINCIPLE #4

Never forget that successful communication starts with an analysis of the intended audience.

You would not address an audience of 40 year old men and women by breezing into the room and saying, *Good morning, boys and girls. Isn't it a pretty day today!* Always know the audience you want to reach. You should know something about their educational level, their income groups, their values and goals.

Be sensitive to any special considerations with your audience. As Brother Mark Twain remarked, "It is indelicate to mention rope in the house of someone who has recently been hanged." Do not violate the cultural or social conventions. **In that context, remember the Korean clothing manufacturer who decided to introduce his line of men's underwear (which had proven very popular in Korea) into the United States. He had the name translated into English and started marketing "Little Pansy men's underwear." Sales did not meet his expectations.**

Preaching to the choir is fine, if you only want to talk to the choir. Putting together a communication without knowing and analyzing your audience is exactly like trying to make clothing for someone without knowing what size they are. You might, just by accident, get it right. But the odds are against you.

THY OCEAN IS SO GREAT, AND MY BOAT IS SO SMALL!

Masonic communication may be more difficult than most. We operate under strictures of ethics which do not concern many others. We also often operate with the necessity of making sure that the right egos are petted, the Venerable Guard (ever ready to criticize anything that differs from their youth--circa 1723) is appeased, and the Appendant and Affiliated Bodies made properly content. May everyone have the luck we have in Oklahoma, where those problems seldom arise!

But even with the best going for us, it is a difficult task. Masonry has become somewhat remote from the experiences of a typical non-Masonic audience. Finding ways to communicate effectively with that audience is not easy, but it is possible.

Just remember this: we must communicate with people "where they are," not where we wish they were. We have to find ways to speak their language.

Masonic language is fine and highly desirable among Masons. It is a foreign tongue to the non-Mason.

GUARANTEED STEPS TO FAILURE
IN COMMUNICATIONS

1) Pass over your newest Master Mason, who also happens to be your best communicator, in favor of Brother Codger because he is a Grand Lodge Officer, a Past Grand Master, or the "grand old man of Masonry" in your state.

2) Load as much Masonic jargon as possible into every sentence. If the audience doesn't understand, they should pay better attention!

3) ALWAYS hold meetings with the public in the Lodge Room. No worse structure for communication can be created than having people sitting down both sides of a room so that, to look at half the audience you must turn your back on the other half.

4) Answer every question with "I can't talk about that, it's secret."

5) In writing news releases or newspaper stories, be sure to put all the Masonic titles into the first sentence. That way if they print it, they may not cut the Masonic titles. And we all know that they are far more important. Start the actual story about paragraph seven.

But you knew that one.

Prepared for a Lodge Leadership Seminar held by the Grand Lodge of Oklahoma

Multiplex Masonry

In Oklahoma, where I live, move, and have my being, we take chili and barbeque seriously--not as seriously as football (which has the status of religion), but seriously. Life-long friendships have been terminated over the question of whether chili should contain beans. In Texas, which takes these things even more seriously, there are reputed to be counties in which it is a hanging offense to barbeque with hickory rather than mesquite.

No one seems to be willing to say, "Some people like chili with beans, some do not, and that's fine." Or, "Barbeque according to the inclinations of your own heart."

I'm reminded of that when I contemplate the various "schools" of Masonic thought. Louis XVI would not have been more haughty toward and contemptuous of a pox-ridden peasant than some adherents of one school are of another.

But Masonry is multiplex. One of the things we most often hear is that a man will find in Masonry what he chooses to seek. That is, perhaps, the greatest strength of the organization. It has many facets; it is not a single path but an interlocking series, rather like a circuit board.

It may be helpful, especially for the new Mason, to review these schools, with their various approaches to the study of Masonry. No value judgements are intended in what follows, and those which may appear are unconscious. The whole point of the article is that a school of thought or study is valid for those who follow it. Each Mason has the absolute right to follow the one(s) he wishes or to create a new one for himself. And no one has the right to sneer, to carp, to criticize, or to hold him up to ridicule for his choice.

The Authentic School - sometimes called the historic or scientific school—is recent, being about 100 years old. The purpose of this approach to the study of Masonry is to separate historic fact from legend and myth. Using the tools of the historian, Masons of this school attempt to create as accurate and unbiased a picture as possible of the actual events in Masonry's past. Generally, students of this school are not interested in the meanings of the symbols of Masonry, but concentrate on that which can be proven and documented. It could fairly be described as a "hard-edged" approach to Masonry.

The Textual Criticism School - Textual criticism is the study of printed material. Masons of this school are generally most interested in the ritual and its evolution. They deal with such questions as, "When did changes come into the ritual? Who introduced the changes? Did the changes spread, or did they remain localized?" Given that what little has been written down appears to have been written after it was already in use by word of mouth, their job is especially difficult. To illustrate this approach, one student of this school is trying to discover if a common phrase in the Blue Lodge ritual, usually thought of as "rights, lights, and benefits," was intended to be "*rites*, lights, and benefits."

The Anthropological School - If the focus of the Authentic School is history, the focus of the Anthropological School is man, and his long path of spiritual and intellectual development. If the Authentic School regards myth as detritus to be swept away, the Anthropological School regards myth as a primary source of information about humanity and human culture. Masons of this school frequently speak of the "ancient origins of Masonry." This is not intended to suggest that Adam, upon becoming aware of his nakedness, rapped a gavel and said "Brethren, be clothed," nor that King Solomon was, in fact, a Grand Master of a Grand Lodge. Rather it suggests that many of the symbols and great themes of Masonry can also be found in the most ancient myths and spiritual expressions. "What," a student of this school would ask, "does this tell us about humanity? Does it reflect some fundamental truth about mankind? Does it speak of some profound intellectual or spiritual need or awareness which is common to all people?" When a Mason of this school speaks of the relationships between Masonry and the ancient Mysteries, he usually is not trying to suggest that they were handed down in an unbroken line, but that similar ideas or images can be found. Masons of this school are usually involved with the symbols of Masonry and their meanings. For them, the symbols, like myths, are markers on the map of self-development.

The Mystical School - I wish I had a different word to use here, simply because "mystical" has developed a bad reputation it doesn't deserve. Throughout the recorded history of thought, "mystical" has referred to a search for a sense of union with the Deity—not the sort of "lunatic fringe" association some people give the word today. The follower of this school usually works very hard to avoid cynicism and skepticism. His attitude is characterized by the words of one of my professors—"I would be deeply disappointed if any of you expected to see an elf when walking in the woods, and just as deeply disappointed if you were surprised when you saw one." He seeks self-development and enlightenment, and usually seeks it through his faith as well as his fraternity. He has a strong sense of the sacred, and is moved to the contemplation of God by such things as a beautiful sunset or a powerful work of art. By contemplating the rituals, the symbols and the teachings of Masonry, he is led to a sense of closeness to his Creator and a sense of the unity of all creation.

The Aesthetics School - This school focuses primarily on the products of Masonry, both written and tangible. Thousands of artifacts have been produced over the years; from vast buildings, to pocket watches, to firing glasses, to painted aprons, to carved furniture, to commemorative china, to jewelry, to costumes, to plays, short stories, songs, operas, and instrumental and choral works. Masons interested in this school include collectors, those who study the influence of Masonry on the popular culture of the day, those who try to understand how the teachings of the fraternity are reflected in what it produces, and those interested in the ways in which Masonic design differs from the designs and motifs of other organizations.

The Rhapsodial School - *Rhapsodes* were men in ancient Greece who specialized in memorizing and reciting the great epic poems. They placed a special emphasis on accuracy of memory, and transmitted the great stories down from generation to generation until they were finally committed to writing. Masons of the Rhapsodial school function in the same great tradition. Their pleasure is to learn the ritual, perform it, and teach it to others.

The Fraternal School - Masons of this approach find their greatest satisfaction simply in being Masons. They enjoy being together, as Brothers, and require little else. They are especially concerned, perhaps, with the obligations of Masonry and many of them are the most committed to charity. But, more than esoteric conundrums, they want the good feelings which come from association of good, like-minded men. And power be unto them!

As I said at the beginning, Masonry is multiplex. There are other approaches, other "schools," and each person is entitled to choose or create as they please. Surely we are obligated to be as tolerant of each other's search in Masonry as we are of each other's religious faith. Surely the fact of the quest is more important than the path.

Chili can be enjoyed with or without beans. And I even know good men who prefer pecan wood to either hickory or mesquite for barbeque.

"Multiplex Masonry" appeared in *The Scottish Rite Journal* of September, 1999

Great Aunt Effie and Moses

She was, physically, a very small woman. Her name was Effie Thompson. She had been married in her teens, in 1896, was widowed before her 21st birthday, and lived the rest of her life with her sister, my grandmother and my grandfather.

She had a very good mind, although both she and my grandmother left school in the 3rd grade. More accurately, I suppose, school left them. Education in the Oklahoma Territory in the last half of the 1800's was a chancy thing, and most schools did not extend past the third grade. Of course, by the time she left the third grade, she had like the other students, learned to read and write (in a beautiful hand) to add, subtract, multiply, and divide, to name the existing states and their capital cities, to quote from memory the first passages to the United States Declaration of Independence and the Constitution, as well as long passages of Milton's *Paradise Lost,* Shakespeare's *King Lear,* Bunyan's *Pilgrim's Progress,* and to do basic accounting as well.

I adored her. Like all the other members of my extended family, she spent long hours reading to me when I was an infant, and even after I had learned to read for myself. There was only one little hitch, and it didn't really bother me. The third grade education had taught her many things, but it had left her vocabulary a little weak, and she sometimes came upon words she didn't know and couldn't pronounce. That slowed her down not a bit. When she came to a word she didn't know, she'd simply say "Moses," instead, and go right on. I can remember, when she was reading Kipling to me, that Moses showed up in India a lot, but it really didn't matter. She read with love, and with feeling, and with a delight in the words, even those she didn't know.

She had, as well, a profound respect for words, and for the right word. I recall once, when on a hot day I remarked that I saw some sweat on her face, she sternly rebuked me, saying "Remember, Jim, animals sweat, men perspire, ladies feel the heat."

With all of that, there was a sense of the flow of the words, of the way they linked. I think, perhaps, it came from memorizing the great poets in her youth, as well as from the old revival hymns with which she used to sing me to sleep. In truth, to this good day, in the drifting stage between sleep and wakefulness, I sometimes hear her voice singing "Will There Be Any Stars in My Crown?" or "When the Roll Is Called Up Yonder."

One of the very few regrets of my life is that she did not live long enough (she died when I was 19) for me to see her do the ritual work of the Eastern Star. Both she and my grandmother were very active in the Star, and Grandmother had that same "feeling" for words as Effie. I'll bet it was an awesome experience to hear.

That, probably, is what set me on the closest thing to a crusade I have—to see ritual well done. Among some people, I have a reputation for not liking the ritual of either the Blue Lodge or the Scottish Rite, and nothing could be farther from the truth. I love the ritual, I strongly believe that it is what make us Masons, and that to take the ritual out of Freemasonry would be worse than neutering it. It would be to tear the heart out of Masonry as viciously as ever the heart was ripped from the chest of a living victim on an Aztec altar. It is powerful, life-changing, spirit moving—but only if it is done well.

And done well is not the same thing as done accurately.

I overheard a couple of Brethren talking after a Degree the other day. They had also talked all through the Degree, but that's a different gripe. One said, "It was a very good Degree; I only counted five mistakes."

It wasn't a good Degree, although it may have been an accurate one. The words were delivered in a series of flat monotones. No meanings were given to the lines at all. It was like listening to music played on an old player piano, same tempo, same volume level, same inflection, no matter what the sentence. Mechanically perfect Perfectly mechanical. Rushed through far too quickly, as if the Brother had to get it out at top speed before he forgot it No wonder the eyes of all in the room glazed over almost at once, the Candidate's included. "It was a very good Degree" but no one listened to it. (The operation was a success, but the patient died.)

It's important, of course, to get the words right, whether you are doing the Fellowcraft Degree or *Romeo and Juliet*. But learning the script is the beginning of the process, not the end.

And so a plea to the Brethren who do the ritual work of Masonry. You are the most important people we have, doing the most important work we have to do. Please remember, it's fine to worry about accuracy when practicing, not when you are doing the Degree. Then, the only thing that matters is the Candidate. The Degree has to work for him, involve him, move him—not the Custodian of the Work, or the Director of the Work, or anyone else. Give it energy and strength and purpose. Look for the meaning of each sentence and make sure it flies into the mind like an arrow to the target. You will be giving him the greatest gift a man can give to another.

And if, every now and again, you forget a word and have to say "Moses," no one who matters will mind.

"Great Aunt Effie and Moses" was published in *The Scottish Rite Journal* of May, 2003

The Old Dog Barks Backward

**"The old dog barks backward
without getting up.
I can remember when
he was a pup."
Robert Frost**

It's easy for those of us who have gotten a little long in the tooth in Masonry to sympathize with the old dog in Frost's poem. There you are, living in a small town, with so little traffic that you can sleep in the street, and, if something needs to be barked at, you can do it over your shoulder without really disturbing your comfort.

Then, without warning, an oil boom hits. There's a lot of traffic, and the drivers don't even see you, let alone understand that the street's your favorite napping spot. Not only that, but there are lots of new, young dogs in town, and they want to *do* things; chase rabbits, tree cats, and generally run around and explore things. What's more, they want you to help show them where the best rabbits and squirrels are to be found.

All of a sudden, we old dogs are not only being asked to learn new tricks, we're being asked to teach them to others.

But that's the reality of Freemasonry in the United States today. It's great news, because it means survival, and not only survival but growth and expansion. Across the United States, Lodges are seeing a growing interest in the Fraternity. Not only is Masonry appearing in more serious scholarly books (for example, Margaret Jacob's *Living the Enlightenment*), but in special after special on the History Channel, the Discovery Channel, and in popular literature and films. It is as if the world were discovering Freemasonry for the first time.

This increased interest is resulting in increased numbers of petitions for the Degrees, and the Candidates who averaged 45 years of age just a few years ago are now averaging in the upper 20's. It is a vast change and challenge for the fraternity. It is a special challenge for us older dogs. For these younger dogs are a whole new breed in many ways.

First of all, most of them know a lot about Freemasonry before they petition. We didn't. If we knew anything, it was that our father or grandfather or someone we liked was a member, and if they thought it was good, it probably was.

Most of our young members do not have fathers or grandfathers who were Masons. But they have checked us out throughly on the Internet. The day this was written, I did a Google search on the word "Freemasonry." The computer came up with more than 2,200,000 different sites. They have read a lot, both good and bad. Some have even watched the Degrees on the Internet. They have made a more informed choice to join the Fraternity than we *could* have made.

But they come with questions, and they expect answers. And it is our fraternal responsibility to find the answers.

The Grand Lodge recently surveyed new Master Masons who were 40 years of age or younger. The results are interesting. Overwhelmingly, they believe in the traditional Masonic values. Strongly. The majority want to learn and participate in the ritual. A majority are willing to be officers in the Lodge.

Eighty percent have education past high school, with about 50% having one or more college degrees. About 3 out of 4 are looking for spiritual growth and/or intellectual stimulation. And they expect the older Masons to be their mentors and guides. Here are some of the things they told us on the survey form:

♦It's frustrating not having men that will teach me what I need to know. Not many Lodges seem to want to teach.

♦I would enjoy most to have a night once or twice a month, when Lodge is opened to have open discussions about Masonry (e.g. history of Masonry). Everybody has something they can add.

♦No one will tell me where I can get more information.

We old dogs in Masonry are going to have to stretch the back, get on our feet, and start helping the young ones get what they are searching for. We don't have to know the answers—they are happy to accept "I don't know, but I'll help you find out." But we do have to be willing to help them look. There are lots of resources.

It takes us a bit out of our comfort zone; we have to do less barking and more leading. But if we are willing to share in their excitement and sense of discovery, we may find it makes us younger to run with the pack. And, after all, the ritual promises them that we will be as willing to teach as they are to learn.

From the Oklahoma Masonic Lodge Education Committee Newsletter
July, 2007

Family

"Blood is thicker than water," one of my friends of the Scottish Rite Bodies remarked a few days ago, "but mortar is thicker than blood."

"That's true," another friend observed, "but I'd be careful where I said it."

In many ways, it *is* true. One reason, I think, that Masons support family values so strongly, almost ferociously, is that we are members of an extended family, and it is a very close one. I've lost track of the times Masons have told me that they are closer to their Masonic Brethren than to their biological brothers. (I'm lucky. My brothers are also Brethren.) I could not honestly say that my Masonic family was closer than my "real" family—my real family is very close—but the ties to my Brethren are every bit as strong.

A couple of years ago, I wrote about the support from my Masonic Brethren when I had to have a knee replaced. About a week after the surgery, the Scottish Rite Bodies of Guthrie, Oklahoma, had a Reunion, and I had to act in two of the Degrees. Nearly 300 of us live in the Temple during a Reunion, and I literally could not dress myself, much less make a costume change. It is an humbling experience when two of your Brethren have to help you dress, but if they had not been Brethren it would have been humiliating, not just humbling.

That's merely an example. The point is that Jimmy and Greg and Tim and John and Clay and Bob and Max and George and Joe and Bill and the others are more than just friends. They are family. We often have keys to each other's homes and vehicles. We call each other, sometimes in the small watches of the night, because we need to hear a friendly voice or just to unload some of the day's "junk" we don't want to impose on family members. As one of the guys, a member of AA, said, "Ten minutes on the phone with a friend beats a stiff drink any day, and I should know."

There are no "invidious distinctions." Nothing but our common bond in Masonry matters. One is a Past Grand Master and a 33°, some have black caps, some red, some white. Some are professional men, some are laborers. We aren't even conscious of those distinctions.

(Not that your Masonic family will cut you much slack, at least in some matters. When the Supreme Council awarded me the Grand Cross, easily the highest honor I will ever receive, the guys pointed out to me that it was a triumph of charity over justice, and sympathy for the mentally handicapped over merit. Clearly, helping me dress is only one way they have of keeping me humble. But they also bought me a white cap box and put a blue "racing stripe" on it to make it into a Grand Cross cap box.)

Unconditional trust—that is so very rare in the world, and it is what my Masonic friends and I share. We share an absolute, unshakable certainty that none of the others could or would deliberately do anything to our disadvantage. In many cases, we are in each other's wills as guardians of children or administrators of estates. Being with each other is a recharging experience. No matter how bad things get "outside," we can always make each other feel better "inside" our shared fraternal bonds.

Does that make us a family, and all of Masonry an extended family? I think it does.

We speak of Family Values—of honesty, love, respect and self-respect, a willingness to see others do better than ourselves, an eagerness to see them successful and happy, a set of shared memories of both happy and sad events. Psychologists tell of the instant bonding when the father is present at the birth of his child. Sociologists tell us how the family is strengthened as they face both trials and triumphs together. Family therapists tell us that a sure sign of a healthy family is a desire to share what they have with others. And what father has not felt closer to his son when, perhaps late at night, the son finds him and shares with him some painful or joyful experience of the day?

But that is Masonry! We teach honesty and love and respect and self-respect and a willingness to see others advance further than ourselves, not just as abstract values but as the ways Masons are to feel about each other. We share both happy and sad memories. If being present when a friend is raised to the Degree of Master Mason is not quite literally being there at his birth, it is very nearly the same thing. We face trials and triumphs together. We are taught to share both our time and our resources with others. And many of us have been privileged, under the promise of the confidentiality of the obligations, to have our Brothers share their secret hopes and their deepest fears and disappointments.

It is surprisingly difficult to write about this family aspect of Masonry. The words seem cold and far from the glowing emotions I want to describe. It may take a composer or a painter to capture this feeling, this tie—fragile as the worn leather binding of a treasured book, tough as the steel prow of an ice-breaker—which binds the Masonic family.

But as we think about the family and the role and importance of family values, it is good to remember that Masonry does not just support and celebrate the family; Masonry *is* family.

And we are, truly, Brothers.

"Family" was first published in *The Scottish Rite Journal* for November, 1998

A Little Sand in The Gears

"Remember, Son, *dying* organizations love rules. Groups that are living and vital and growing don't have time to make rules, they're too busy doing things. That's my greatest fear for Masonry."

My father, Jack N. Tresner, Sr., 33°, loved Masonry with a passion and was especially active in the Scottish Rite. He was, among other things, Chairman of the Advisory Conference, Wise Master of Rose Croix, and Director of the 33° Conferral Team where he took the role of Grand Commander. The welfare of Masonry was much on his mind in his final days. He had been very active in business as the president of an insurance company and in the church where he served on the International Board of Church Extension of the Christian Church, but his family and Masonry were his two great loves.

Not long before his death, we had the last of many conversations about Masonry. He was deeply worried about the future of the fraternity. He had watched it decline from the most active, energetic, positive organization in the community, attracting so many good men each year that it was difficult to find time to perform the Degrees, to an organization which, each year, lost so many men that it had only half its former membership. I had learned long ago that he was a man of extraordinary insight and wisdom, and I listened carefully to what he had to say.

"Why does that happen?" I asked.

"Dying organizations turn inward," he said. "When I joined Masonry, our rules, our Constitution and Code, filled a little booklet, about 3" X 5" and about 20 pages long. Now the pages are 8 ½" X 11" and they fill a three-ring binder. And there are so many new rules each year that it *takes* a three-ring binder to keep current. Other states are the same way.

"When I joined Masonry in 1941, I was really impressed by how the leadership kept finding new things for Masons to do. I watched that change."

"Why," I asked, "what happened?"

"Old men:' he answered. "I don't mean age. Some men are old and crotchety at 20, some are young and vital at 80. You want to watch that, by the way. You can tend a little to the crotchety side yourself if you're not careful. But the fraternity fell into the hands of these old men, of whatever age. All they wanted to do was control others—tell others what they had to do and what they could not do. There's something they didn't like, so they made another rule. They're the moss-backs, like the old turtles that hide under the logs in the stream and snap at everything that goes by. I've spent the last 20 years trying to scrape a little moss and carry a little sand."

That last allusion escaped me.

"That was one of your grandfather's expressions. When an organization, any organization, is alive and vital, its leaders judge their success by how much gets done. When an organization is dying, they judge their success by how smoothly things go. I actually heard the Worshipful Master of our Lodge say that he had a good year-*nothing happened."*

"Jim, the only smooth ride in the world is the ride down when you fall off a cliff. It's as smooth and easy as anyone could want, until you get to the bottom. Then it's fatal. It's natural for leaders to want a smooth ride—and the. cruelest thing you can do is to give it to them. Every now and then, you need to sprinkle a little sand in the gears. I know you always wondered why I appointed"—he named an individual—"to the company Board of Directors."

"I certainly have wondered!" I said. "He does nothing but challenge you."

"That's why. I don't dare let the ride get too smooth, even for me. He is my sandman. I've tried to do the same thing for Masonry. But I can't do it any longer. If you love Masonry as much as I think you do, you've got to sprinkle the sand, now.

"You don't have to cause problems, I don't mean that. Sometimes the most effective sand you can use is just to ask *Why?* Why do we have that rule? Why do we do something? Why does it have to be that way? We promise to whisper good counsel in the ear of an erring Brother—why do we try to find a way to throw him out of the fraternity? We say that Masonry has some of the greatest lessons the world has ever known—why don't our people even take the trouble to learn the *meanings* of the words of the ritual so they know what those lessons really are? We say that Masonry is important—why won't we set the dues high enough to really support the Lodge and its activities?

"I'm not asking for a promise, because there's a price. The mossbacks won't love you. You won't win any popularity contests. But maybe Masonry will wake up and decide to live again."

And, even though he did not ask for a promise, I promised.

All this went through my mind again during the recent Scottish Rite Leadership Conferences. I listened to many younger Scottish Rite Masons, especially the Scottish Rite Fellows, talk about changes; some fair amount of sand was tossed around. Some of the ideas bothered me a little. (Dad was right, I do tend toward the crotchety.) But that's all right. They were thinking; they raised questions and addressed issues; they challenged us. God bless them all!

One of the suggestions was that the *Scottish Rite Journal* publish some controversial articles; articles which raise issues and eyebrows. And the leadership agreed! Not only is this article being published, but you will find the first essay in a series titled *"Essays from the Edge"* on page 37. It is almost certain that there will be articles in this series which will annoy me, and possibly you. But (not indulging in the temptation to point out it is only the irritated oyster which produces a pearl) that annoyance is good for us. Brethren whose articles appear in the series *"Essays from the Edge"* do a service by making us think, by sprinkling a little sand in our mental gears.

The fall off the cliff, while smooth, really isn't comfortable. And a few bumps on the way are a lot better than that sudden stop.

"A Little Sand in the Gears" was published in *The Scottish Rite Journal* for July, 1998

"Fan My Brow And Call Me Moses!"

I'm watching the death with sadness.

Certain phrases which I used to hear often in my youth have all but disappeared, used now only by the elderly. I suspect they always were regional, indigenous to the South and to the West; and to that strange and rich combination of South and West which is Oklahoma.

Today, their substitutes usually involve vulgarity or profanity, but these folk expressions were attempts to avoid those two extremes. Most of them were. expressions of surprise or amazement such as "I do declare!" "Rain and snow in Beulah Land!" "My sainted aunt!" "I'll be hornswoggled!" (meaning bamboozled, tricked). "Well I swan!" ("swan" being a substitute for "swear," something the user would never do). "I swan to Josephus!" "Great day in the morning!" "Well crown me with glory!" "Heavens above!" And my personal favorite, "Well fan my brow and call me Moses!" There is no doubt these phrases fall strangely on the modern ear. But they have a richness and texture I miss.

As Masons, we are the inheritors of some astonishingly beautiful language. It was crafted, rather than written, at a time when the sound of a phrase was considered as important as the information it communicated. It is important not to lose sight of that beauty. Listening to the words of the ritual, delivered by someone who understands what he is saying and is willing to let the words sing, is like listening—sometimes with the sound of a vast organ and sometimes with the sound of a harp—to a chorus of the great men who have gone before us. It is the sound of our legacy, echoing in the corridors of time.

The rituals of Masonry are not "how to" manuals. They are not designed primarily to convey information, especially not in the telegraphic fashion popular today. They are intended to produce insight, and insight does not come by following a set of instructions. The Degrees of Masonry are like symphonies, each note dependent upon the ones before to create an intellectual and emotional context in which insight can occur. You can force yourself to learn, but you cannot force yourself to understand. Understanding comes when it comes, not when it is demanded. The Degrees of Masonry create a context in which understanding is possible. They are not a factory into which you can put raw materials and from which comes a predictable, designed-to-specifications product.

The following are passages from various Masonic rituals. They are not esoteric in the Oklahoma work, and I offer apologies to any Brother whose work regards them as esoteric. Read them aloud, slowly. Let the words trickle through your mind like the drops of a warm spring rain. Bathe in the glory of the language.

"You have this evening, my Brother, pressed beneath your feet, transmounted and transcended all the powers and passions of the senses and sciences of man."

"But is this the end of man and the aspiring hopes of all good Masons? No, blessed be God, we pause not at our first or second steps, but, true to our principles, look forward for further light. As the embers of mortality are feebly glimmering in the sockets of existence, the Holy Bible removes the dark shroud, draws aside the sable

curtain of the tomb, and bids hope and joy to arouse us. It cheers our drooping spirits and points beyond the bounds of time to the breaking light of a resurrection morn, and bids us turn our eyes of hope and confidence to the opening scenes of eternity."

"It was our mother's evening hymn that lulled us to sleep in infancy; and the mellowing tides of old cathedral airs, vibrating through aisles and arches, have stilled the ruffled spirit and, sweeping away the discordant passions of men, have borne them along its resistless current, until their united voices have joined in sounding aloud the chorus of the heaven-born anthem, 'Peace on earth, good will toward men;' but it never sounds with such seraphic harmony as when employed in singing hymns of gratitude to the Creator of the universe."

And from the memorial service, consider the following: *"Soft and safe to you, my Brother, be this earthly bed; bright and glorious be your rising from it. Fragrant be the acacia's bloom which here shall flourish. May the earliest buds of spring unfold their beauties o'er your resting place, and here may the fragrance of the summer's last rose linger longest. Though the cold blasts of autumn may lay them in the dust, and for a time destroy the loveliness of their existence, yet the destruction is not final, and in the springtime they shall bloom again. So, in the bright morning of the world's resurrection, may your mortal frame, now laid low in the dust by the chilling blasts of death, spring again into newness of life and unfold in immortal beauty in realms beyond the skies. Until then, dear Brother, fare thee well. Fare thee well."*

There is more, much more, but the point is clear—those who approach the Degrees of Masonry as they would a cookbook or the instructions on an IRS form will be frustrated and disappointed. Those who approach the Degrees of Masonry as they would a work of art, with open mind and heart ready to be moved and made glad, will find the reward they seek.

And, who knows, when that moment of insight and understanding strikes, they may even be motivated to say, "Well, fan my brow and call me Moses!"

"Fan My Brow and Call me Moses" was printed in *The Scottish Rite Journal* for October, 2003

Prepared

Interesting word, "prepared." We all know its typical meaning of "to be ready for." But to really understand its meaning, especially in Masonry, it's useful to go a little deeper. It is important to remember that, when the ritual was being developed, Latin and Greek were taught in what amounted to grade school so that even when "English" words were being used, most Brethren knew and automatically thought of the Greek and Latinate forms and the derivations of the word.

And those make "prepared" especially interesting.

It's a combination of two words. "Pre" had the same meanings it has now of "before," or "in advance." The word "pare" has remained in English also, as when we speak of paring an apple, or a cheese, or a budget. To pare something is to make it ready for use by trimming away that which is useless, or unnecessary, or a hindrance, or prevents one from getting the full value or use of the thing. It can also be thought of as reducing something to its essentials. To "prepare" is to do that before the actual moment of need or use.

There is an obvious similarity of idea between the meaning of "prepare" and the phrase from the description of the common gavel; ". . .divesting our minds and consciences of all the vices and superfluities of life. . ."

So what does it mean that a man is first prepared to become a Freemason in his heart?

Again, we need to understand that phrase as it would have been understood in the traditions of the 1700's or earlier. People were not exactly certain what the function of the brain was—in fact our entire knowledge of human anatomy was very spotty. William Harvey had discovered the circulation of the blood only about a hundred years earlier, and it still was not accepted as factual by many doctors. The general belief was that knowledge and especially memory was located in the heart. (We still speak of memorizing something as "learning it by heart.")

So to be "pre-pared" in the heart means that the person has trimmed away those things which stand in the way of knowledge and memory—such things as fear, prejudice, anger, and superstition.

And where does this take place? In general, it takes place throughout life, but especially it takes place in the preparation room.

The preparation room in most states and most Oklahoma Lodges is little more than a dressing room where the candidate receives the appropriate costume and is interviewed by the Senior Deacon, but originally (and still in most of the world) it was and is much more. The ceiling of the room was painted black, and the walls were hung with heavy black velvet curtains to exclude as much sound as possible.

The only furniture in the room was a simple wooden table and chair. On the table were a lighted candle, a skull, the books of various religions, paper, pen and ink, and often an hour glass which the Candidate's guide (in most traditions the Senior Deacon) would turn just before he left the Candidate alone in the room.

The candle provided the only light, and usually the Candidate heard the door being barred and then fastened by a heavy lock as the guide left. Hanging against the wall were painted admonitions. We have record of only a few, but they included such things as:

Woe unto those who seek knowledge for which they are not fitted.

Death followeth thee at every step, and thou knowest not the hour of his coming.

Think! Learn! Be Silent!

He had been told to use this space and time to prepare himself for the journey which was to come, and to take pen and paper and answer one of the questions written on a parchment next to the skull. He was then to knock thrice on the door to alert his guide that his answer had been written. Typical questions might include:

What does it mean to be a man?
What is truth?
Where is truth to be found?
What does God expect of man?

When he had written his answer, he signaled the guide, who took the answer to the Lodge where it was read to the assembled Brethren. The Candidate remained the in preparation room, alone with his thoughts for about an additional half hour, and was conducted thence to the door of the Lodge----

----where he entered, duly and truly prepared.

"Prepared" appeared in the newsletter of the Masonic Lodge Education Committee of the Grand Lodge of Oklahoma in September, 2007

Sex as Symbol

At the risk of being accused of controversy, or even poor taste, it is useful to explore the concept of sex as it appears in symbols.

You may have seen material on anti-Masonic sites which suggests that the combination of the square and compasses symbolizes the union of man and woman (which shows that anti-Masons have a fertile, if prurient, imagination), or that the obelisk is a Masonic sexual symbol (the obelisk is not a Masonic symbol, although it and other Egyptian images are sometimes used as decoration on Masonic artifacts, and the obelisk was not a symbol of sexuality for the Egyptians but rather a symbol of resurrection, partaking of the same symbolism as a pyramid). Some have even suggested that the apron was intended as a symbol of sexuality.

Those suggestions can be dismissed with no thought other than a mild amazement at the ignorance involved. But the concept of sex or sexuality, not as a matter of human reproduction but as a metaphor for the great power of life itself, and even as the energy of the universe, is worthy of consideration.

In order to consider it, however, it is essential to rid our thinking of the puritanical concept that sex is, somehow, dirty. That "dirty" applications can be made of it, or "dirty" (i.e. animal) thoughts can be thunk about it are obvious. But it has also inspired some of the greatest art and most profound thought in human history.

Sex represents the almost incredible power of life to exist and to express itself. The force of life must have staggered early man, as it staggers us. One need only look at a tree seedling forcing its roots into a rock, or observe the ferocity with which a mother—human or animal—defends her young, to realize that something extraordinary is at work.

From early times, Deity has been associated with the life force symbolized by sex. Egyptian belief included the creation of the world by the sexual self-stimulation of a god. Archeological finds have clearly established that the popular religion of the Israelites during much of Biblical history, included a belief in Asherah as the wife-consort of Yahweh.

Venus (Roman) or Aphrodite (Greek) was a goddess associated with sexual energy and the power of life, just as Bacchus (Roman) or Dionysus (Greek) was the god representing the same thing in an even more fundamental and raw-energetic way. He was sometimes shown riding a leopard as a symbol of the generative force of life.

Even in Christianity, there is an interesting echo in the Nicean Creed, perhaps the most widely used credo in Christianity. In the translation used by the Anglican Church a passage reads ". . . And in one Lord Jesus Christ, the only-begotten Son of God. Begotten of his Father before all worlds, God of God, Light of Light, Very God of Very God, Begotten, not made, being of one substance with the Father by Whom all things were made . . ." "Begotten" is the past participle of "beget" which means "to produce through procreation."

Throughout religious art, but especially in stone carvings adorning buildings and in book illustrations, figures are seen in a sort of frame known as a *vesica piscis*. The *vesica* (for short) is formed by the intersection of two circles.

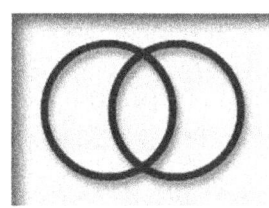

It represents the intersection of the two worlds, but also the entrance to the womb, as the entrance of life into the world. Interestingly, the shape was used as the shape of the official seal of many of the medieval universities.

In Hinduism, many works of art portray sex or semen as representing the universal energy.

In one way or another, the idea of sex as a manifestation of divine energy or power is found in almost every religion.

Essentially, it seems to me, the concept of sexuality as Divine energy is used primarily to symbolize four things. The first is the process of pouring energy into the world or universe, of creating living matter from dead matter, of the continual re-creation of the world. The second is the pouring of that energy into the individual, or the establishment of a connection between the individual and the energy of the universe. The third is the power of life, and the power of life to create new life. The fourth is the combination of two things to create a third thing which represents the equilibrium of the others.

I've already suggested one or two examples of the first meaning. Another good example is found in the Bible in the *Song of Solomon* or *Song of Songs*. As one of my professors of Biblical literature remarked, it is either a powerful and skillful metaphor for the energy of the Divine, or the most pornographic work of the ancient world.

As examples of the second meaning, consider the fact that nuns are considered to be the brides of Christ. I am not suggesting anything of a carnal nature, but that the symbolic marriage is a joining, making of two, one.

The Abbess Hildegard of Bingen (1098 - 1179) is considered one of the most brilliant women who has ever lived. Powerful mystic, advisor to kings and popes, theologian, physician, fine painter and writer, she is also the very first composer in history whose name has come down to us. According to the musicologist Bruce Holsinger, *"not only the texts but Hildegard's melodies were an expression of sexuality centered around the female body, womb, and virgin community. The act of singing Hildegard's music would have connected the worship of God with the physical pleasure of singing as an enactment of sexual fulfillment through God's love."*

The Native American mythic tradition has many stories of maidens who married or coupled with supernatural males to bring food, medicine, or other benefits to their people by the connection thus established with the divine.

St. Teresa's description of her central mystical experience does not involve sex, but rather an angel thrusting a golden spear into her body, thus producing both agony and ecstasy; but the description nevertheless conveys a powerful feeling of divine sexuality.

Examples of the third meaning--the power of life and the power of life to create new life--are to be found everywhere. Noah is to take a male and female of every species into the ark. Virtually every culture holds childbirth to be a powerful spiritual event (although often one requiring ritual purification after it is complete). Nearly every society has treasured its children, holding them to still possess some trace of the divine energy or nature they have just left.

Examples of the fourth meaning--the combination of two things to form a third which may be an equilibrium of the two--are found throughout alchemy and Freemasonry, as well as in other disciplines. The androgen, a human half male and half female, is a typical example. The alchemical union or marriage of the King and Queen is another. The lesser lights--the combination of the sun (Apollonian consciousness) and the moon (Dionysian consciousness) to form the Master (the complete human being) is one example from Freemasonry.

There are many other references we could trace, but, for the moment, it is sufficient to remember that the great mystery of the energy of life permeates all esoteric thought. It is hardly surprising that its manifestation as sexuality should appear among mankind's most sacred images.

This material originally appeared on the Masonic website, **The Sanctum Sanctorum**

Pigeons in the Rocket

It had been raining the day last September I went to photograph the presentation of a check to the Oklahoma State Teacher of the Year by the Masonic Fraternity, but the rain had stopped, leaving a pleasant, cool and overcast day. The event is held at the fair grounds, during the State Fair. There was a courtyard outside the building, where I wandered to get some air and sacrifice a pipe-full of tobacco while waiting for the program to begin.

In the courtyard was a steam locomotive and also stages of one of the rockets used in the early space program. Pigeons had obviously been roosting on top of the cab of the locomotive, and, as I watched, two pigeons flew into the rocket and perched in one of the openings. One of them added to the droppings which stained its sides.

It was a sobering moment.

The steam locomotive was once the most powerful force in the world. It shaped the economies of nations, affecting hundreds of millions of people. It roared across the country on its iron tracks like mankind's rush toward progress or the headlong flight a demon toward the blackest pit of Hell—and it was compared to both in the press. Towns flourished or died, depending on the location of those tracks. Sociologists tell us that it was the first invention which completely reshaped the countryside and the lives of the people. It even affected the genetic pools, allowing people from distant areas to meet and marry. It was the symbol of the 1800's.

It was sitting there, a museum relic of lost power and importance.

And it was a home for pigeons.

The rocket seemed far too modern to have suffered a similar fate. How many millions, myself among them, were glued to the television sets when that mighty form thundered into the skies, as unwieldy and improbable as if an Egyptian obelisk had suddenly flung itself toward the stars. It was the symbol of all we hoped would change the world for the better. It was science elevated past an art form and into an inspiration. It carried our hopes and fears with it. In the taming of all that raw power we felt a foreshadowing of a better life that science and technology could bring. Surely nothing was impossible to us.

But it had been passed—replaced by something better.

It was sitting there, a museum relic of lost power and importance.

And it was a home for pigeons.

Freemasonry, in the 1700's. was quite literally one of the most powerful forces in the world. Scholars are just now beginning to realize what a critical role it played. It was in the Lodge that men learned the rudiments of self-rule and democracy. No one elected the kings, princes, and cardinals who ruled their countries. But in the Lodge, men elected their leaders, wrote their own by-laws, changed them at will. It was the school from which democracy sprang. Freemasonry grew like wildfire because it was the guardian and carrier of the great ideas of the Enlightenment—freedom of thought and action, freedom to learn, freedom to do something important, equality, limitation only by one's own merit and ability. It was, quietly, a school for rebels.

In the 1800's Freemasonry changed and accepted another important role. It was the guardian of persons and values. When there were no governmental social programs, no "safety net," Freemasonry performed that function in every town and village in America. We cared for the widows and orphans. We funded civic improvements. We brought together, in the Lodge, the leaders of the town and gave them a forum for working out the ideas which built America's social fabric. We were there with the inspiration, the leadership, and the plain hard work to make things happen. We WERE the community, at its finest, working and planing to build a better life for everyone.

"Philanthropy" literally means "the love of mankind." We were among the foremost philanthropic organizations in the world. We demonstrated by word and deed that we loved and cared for mankind.

That was at least as true in the first half of the 1900's as it was in the 1800's.

But sometimes, as I look at Masonry, I am forced to wonder if we, too, may become a museum piece of past power, glory and usefulness.

In 1850, Emerson wrote, "Every hero becomes a bore at last." I remember them—the men who fought in the First World War—from my own youth. One tried to be polite—one had been taught to be polite to one's elders. But oh, how tedious were their stories, told endlessly, of battles and encounters. How little important they seemed to a six-year-old boy! They truly were heroes—I realize that now. They did vital and important things at great sacrifice. But they seemed to me then as quaint and curious shadows, with no relationship at all to the things in which I was interested. And I tried, as quickly and politely as possible, to be somewhere else. And I now realize how it must have hurt and confused them. They had a great and important history, they had done vital things without which my world would not have existed. And no one seemed to care.

I cannot help but wonder if Emerson's truism is true of organizations as well. Is Masonry, like a hero, doomed to become a bore at last? Are we a quaint and curious relic of past importance?

I know something of our history and I revel in it. It is a proud heritage. But most Masons, myself included, when we talk of Masonry, speak of what it HAS DONE, not what it IS DOING.

Do we still love mankind?

Is Masonry, like a tidal wave, bringing its still great economic power and prestige to the fight for social justice and the improvement of the lot of humanity?

Are Lodges, outraged by second class education being offered in the public schools, taking strong, vocal public stands in support of excellence in education and going to school board meetings, and generally raising a ruckus until the situation gets better? Do Lodges form volunteer pools to help serve as assistants in reading classes—just sitting there listening so a child can read to them and they can share stories with the child? *(Yes, I know of some—and there are surely others.)*

Do Masonic organizations decide to do something to take the streets back from the punks and gangs, and help form neighborhood watches and patrols, and then go to Town Council meetings with both an offer of help and a demand that things change for the better? *(Yes, I know of some—and there are surely others.)*

Are there Lodges or Masonic organizations which are trying to do something about AIDS, and childhood crack addiction, and illiteracy and teen pregnancy? *(Yes, I know of some—and there are surely others.)*

Have Lodges have gone to drug rehabilitation centers, where mothers and their children are living while the mothers try to beat a drug habit, and talked with the social workers to find out what the kids wanted, and bought them Christmas presents, and delivered them on Christmas eve, dressed as elves, and then tried not to weep as they saw the suddenly-kindled Light in the eyes of the mothers and the children? *(Yes, I know of one—and there are surely others.)*

We are justly proud of our charities—but how much of that is OUR doing, and how much is from funds our fathers and grandfathers established and endowed? We are proud of how much we give—but it amounts to less than $1 per Mason per day. And about 70¢ of that comes from the endowed gifts of Masons before us. Are we still charitable men? *(Yes, for new funds are created, new endowments built. It is less easy today, but it is done. The Language Clinics are a prime example.)*

It can be argued that we do less than we once did. In many ways that is true. Anyone who tries to raise funds for charitable purposes knows that it is getting harder to do. In some ways, perhaps, we run the risk of becoming "likers" rather than "lovers" of mankind.

But it doesn't have to be that way!

Masonry has some of the finest teachings ever written for living good, productive lives, if we will only teach and live those principles. We CAN make a difference in the world. We can ACTIVELY oppose injustice and intolerance and religious bigotry. We can be the dynamic center of the community again. It won't be easy. It will take money and commitment and damned hard work. It will take a refusal to listen to the voices in the Lodge who say "It won't work." It will take a teeth-gritting determination that Masonry will stand for **excellence *in everything*** and will not tolerate the "good enough" in anything. It means getting our hands dirtier and our hearts cleaner. BUT WE CAN DO IT.

If we do, then far from becoming a bore at last, we will become like the Constitution—echoing a rich heritage from the past and serving as the guiding principles for the future. We can again shape the world into a better place for everyone. We know how to do it—we've done it before.

I really believe that will happen. I really believe that Masonry will revitalize itself and become not a museum piece from yesterday but a blueprint for tomorrow. I know we have it in us. We can choose our destiny.

But it is well not to forget the pigeons in the rocket.

"Pigeons in the Rocket" was published in the *Scottish Rite Journal* for May, 1998

Our Really Rather Radical Brother, Albert Pike

Albert Pike, a radical?! Yes, or at least a liberal when it came to social issues.

I don't mean to suggest that Pike was a Northern Liberal of the 1990's. He wasn't. But he certainly was a Southern Liberal of the 1860's. And nowhere does this attitude come across more clearly than when Pike is speaking of Labor, and the relationships between Labor and Management.

Pike was keenly aware of the poverty in which most of the working men and, especially, women of his time lived, and how easily they could be seen as dispensable by an industrial system which was becoming less and less humane as he watched. Pike had seen both sides. He had literally split rails in exchange for room and board when he first came to Arkansas. He had, by hard work and self education, made himself into a prominent lawyer and a wealthy man, before the Civil War. But he never forgot his sympathy with the laboring men and women, and he not only wrote it into the Scottish Rite, but into his essays and poetry as well.

> While every ox and horse can find work, and is worth being fed, it is not always so with man. To be employed, to have a chance to work at anything like fair wages, becomes the great engrossing object of a man's life. The capitalist can live without employing the laborer, and discharges him

> *whenever that labor ceases to be profitable. At the moment when the weather is most inclement, provisions dearest, and rents highest, he turns him off to starve. If the day-laborer is taken sick, his wages stop. When old, he has no pension to retire upon. His children cannot be sent to school; for before their bones are hardened they must get to work lest they starve.* (M&D 179)

In the lecture of the 20°, Pike draws the duties of employer and employee in stark terms which sound much more as if they were written in the middle of this century than in the middle of the last.

> *As Master of a Lodge, you are to inculcate these duties on your brethren. Teach the employed to be honest, punctual, and faithful as well as respectful and obedient to all proper orders; but also teach the employer that ever man or woman who desires to work, has a right to have work to do; and that they, and those who from sickness or feebleness, loss of limb or of bodily vigor, old age or infancy, are not able to work, have a right to be fed, clothed, and sheltered from the inclement elements: that he commits an awful sin against Masonry and in the sight of God, if he closes his workshops for factories, or ceases to work his mines, when they do not yield him what he regards as sufficient profit, and so dismisses the workmen and workwomen to starve; or when he reduces the wages of man or woman to so low a standard that they and their families cannot be clothed and fed and comfortably housed; or by overwork must give him their blood and life in exchange for the pittance of their wages: and that his duty as a*

Mason and Brother peremptorily requires him to continue to employ those who else will be pinched with hunger and cold, or resort to theft and vice; and to pay them fair wages, though it may reduce of annul his profits or even eat into his capital; for God hath but loaned him his wealth, and made him His almoner and agent to invest it. (M&D 330)

Rough stuff, that! One wonders what Pike would think of this day of down-sizing and exporting of jobs.

To Pike, work was a blessing and a benefit in and of itself.

Sympathy with the great laboring classes, respect for labor itself, and resolution to do some good work in our day and generation, these are the lessons of [the 22º], and they are purely Masonic. Masonry has make a working-man and his associates the Heroes of her principal legend, and himself the companion of Kings. The idea is as simple and true as it is sublime. From first to last, Masonry is work! (M&D 340)

[Nature] scorns the man who sits screened from all work, from want, danger, hardship, the victory over which is work; and has all his work and battling done by other men; and yet there are men who pride themselves that they and theirs have done no work time out of mind. So neither have the swine. (M&D 341)

To toil, whether with the sweat of the brow, or of the brain or heart, is worship--the noblest thing yet discovered beneath the Stars. Let the weary cease to think that labor is a curse and doom pronounced by Deity. Without it there could be no true excellence in human nature. (M&D 342)

There is much more on the topic. Pike reminds us that all work is equally dignified, simply because it is work. He challenges us never to forget that wealth is nothing more than another tool with which to work, not an excuse for luxury and idleness. He insists that each Mason has an absolute obligation to find some work to do.

Yes, for his time and place (and even for our own) Brother Pike was really rather radical, He truly believed in equality and in human dignity; he cared about compassion; he campaigned for economic justice.

And, above all, he *worked* to bring them about.

This material first appeared in *The Scottish Rite Journal* for September, 1996

Ritual: Who Needs It?

The short answer is, "we do."

To explain why takes a little longer.

In a very real sense, it is the ritual of Masonry which makes Masonry work. Ritual is the channel through which Masonry teaches. But it is more than that.

Because ritual is so important to Masonry, it's worth taking a little time to talk about the nature of ritual itself, and why it is central to the Masonic experience.

First of all, ritual is a virtual necessity to all humans, in fact to nearly all animals. This is so true that all human brains come "hard-wired" to respond to ritual. (Amazing, in its own way. Very few things in human beings are instinctive —almost everything is learned behavior. But the response to ritual has been located by brain anatomists in the oldest and most primitive part of the brain, just above the brain stem, in the same area which controls alertness and the emotions. It is as "natural" to us as love, or aggression, or cooperation.)

All of us engage in ritual all the time—we just don't always recognize it. Most of us have a morning routine, for example. Some of us shave before showering, some of us shave after showering, and some shave while showering, but whichever it is, we usually do it the same way. A few people even have morning routines so exact that they always put on the right sock before the left sock. This morning routine is a ritual.

Most of us shake hands when we are introduced to someone—that is a ritual. Pledging allegiance to the flag is a ritual. Bowing the head during prayer is a ritual. Making coffee in the morning is a ritual. Starting a meal with soup or salad and ending with dessert is a ritual. Our lives are filled and surrounded with rituals from birth to marriage to death.

Why?

Ritual gives us a framework to organize events.

We don't deal well with chaos. We make lists of things to do, to buy, to read. Ritual does the same thing for us. By doing things in a given order (which is the essence of ritual) we make sure everything gets done. Even churches which try to make a point of not using ritual, use ritual in that sense. The order in which hymns are sung, the collection is taken, the sermon is given, and prayer is offered seldom changes for a given congregation. The primary reason most of us have a morning ritual is to make sure that we don't overlook shaving, or brushing the teeth, or some other aspect of preparing for the day. Ritual provides a sort of mental checklist for many of life's activities.

Ritual helps us in our relationships to others.
  Almost all families have family rituals—things they just do in certain ways. Those rituals might include such things as making it a point to eat together on certain days, calling at certain times of the day, giving certain kinds of gifts; there are thousands of possibilities. Those rituals strengthen the unity of the family. Other rituals relate to those outside the family. Shaking hands when we meet, taking turns talking in a conversation—almost all the things we classify as polite (or consider a person as rude if he doesn't do) are matters of social ritual. They help to make everyone comfortable and help situations move smoothly.

Ritual is a powerful teaching tool.
  In fact, it was probably the very first teaching tool. We know of hunting rituals among some tribes, whose purpose was to teach the young man how to hunt effectively. Mnemonics (phrases which help us remember things, such as "Thirty days hath September, April, June and November...") are rituals, as is learning the alphabet by singing the alphabet song. The military developed many rituals (patterns of repeated behavior) to teach recruits how to maintain weapons.

Ritual helps give us a sense of identity.

It may seem strange, but people often define themselves by their actions (I'm a salesman, a mechanic, a professor, a millwright, etc.). That's not limited to what we do for a living. Our rituals, our actions, give an underlying sense of reality to our lives. We feel "right" or "complete" when we follow certain rituals.

Ritual helps us prepare—helps us "get in the mood" for what is to follow.

Whether the event is a church service or a football game, most repeating events have a ritual of some sort which helps set the emotional tone. And we would have a strong sense of "wrongness" if those were violated—if a church service started with band music and cheerleaders or a football game started with a liturgical procession, for example.

Ritual lets us condense a lot into a little time.

Ritual enriches an experience by concentrating it. Rather than involving a full exposition, like a lecture, ritual makes references to things and leaves us to think about and fill in the details for ourselves. To illustrate with a portion of church ritual, consider just the last line of the Doxology—"Praise Father, Son, and Holy Ghost." The concept of the Trinity is a very hard concept to "wrap the mind around." Rather than giving the many hours of discussion which would be necessary to explore the topic, the ritual simply mentions it, and leaves it to us to do the thinking if we are so inclined.

The ritual of Masonry involves all these and more.

The rituals of Masonry—the opening and the closing, the Degrees, even the ritual of voting—organize the events and make sure that everything happens that is supposed to.

It helps us define ourselves as Masons and strengthen the fraternal ties which bind us together as Brothers. And that effect is international and cross cultural. We know we have shared experiences with Masons from all over the world.

It is a teaching tool—the lessons and values of Masonry are taught through ritual and symbols.

It helps set the tone and mood of the meeting-it helps us set aside the concerns of the outside world and focus on the great truths of human and spiritual nature.

Masonic ritual obviously condenses experience. It contains elements which raise important questions but which are deliberately left unexplored because it wants the Mason to think them through for himself. To give just a few examples:

Why are the three ruffians fellow countrymen of the man they murder?

Why does a murderer mark a grave so it can be found again if necessary, when the very last thing a murderer would want is for anyone to find the grave of his victim.

Why is there a rubble heap at the Temple when we are told that all the stones are cut and finished in the quarries and fit perfectly without further adjustment?

Masonic ritual gives full range to Masons to explore their own interests. Many of my best friends love learning and performing the ritual. My own interests deal with interpretation of the ritual and the symbols it uses—and especially with the effects the ritual is designed to produce in the minds of initiates and the ways in which those effects are produced.. Others are especially interested in the history of the ritual and the way it has changed and evolved over the years. One Mason I know is interested in the ritual from the standpoint of a cultural anthropologist, and enjoys tracing the ways the ritual relates to the great initiatory traditions of history.

And the ritual is large enough and complex enough to accommodate all those interests, and many more.

So, again, the answer to the question "Who needs ritual anyway?" is "We all do." The ritual of Masonry meets many needs and many interests. It is not the same thing as Masonry—any more that a sermon is the same thing as a church—but it is a primary way we teach and learn. It is the glue which holds us together. It is important.

It makes us, us.

"Ritual, Who Needs It?" was first published in *The Scottish Rite Journal*, March, 1999

The Tragedy of the Third Degree

There are some interesting implications in the tragedy of the Master Mason Degree, but to discuss them we have to clear up some contemporary confusion with a couple of terms. I sometimes think it may be caused by the fact that American intellectual and emotional life has become so very shallow over the last hundred years, that we have robbed many words of their once considerable power. It probably seems nit-picking on my part, but we have so few words of real strength that it bothers me to see them beggared. I heard someone refer to a hamburger as "awesome" a few days ago. Really? Were they truly so struck by the grandeur and inexpressible power of that hamburger that they were as incapable of speech or thought as they would be in the immediate presence of the Deity? "Tragic" or "tragedy" and "hero" have suffered the same fate.

A local television station referred to the accidental drowning of two teenagers a few days ago as a tragedy; in fact they used the words "tragedy" and "tragic" several times in the story. I'll grant without argument that it was a terrible misfortune, but it was not a tragedy. That does not make it any less an event, nor entitle those left behind to any less sympathy—it simply means that one should not call a trombone a violin. They are both excellent instruments, but they are not the same instrument.

Likewise "hero." The term is now used to describe the actions of a person which earlier in my life would have been expected, not exceptional. Some newspapers and broadcast media referred to a boy who jumped into the lake to save his younger brother as a hero. He (and all honor be unto him) declined the term, saying that he was only doing what was natural.

So wherefor this wandering? Because the story of the second section of the Master Mason Degree can only be understood if one realizes that it is a classical tragedy, given in the format of a Medieval Mystery Play, and that was fully known and understood by those who created it, and who first saw it.

There are very specific rules of classical tragedy.

- ✦Everything which happens must be motivated by the character of those involved; chance, accident, or coincidence must play no part in it.
- ✦Given the opening situation and the character of the people, the action and events must be predictable and inevitable. Once set in motion, a tragedy unwinds, in Cocteau's terms, "like an infernal machine." We know what is going to happen, we wish with all our might that it not happen, and it happens.
- ✦The tragic hero falls, not by chance, but because of a flaw in his character of which he was unaware.
- ✦Because of the tragic flaw, he crosses some invisible line or offends against some divine principle which leads to his fall.
- ✦After the action of the fall, it is permissible that chance or circumstance may lead to the discovery of the act, although such chance was generally understood to be the working of Divine Will.
- ✦He is destroyed by the fall, but, in the process, comes to a fuller understanding of himself and his own character.

As a side note, I mentioned that the format was that of a Medieval Mystery Play. These were still being done in many parts of England at the time the Master Mason Degree must have been written. By definition, a Mystery Play involves a minor character or event mentioned, but not elaborated upon, in the Bible; treats the story as an allegory to make some moral or ethical point; concludes with a moral lesson.

So, does the story of the Master Mason Degree qualify as a tragedy? Yes, the action comes about because of the character or personality of those involved, there is a tragic fall and death, and the hero comes to a new understanding of himself.

And who is the hero. Most people will answer "Hiram," but that is not true. Hiram's death is not tragic. He does not fall as the result of a tragic flaw: he does not fall at all. He dies, and dies because of his character, but that is not at all the same thing as a fall.

No, the hero of the Third Degree is J___lum. His tragic flaw is impatience and, especially, lack of faith and trust. He comes to insight into his own character, and into what his character should have been, when he considers the integrity-unto-death of Hiram. Having attained that insight, he pronounces his own sentence and accepts his own death.

Since, in a tragedy, it is the tragic hero from whom we are to learn, it may cast a somewhat more complex light on the lessons of the Third Degree.

Up to this point, we have been dealing with more or less objective fact as to the structure of a dramatic form and the events in the plot of the Degree. Now we enter interpretation, so it is time for the usual warning—there are no official or "right" interpretations of Masonry. Any interpretation is valid only for the person who finds it useful. So what follows is of no authority whatsoever.

If we see Hiram as the hero, the one from whom we are to learn, then about the only lesson is the importance of integrity, even to death. True and important, but somewhat obvious. If we see J___lum as the one from whom we are to learn, the lessons include these:

✣ putting our own self-interests above the goal which is to be achieved (selfishness in any form) leads to poor decisions and destruction;

✣ giving way to our animal side, even for an instant, leads to consequences which may be impossible to undo;

✣ ALL positions in life are positions requiring integrity and honor, from the lowest worker in the quarry to the designer of the building;

✣ since the building of the Temple represents the building of our own lives, we must be careful not to subvert that building for short-term goals;

✣ there is no such thing as an unimportant action or decision, there are only actions and decisions whose importance is not known or understood;

✣ of all wrong actions, the most wrong are those which violate what should be our own insight and understanding;

✣ if we spend much time thinking about what is "due to us," or "what we've earned," we are almost certain to become resentful and impatient.

Once we truly develop a sense of integrity, we accept the consequences of our actions.

There is more, of course, but at least it may be clearer why the identity of the tragic hero in the Degree makes a difference.

This material originally appeared on the Masonic website, **The Sanctum Sanctorum**

Using Masonry

It is true, of course, that we are not supposed to "use" Freemasonry in most of the usual senses of the word. We are told, rightly, that we are not supposed to use it to get ahead in business or social life. Masonic Brothers are not a gathering of prospects for our commercial services, our political ambitions, or any similar agenda.

There is a sense in which we speak of using Freemasonry which is not objectionable. Many men give their wives copies of their state's list of Lodges, with the suggestion that they keep it in the car and, if they run into trouble in a town, they contact a local Lodge or Mason (although both the need and practice have been diminished by the ubiquity of cell phones). Many men put Masonic emblems on their automobiles for a similar reason. Some men use Masonry as their primary conduit for charitable giving, or as a source of help and support for various civic projects. These are good and useful.

But all these things are ways of "using" Masons and the relationships between Masons. They really are not ways of using Masonry itself.

Using *Masonry* suggests deriving a benefit from the Degrees, the allegories, and the symbols and lessons which comprise Freemasonry. While there are many such benefits possible, I would like to suggest four primary ones. Some Brothers may be surprised that fraternalism, brotherhood, and friendship are not included in the list. Those are very important, and the things I treasure most, but, again, they derive from Masons and our interactions with Masons, not from Masonry itself. Apologies are also offered for the number of personal pronouns used here, but, as we will see, the topic is inherently a personal one.

Tradition and "Connectedness"

While some generations and some political movements (e.g. China's "Cultural Revolution") have tried to discount the past or at least sever intellectual and emotional ties to it, such attempts have always failed. There appears to be in mankind a need to feel that he is a part of a longer picture, as well as a larger one; that he has "roots." Even the youth movement in the 1960's in America, when young people actively distanced themselves from their parents' values, hopes, ideals, institutions, and life styles soon gave way to a seeking for connectedness to something more permanent. It is true that Freemasonry lost a generation, as did almost all organizations—but one of the interesting phenomena of the present is the rate at which the children of the '60's generation are joining the Fraternity, and often then bringing in their fathers.

An important benefit of Masonry is the feeling that we are part of something permanent. Few Masons seriously believe that George Washington heard the same ritual words as we do today, or that a Lodge meeting in the time of Mozart was conducted as it is now. But we do feel that the traditions, the values, have largely remained unchanged. Even if it is at a very basic level, Freemasonry lets us feel that some things are long-lasting. It is a sort of emotional and spiritual anchor to windward; not just a grounding in ethics and morality, but also in permanence.

Intellectual stimulation

A second benefit which Masonry can confer is exercising the mind. The most obvious way is by memorizing the ritual. There is evidence that learning actually changes the architecture of the brain. Those who exercise the mind develop it just as they would develop a muscle with the proper workout. Memorizing material seems to keep the mind more alert and focused. One physician has remarked, anecdotally, that he seems to see a slower onset and progression of memory loss associated with ageing among men he knows to be active participants in the Masonic rituals.

But the intellectual stimulation of Freemasonry goes far beyond the learning of ritual. There is the pleasure of learning the symbols and allegorical systems of Freemasonry. Many educators have asserted that learning additional symbol systems makes it possible to think more freely and creatively in all the other symbol systems we know. And that is a matter of common experience. Our language is a symbol system. If that is the only symbol system we know, we will have a difficult time in dealing with mathematics (numbers are a separate symbol system) and will be very limited in what we can do in music (musical notation is a third symbol system). A person who knows a language, mathematics, music, and the visual symbol systems of art is simply equipped to think about more things and to think about them in more complex ways.

Intellectual stimulation is one of the most "useful" benefits of the Fraternity.

Speculation

The last two "uses" of Freemasonry are controversial in some quarters. There are some highly-respected Masonic writers who insist that it is not appropriate to go beyond the meanings for the symbols as given in the rituals when studying Freemasonry. But the use of Masonry is different from the study of Masonry. Speculation on the symbols of Freemasonry—their relationships to each other—the interplay of allegories—may be, in Poe's terms, "linking fancy unto fancy;" but it also stretches the mind and exercises the imagination. That is an important benefit in and of itself. Such speculation may or may not tell you about Freemasonry, but it does let you use Freemasonry to learn about the interplay of ideas. For that purpose, the question is not "Are my conclusions valid?" but rather "Have I broken new ground in my own thinking?" The validity of such speculation is not found in historical verification or the agreement of experts—it is found in a broadening of your own mental landscape. It is more than the intellectual stimulation mentioned above. If intellectual stimulation could be compared to a workout in a gym, speculation could be compared with jogging cross country and seeing new lands.

Which leads us to the fourth use.

Creation of your own Life-Myth—your own Hero's Journey

Joseph Campbell, the great 20th Century expert on mythology and comparative religion, suggested in both his books and his lectures that the function of mythology was to give us a way to relate to our own nature and find a way to put ourselves in accord with the world, both physically and spiritually. For those who choose to use it that way, it can be one of the greatest benefits of Masonry. It is, I think, what the late Rev. Forrest Haggard, PGM, 33°, Grand Cross and Blue Friar meant when he used to tell me that one had to decide whether Masonry was the can or the contents of the can.

The ritual of the Fraternity seems clearly to have been structured around the great quest or hero's journey myths. The young man comes to the cave of initiation. He is met by the spirit guide or psychopompos (Senior Deacon) who leads and assists him on the journey. He meets and overcomes obstructions, is supplied with the materials or weapons needed to successfully complete the journey (tokens and working tools) and finally penetrates to the heart of the mystery (the altar) where he often encounters someone representing his father or a father figure (the Worshipful Master). In the process, he gains knowledge of himself and is transformed.

Even if the candidate does not understand the symbols or know any of the history, the ritual still has an effect upon him, often a profound effect.

But by using the mind, and by using the symbols, we can create for ourselves a life-myth, an opportunity for insight, which can be much stronger. That is using Masonry.

As an example (and it is an example which works for me but may not work for you—as we have said, it is an individual creation) consider the pillars Jachin and Boaz. What do they "tell" us?

In Oklahoma, the non-esoteric portion of the Fellow Craft gives us information taken primarily from the accounts of the Temple of Solomon in the Biblical book of First Kings. We are also told that the names mean "strength" and "establishment" although some traditions give the meanings as "strength" and "wisdom." And we know that they were either bronze or brass—some scholars suggest that the ancient Hebrew word did not distinguish between the two. In either case, they would be a mixture of a sun metal (copper) and a moon metal (zinc or tin). That calls to mind the lesser lights, representing the sun, moon, and Master of the Lodge; and since the Master of the Lodge can symbolically represent the candidate, it suggests that the sun/moon—male/female —Apollonian/Dionysian consciousnesses—must be in proper balance within the person. But the two pillars with the Fellow Craft standing between them also strongly suggest the three pillars of the Tree of Life, which would make the Fellow Craft the middle pillar or the pillar known as beauty, harmony, or balance.

On the other hand, the pillars are standing at the door, so what about portal guardians from other traditions: what insight might I gain from those. What if I also think about them as the demons/portal figures often found in Buddhist shrines? Then the pillars would represent "fear" and "desire" or "self-centeredness," which I must overcome before I can enter the place beyond them, which represents a place of enlightenment.

Thus I can "use" Masonry to constantly remind myself that if I want to have a meaningful and productive life, to be of benefit both to myself and others, I must maintain a balance in my mind and spirit. I must not give way to self interests or place my interests above those of others; I must not be afraid of shadows or the unknown; I must be master of myself, not a slave to my passions; and I must always remember that, no matter how far I think I have come, I have only started the journey.

That, for me, is a use of Masonry. My best wishes to you in finding your own uses.

This material first appeared as a *Short Talk Bulletin* for January, 2008, published by the Masonic Service Association of North America

Faded Plastic Flowers

On one of the back roads I sometimes take between Guthrie and Edmond, there is a small country cemetery. On a grave by the fence near the road is an old stone. Wired to the stone is a bouquet of plastic flowers, now faded nearly to a yellow-white. When I first noticed them, over five years ago, more of the original colors were left—white lilies, red and pink roses, none of which could have looked real even when new.

But someone had taken the trouble. Someone had cared enough for the person buried there to buy those flowers, sharing the little money they had with the memory of the dead, fixing them carefully in place—wired down tightly against the chance of wind and rain.

One wonders how someone could have cared so much then, and not cared enough since to replace them. Perhaps that person, too, is now dead; perhaps he or she lives in another state. Or perhaps, like most Americans, this person has come to fear death so much that to return is too uncomfortable. I hope the memories are brighter; less faded than the flowers.

We have come to a strange relationship with death in this country. As a culture, we have come to shun it, to fear it, to treat it as an enemy to be fought at all costs. What should be the supreme culmination of life, the great and joyful transition to the next existence, has become dirty—a thing not to be talked about. No Victorian maiden aunt ever felt more uncomfortable about the mention of sex than the typical American now feels about the mention of death.

Those plastic flowers are, in a haunting way, a perfect allegory for contemporary attitudes toward death. Real flowers bud, bloom, wither and die. It is natural and accepted. We may miss the blossoms, we may wish they still bloomed, but no one feels cheated by the process of nature. Plastic flowers, like plastic death, just fade, silent and forgotten. They are not part of a great cycle, created by a kind and loving God. We have allowed our grave decorations, and our relationship to death, to become artificial and ugly.

Masonry has much to say about death. The ritual was written at a time when death was not an enemy to be feared (or, even worse, a social indiscretion to be apologized for). Our culture as a whole understood death in a different way. Poets, writers, and others pictured death as gentle and natural, and not as some sort of calamity.

Masonry belongs to this latter tradition, and it is one of our great strengths. The Mason is taught to greet death as an approaching friend, not as the final enemy. In this, Masonry is more in tune with the rhythm of the world, more natural, than most of our contemporary thinking which hides dying away in the sterile walls of hospitals. In Freemasonry, we learn to look Death in the face, and we find there the welcoming faces of those we have loved and lost. Consider these passages from various Masonic rituals.

> *"Nature will have its way, and our tears will fall upon the graves of our Brethren, but let us be reminded by the evergreen, symbol of our faith in immortal life, that the dead are but sleeping, and be comforted by the reflection that their memories will not be forgotten; that they will still be loved by those who are soon to follow them; that in our archives their names are written, and that in our hearts there is still a place for them."*

> *"Death is the final friend, who carries us into the more immediate presence of God."*

> *"Only he who has overcome the dread of death shall be entitled to advance in knowledge."*

Masonry's interest in death is not morbid. Our ancient Brethren knew that if a man does not come to terms with death, he will spend his life in the living death of fear. It is only when death holds no terror for us that we can truly live freely and creatively.

It is surely true that a major purpose and goal of Masonry is to allow men to live creatively and vibrantly. Masonry is an affirmation of life in all its glorious diversity—a life of sharing, not greed; of love, not hatred; of compassion, not narrow indignation; of growth, not of stunted confinement; and, especially, of trust and confidence, not of fear.

From the first steps the candidate takes as an Entered Apprentice, to the words of the Senior Warden at the grave, to the great cry of Constans "My trust is in God!" in the 27° when he is surrounded with impossible obstacles, to the vows of the 32°, Masonry teaches that we have nothing to fear, if only our faith is well-founded.

Never was that lesson needed more. Today the world encourages us to fear and dread. Bombs in the hands of terrorists, whether placed in Olympic parks, aboard air planes, or outside abortion clinics, strive to fill us with the fear which means surrender of our lives to doubt and panic.

Terrorists are so called because they seek to inspire terror. If we give into that terror, we become their accomplices as well as their victims.

But Masonry says "NO!" "Live in hope and not fear. Let no one circumscribe your life. Let your monument not be faded plastic flowers but confident living—building in others the memory of a man who did not fear to die and, especially who did not fear to live.

"Faded Plastic Flowers" was published in The Scottish Rite Journal for January 1997

I Had It Good

No, when I was growing up I had it **GREAT!** My family was all anyone could ask. My father was—and my mother is—highly gifted and thoughtful. They had a wonderful ability to make anyone feel instantly comfortable and at home.

Evenings followed a predictable pattern. My father would come home from the office about 5:15 in the afternoon. He would mix a spirited refreshment for Mother and himself, and fix soft drinks for us children, until we were old enough to handle something a bit stronger. We'd all gather in the den and discuss the events of the day.

Usually at least one of my parents' friends would stop by for a refreshment during that period, and they were always welcomed. Family and friends all used the back door; if the front bell rang, you knew it was a stranger. If someone had a special problem they wanted to discuss for a few minutes, he and Dad would go into the living room. I used to notice how many people went into that room looking tired and worried and came out looking relaxed and hopeful.

Later in the evening, the family almost always had dinner together (Mother is a great cook), and the discussion continued. Sometimes it was about school, but usually it was about what I now know were ethics and philosophy and religion. And, as I grew older, Freemasonry. We learned the basics of all those things as we learned how to handle alcohol or human relationships, naturally and by example, without ever knowing we were learning anything at all.

Once, after I had left home for college, I realized that I had never, literally never, heard either of my parents' voices raised in anger—at us, at each other, at anyone. Thinking I must be mistaken, I asked Mother about it.

"No," she said, "we decided when we got married that anger simply gave hurt and accomplished nothing, so we agreed that if either of us started to feel anger, we'd stop the conversation until later when we could pick it up calmly."

There was not a moment in my childhood when I did not feel loved and cared for.

I have a good friend called Terry. Terry's home was a continual battlefield. There was alcohol in his home, too, but not in moderation. Both his parents drank to the point of intoxication, almost every night. Verbal abuse was constant. Physical abuse was frequent. He was getting his own breakfast by age six. His mother was usually too drunk to get out of bed. He has a bridge in his mouth, replacing the teeth his father knocked out when he was 12. When he was 14, his mother left with another man. Today, Terry has no idea where she is. When he was 15, his father threw him out of the house. He's been on his own since then. There was not a moment in his childhood when he felt loved and cared for.

Yet, he has done well. He has a good marriage with a charming and accomplished lady. They have a son and daughter, nearly grown. But it wasn't easy for Terry. He had to learn how to be a human and then how to be a father. Over the years, it has been a joy to watch him grow and develop.

Paul is a DeMolay in a town not far from Guthrie. Paul is on his third stepfather. His mother changes husbands more often than most people replace automobiles. (There have been several "special friends" between the husbands.) He's a big, good-natured kid of 18, getting ready to go to college on a football scholarship. I was surprised one night after a Chapter meeting when I went back in the room to turn off the lights and found him sitting alone, crying with the most racking sobs I've ever heard from a human being. I went over and sat down by him and he threw his arms around my neck and sobbed even harder. When he had calmed down a little, I asked him what the matter was. He said, "We had a degree tonight, and it always gets me when they talk about filial love. They just don't know how much filial love can hurt!"

He'll reach the minimum age to petition the Lodge next year, and I've promised to get him a petition. I hope Masonry can teach him how to love and that love doesn't have to hurt.

My friend Burt doesn't know his father's name. He knows his mother, but they don't communicate. The child welfare people took him away from his mother when he was a young child. He lived in a series of foster homes until he was 18. He's 30 now, with a good job. But he can't form permanent relationships. We've been friends for nine years, the longest friendship, he tells me, he's ever had. He's very smart, but he primarily uses that intelligence to manipulate others.

I'd give anything if I could somehow magically give Terry and Paul and Burt the sort of family I had—the sort of love and security and consideration and positive feelings I simply took for granted. I can't. All I can do is be the best friend I can possibly be, and try to help them over the rough places each has to face.

When we talk about family values, we have to take each family where it is and as it is, whether we like it or not. Often we don't like it at all—often we want to go in and tear a family apart and shake it up and shout "You're doing nothing but hurting yourself and every else. Stop it!" But that doesn't work, either.

My father told me many things which have been of great value to me, but one of the most valuable was this: "Remember, at any given moment, each person is doing the very best he can at that moment and under those circumstances. No one deliberately does less than their best. It's just that their best varies a great deal."

If we, as Masons, truly care about families and truly what to help preserve "family values," we have to accept families as they are. You don't restore a perfectly preserved building; you don't tune a well-running engine. We must assume that a family, no matter how troubled, is composed of people doing the best that their experiences, their personalities, and their resources allow them to do. If we are truly to care about the family, we must be willing, personally and corporately, to help improve those things, rather than to stand by in Olympian approval or disdain.

If we believe that love within a family is important, we must be willing to teach love, and precept and example.

If we believe that mutual support is important, we must be willing to be supportive.

If we believe that trust is important, we must be willing to trust, have that trust violated, and trust again.

The Scottish Rite teaches that we make a difference in the world one person at a time, and that each action we take echoes to eternity. There must be as much celestial condemnation for the man who passes a wounded family by as there was in the story of the Good Samaritan for those who passed by ignoring the wounded traveler at the side of the road.

It's simply a matter of caring, and Masons have promised to care.

"I had it Good" was published in the November 1997 issue of *The Scottish Rite Journal*, an issue dedicated to the question of family values.

Abe Lincoln's Axe

The story is told of a historian recording folk history in Illinois in the 1970s. Several people in the countryside had told him of a farm family which had the axe Abraham Lincoln used when splitting logs for a living as a young man.

The historian finally located the farm, and found the farmer in the yard splitting wood for the living room fireplace. He asked him about the story.

"Yes," said the farmer, "it's true. Abe Lincoln lived around here as a young man, and he worked for a while splitting wood for my great-great-grandfather. Happened he'd bought a new axe from a peddler the day before Abe Lincoln came to work here, and he gave it to Lincoln to use. We've kept it ever since."

"That's a real historical treasure," said the historian. "It really ought to be in a museum. Would you mind going into the house and bringing it out so I could see it?"

"Oh, we know it's important," said the farmer. "I take it to the school from time to time and tell the kids about it and Lincoln. Seems to sorta make him real for them. But I don't have to go into the house. I've got it here."

He handed the horrified historian the axe he had been using.

"You mean you're still using it?!"

"Sure thing. An axe is meant to be used."

The historian looked it over carefully. "I must say, your family has certainly taken good care of it."

"Sure, we know we're protecting history. Why, we've replaced the handle twice and the head once."

In many ways, Masonry is like Abe Lincoln's axe. All of us tend to assume that Masonry has always been the way it was when we joined. And we have become fiercely protective of it in that form. But, in fact, we've done more than replace the handle twice and the head once.

When Bros∴ George Washington, Benjamin Franklin, and Paul Revere (and other Masons of their era and for decades to come) joined the Fraternity, they did not demonstrate proficiency by memorizing categorical lectures. Instead, the same evening they received a Degree they sat around a table with the other Brethren of the Lodge. The Brethren asked each other questions and answered them for the instruction of the new Brother. They asked *him* questions and helped him with the answers.

The discussion continued until they were confident that he understood the lessons of the Degree. They then taught him the signs and tokens, and he was proficient. In many cases, he took the next Degree the next night .

The Custom of allowing 28 days to pass between Degrees came about for no other reason than the fact that most Lodges met every 28 days, on the nights of the full moon. There was no mystery behind that. Very few horses come equipped with headlights, and only on nights of a full moon could people see well enough to leave
their homes in the country and come into town for a meeting safely.

As to other changes, for instance, the names of the three ruffians have changed at least three times since the Master Mason Degree was created around 1727.

More importantly, the nature and purpose of the Fraternity have changed radically over time. It certainly is no longer a protective trade association, nor a political force amounting almost to a political party, but it has been those over its long history.

So, yes, Masonry changes. It changes fairly frequently and sometimes dramatically. Far from being a bastion of conservative resistance to change, through most of its history it has been a major agent of change agent fostering revolutions in political life (the American revolution, for example) and social life. It created homes for the elderly and orphanages, and then worked for the sort of social legislation to make those widespread. It sought economic development for states and communities. Until the late 1940s and 50s, it was one of the most potent forces for change in America.

And Masonry is like Abe Lincoln's axe in another way. For, although the handle and head had been replaced, that axe was still used by Abe Lincoln in truth if not in fact.

The farmer used the axe to teach. He told children about it and about Abe Lincoln. He helped make the past real to them so that they could learn the great values of honesty and hard work which Lincoln typified so well. It's the same with Masonry. In spite of the many changes which have already happened and the changes which are bound to happen in the future (Masonry, like any living thing, must change and grow or die), it is still the same. Its essence—the lessons it teaches, the difference it makes in the lives of men, that great moment of transformation which is the goal of Masonry, when a man becomes something new and better than he was when he came in the door as a candidate—that essence cannot and will not be lost, as long as Brothers meet in the true Masonic spirit, to work and learn and study and improve themselves and the world.

That's Masonry. And like Abe Lincoln's axe, it was meant to be used, not to rust away in a museum case. That use keeps it bright and sharp and Masonic, no matter how often the handle and head need to be replaced.

"Abe Lincoln's Axe" was published in the February, 1996 issue of *The Scottish Rite Journal*

Before the Flood

It was in the early 1970s. I was teaching at a college in Eastern Oklahoma, which meant a two-hour drive to Guthrie, Oklahoma, for rehearsals for the Scottish Rite Easter Pageant.

To wile away that time, I used to listen to the religious radio stations, most of them broadcasting from Texas. There were the usual offers on some of the more "primitive" of them. One program offered three magic prayer cloths, available for a love offering of only $5. The red cloth would bring answers to your prayers for health or the curing of illness. The yellow cloth would bring answers to prayers for spiritual healing. And the blue would bring prayers for financial security. An autographed picture of Christ was offered by another radio "minister." A third guaranteed a bottle of "healing oil."

But the one which nearly caused me to wreck the car, and which makes me regret to this day that I didn't pull over, write down the address, and send in my money, went as follows (after the usual poorly recorded Hammond organ music, of course):

"Now, dear Brothers and Sisters in radio land, I'd like to tell you about a special offer we have for you today. As you know, in our radio ministry, we try to touch every aspect of your life.

"Many years ago, my father became concerned with the need for a Christian laxative, one that didn't rely on all those harsh and harmful Godless chemicals, but was natural.

Now, my father was a Methodist Bishop [I'll just bet!], *and so he wrote* to *all the Methodist missionaries serving in Africa, and he asked them to talk with the witch doctors of the tribes to whom they were ministering, and ask them what they recommended for irregularity, and to collect samples of the herbs and send them to him.*

And then he personally experimented until he found a combination which was safe and effective. And then, when he decided to make it available to the friends of this ministry, we had to decide what to call it. And since it's all natural, and nature is very old, we looked in the dictionary to find a word which means "old," and we decided to call it "Antediluvian Herb Tea." [Close, "Antediluvian" actually means "before the Flood."] *And I'm happy to tell you, that we can send you a one-pound package of Antediluvian Herb Tea in exchange for a love offering of only $10."*

Honest! That's what he said, as accurately as I can reconstruct it from memory. And somehow, the image of a Christian laxative, the name of which means "Before the Flood" recommended by leading witch doctors, personally tested by a Methodist Bishop, and available tor a love offering, has remained with me throughout the years.

The point, of course, is not that a charlatan can pose as a preacher. The point is to illustrate and underscore Albert Pike's statement, "TRUE RELIGION CONSISTS IN THE EQUILIBRIUM OF GOD'S TWO GREATEST GIFTS TO MAN—FAITH AND REASON." The Rite teaches over and over again that we must never shut off the brain, not even when we are dealing in the area of faith. God has given to man the ability to think, to plan, to evaluate, to make choices. So far as we know, He gave that ability to no other creature. It is a gift and a responsibility.

Abalard, the great Church father, taught that doubt and question were essential if man were to come to a true and strong faith. Pike echoed his thoughts. That does not mean that the Mason should be a skeptic. Faith is essential to the Mason. That great truth is taught in every Degree of Freemasonry from the Entered Apprentice to the Thirty-Third. The difference is between a "child-like" faith and a "childish" faith. The "magic" prayer cloths, the autographed picture of Jesus, the herb tea—these are childish at best. Both the Bible and Freemasonry teach that faith should be child-like.

And unafraid, children ask questions.

Article reprinted from *The Oklahoma Scottish Rite Mason,* February 1996.

The Imposition of Ashes

It was my freshman year at the University of Oklahoma, and it was Ash Wednesday. That evening my friend Dale and I went to St. John's Episcopal Church for the imposition of ashes, a ritual in which the congregation kneels at the altar rail while the priest makes a cross-shaped mark with ashes on the foreheads of those kneeling. It is a solemn and beautiful service. Father Frank, a man small in stature but large of heart was officiating, carrying the powdery ash in a silver container, about the size of a shallow cereal bowl, with his left hand, and marking the sign of the cross with his right thumb after dipping it in the ash.

As Father Frank paused in front of Dale (actually the priests' names and Dale's name have been changed out of respect for their cloth—Dale having later become a priest himself) and reached for his forehead. There may have been a little ash floating in the air, but, whatever caused it, Dale snoze a mighty sneeze.

Instantly, the bowl emptied as the ash took flight, covering everything with a soft grey patina. Father Frank, who had reflexively squinted his eyes as the powder flew at them, looked up with a white circle around each eye in his otherwise grey visage, looking like a pale copy of Al Johlson in blackface. Dale was kept from arising and running only by the press of those standing behind him. The congregation was making a masterful effort to suppress its mirth, but there were not infrequent explosions of laughter, instantly suppressed.

"It's all right, my son," said Father Frank. "Just wait a moment." He departed toward the sacristy and a moment later Father Don appeared. He was a young priest, serving as Curate for a while to gain a little experience before going to a church of his own. A football player in high school and college, he carried the refilled bowl of ashes in a massive hand. As he stopped in front of my friend, Dale took on a look pure terror. It was obvious that another sneeze was coming. He quickly turned away to his left. Father Don saw the expression and correctly interpreted it. He quickly turned away to his right. And so, of course, the bowl was perfectly exposed when Dale loosed a second mighty sneeze, emptying the bowl and bestrewing Father Don with the contents.

That was more than the congregation could take; laughter became general, and prolonged, and nearly

But I Digress...

hysterical. Father Don looked down at Dale, rather like a grey mountain inclining its peak. "Well, Dale," he said, "You've taken out the priest and the curate. Would you care for a shot at the altar boy?"

But then he raised his considerable voice and said to the congregation (and this is the reason I bring the whole thing up), "Remember, now, this is the season that teaches us that, no matter what we've done, we can start fresh. If you will all go back to your seats for about five minutes, we'll pick up where we left off."

To me, one of the most valuable lessons of Freemasonry is that you can begin again. I don't mean in the sense of forgiveness of sins—that's a matter for a church, not a fraternity. I mean the simple idea that we really can start over; we don't have to carry the emotional baggage of the past.

Many of us see that symbolism in the Fellowcraft Degree, when the young Entered Apprentice passes between the two pillars. The tradition is that they were hollow, and that the archives of Israel were stored inside. The symbolism is that the Entered Apprentice can rid himself of the past, can deposit the past in the pillars and leave it there, as he passes between them toward the winding stairs.

You'll find the same idea, symbolized in many different ways, in several of the Scottish Rite Degrees Sometimes the symbolism is of death and rebirth, sometimes of passing from one apartment to another, sometimes of washing the hands, and there are others. Most of them carry additional meanings as well, but the background lesson is simple: whatever the errors, the mistakes in judgement, or the lapses of the past may have been, you can put them aside and go on. It is behind the general Masonic tradition that whatever negative a man may have done is irrelevant once he becomes a Master Mason.

Albert Pike said it beautifully. *"The Mason does not sigh and weep, and make grimaces. He lives right on. If his life is, as whose is not, marked with errors, and with sins, he ploughs over the barren spot with his remorse, sows with new seed, and the old desert blossoms like a rose."* (Morals and Dogma, 163) My Father was wont to phrase it more bluntly: "Neither God nor nature forces a man to make the same dumb mistake twice."

It's an important message. The goal of Masonry is that Masons lead good, happy, helpful, productive lives. We are to benefit others and ourselves, and, through a progress of growth and self-discovery, learn how to be of benefit at ever higher levels of mind and spirit. But while we cannot do that without learning from the past, neither can we do it by lugging the past with us. If we are to living positively, we must keep the knowledge and insight, and leave behind the negative feelings.

The ashes of the past are just that, the ashes of the past. We bear their marks—the things they taught us—upon our brows, but we leave the burdens behind as we continue to climb the stairs.

The Imposition of Ashes was first printed in *The Scottish Rite Journal*

Masonic Symbols Don't Mean

Notes on Thinking with Symbols

If you were to ask many Masons to name the most unusual thing about Freemasonry, they would probably say, "It uses a lot of symbols." It certainly does. Masonic rituals tell us such things as, "the symbol conceals; it does not reveal" "Masonry consists of a course of hieroglyphical and moral instruction, taught agreeably to ancient usages, by types, emblems and allegorical figures." "No man may be said to understand Freemasonry without an extensive and profound study of its symbols." The symbols are the life-blood of the Fraternity. We identify ourselves by wearing the square and compasses, or the double-headed eagle, or the crown and cross. Most of us have looked at a Masonic symbol and wondered aloud, "What does that mean?" The Masonic Service Association publishes several Short Talk Bulletins and Digests dealing with symbols, but even those only scratch the surface.

The reason is that the surface is deceptive. Symbols usually don't "hold still." Granted the complexity of symbolism, they can't.

There are two ways to approach the study of symbols and symbolism.

One is to learn a list of meanings associated with symbols; the other is to think about *how* symbols work—what happens in the mind. (In either case there is a third element, beyond the scope of this work, but critically important. That is a general knowledge of myth and man's use of symbols through the ages. A list of resources is provided after the glossary.) Both are useful, but in this discussion we are going to concentrate on the "how." So we need to lay some groundwork. (An essential book on the subject is Alfred Korzybski's *Science and Sanity,* in which he created the science of General Semantics. A second essential book is *The Meaning of Meaning,* by C.K. Ogden and A. Richards. Most information in this lecture was either lifted from or heavily influenced by those two books.)

Man is a symbol-using critter
(and we are using "man" in the classic sense of "humanity"). Virtually everything we do involves that manipulation of symbols. Remember, words are symbols (if you doubt that, try sitting on the word "chair"), as are numbers, musical notations, smells, sounds, touch, and images. In fact, if you can think about something, you are using symbols to do it. The brain can only manipulate symbols, it doesn't have hands to manipulate real objects. If you plan the perfect house, or think about what to have for dinner, or recite the Pledge of Allegiance, or pray, or plan a business strategy, you are manipulating symbols. There simply is no other way to do it.

So what is a symbol? The fact that you can't sit on the word "chair," or nourish yourself by eating a picture of a turkey dinner, or add football player number 7 and football player number 9 and end up with football player number 16, or buy a soft drink with a dollar sign, gives us a clue. A simple "down and dirty" definition is: *A symbol is something which makes us think of something else, consciously or unconsciously.* Unconsciously, because some symbols do not work at a conscious level. Smells are a good example. For many of us, the smell of baking and vanilla are strongly linked with pleasant childhood memories of home and Christmas; we react with pleasure to the smells, even if we don't consciously know why, and even if we are not consciously aware of the smell. Semanticists and symboligists divide symbols into many categories, including signs, signals, symptoms, referents, emblems, icons, trophies, signets, logotypes, ensigns, types, and attributes (there is a glossary at the back for those interested in the differences) but with rare exception, the principle is the same. A symbol makes us think of something.

And so, Masonic symbols don't mean anything;
no symbol does. To slightly paraphrase one of Korzybski's great insights: ***Meanings are in people, not in symbols.*** (Original: "Meanings are in people, not in words.") Symbols do not have meanings—they arouse a meaning in the mind of the person who encounters a symbol. That can seem counter-intuitive. It certainly seems as if symbols have meanings; we ask all the time "What does that mean?" and someone tells us.

But if we remember for a moment that words are symbols and we think of a time we have heard someone speaking a language we don't understand, the fact becomes obvious. We have to *learn* a language, we have to learn to read musical notation, we have to learn to add and subtract. If the meaning were in the symbol, we would know it automatically.

Consider the sets of symbols here. Do they mean anything?

Not unless you know how to read Egyptian hieroglyphs, or Mayan glyphs.

Meanings are in us, not in the symbols we use, and we have to learn a meaning for a word, just as we do for any other symbol.

PRINCIPLE 1 - MEANINGS ARE IN PEOPLE, NOT IN SYMBOLS.

The noted semanticist, H. Dumpty...

... (as cited by Professor Lewis Carroll in *Through the Looking Glass, and What Alice Found There*) makes the next important point.

"When I use a word," Humpty Dumpty said,

in rather a scornful tone, "it means what I choose it to mean — neither more nor less."

"The question is," said Alice, "whether you can make words mean so many different things."

"The question is," said Humpty Dumpty, "which is to be master — that's all."

When interpreting the meaning a symbol is supposed evoke, the critical question is this: *what was the intent of the person using the symbol?* With very few exceptions, it simply isn't true that a symbol "only means one thing." Those few exceptions almost all involve symbols which are invented for a specific purpose (most often for use in science and mathematics, or in art forms such as music or dance) and used by a small group of people. If one assumes that symbols which arise from the popular culture or history, or especially from differing cultures, can only mean one thing, serious consequences can arise.

No one justly bearing the honorable title of "human."  or the even more honorable title of Freemason will argue that to burn a cross in a person's yard for the purpose of intimidation, or expressing racial hatred, is a completely reprehensible thing to do. But it is not true, as several pundits contended on the television talk shows, that "a burning cross only means one thing—hatred and the KKK."

Not so.

The symbol of the burning cross *(crux flamant)* either with four equal arms as shown here or with the longer lower arm of the Latin cross, developed in the Middle Ages. It was used to represent zeal and devotion, and sometimes as a symbol of the Pentecost. The alchemists used a burning cross to represent purification and refining, both spiritual and physical. Somehow, none of these seem to suggest racial hatred and persecution.

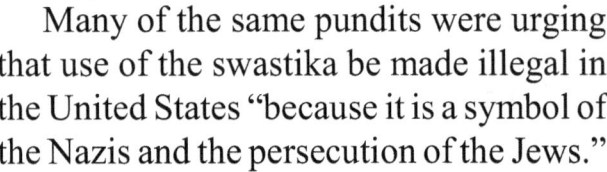

Many of the same pundits were urging that use of the swastika be made illegal in the United States "because it is a symbol of the Nazis and the persecution of the Jews."

But to do that would be to outlaw a symbol which has deep and sacred associations for both Hindus and Native Americans, and which in somewhat altered forms, has been sacred to most of the religions on the planet. The pundits may have only one meaning for the symbol, but the world at large has many more.

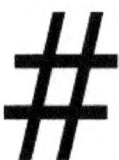

It is obvious in our own experiences that symbols can be used to suggest a variety of things. Take the octothorn. Does it mean "sharp" as in "raise a musical tone ½ step?" Does it mean "number" as in "Garfield Masonic Lodge #501 ?" Does it mean "pound" as in "It weighs 12#?" Yes. It also means "gridiron" and "graph." It also means "tic-tac-toe." Are all meanings equally right? They can be. Are all meanings equally right all the time? No. It depends on the intention of the person who used the symbol, an intention which can usually be inferred from the context. If you are reading the title of a piece of music on a CD, "Bach - Prelude and Fugue in C#" probably means C-sharp, not C-pound.

PRINCIPLE 2 - SYMBOLS MEAN WHAT THE SYMBOL-USER USES THEM TO MEAN.

Anti-Masons violate that principle as a matter of course.

"Look!" they cry in delighted horror, "That's a *pentagram*! That's a sign of witchcraft, a sign of the devil, that is. I *told* you them Masons was devil worshipers." If the anti-Mason wants to use a five-pointed star to represent the forces of darkness, he has every right to do so. I have every right to use the word "dog" to mean "cat" if I wish. I do *not* have the right to insist that every time someone else says "dog," they are talking about a feline. No one has the right to assert what someone else has to "mean" by any symbol.

When they see the symbol drawn with two points upward, they are even more certain they have discovered satanic dealings. "Everyone knows," they aver, "that's a symbol of the horned devil, Baphomet."

Thus, of course, it is not surprising that many anti-Masonic sites on the Internet make much of the

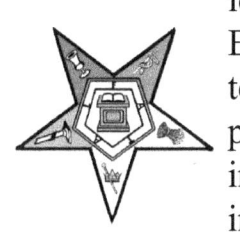

identifying image of the Order of the Eastern Star. They have even been known to insist that the ONLY meaning of a five-pointed star, with two points upward, is to indicate worship of and magical practices involving the demon Baphomet. I would respectfully draw their attention to the Congressional Medal of Honor.

Because this is a critical point in learning to think symbolically, it is worth spending a little time on it. It is also a good example of why a knowledge of the history of symbols used by humanity is important.

At first thought, it seems strange that we would draw a star with five points. It isn't easy to do. It would be much easier to draw a star with four, six or eight points- simply folding a piece of paper or parchment would give you the design. It would be even easier to draw a star as a point or a disc with or without rays. That is the way they appear to most people as we look at the night sky.

There are stars drawn with even numbers of points, of course; but the five-pointed star is very old. This tomb painting from ancient Egypt clearly show five-pointed stars. That may give us a clue.

For the ancient Egyptians, immortality was a complex concept. There were, by some accounts, 9 immortal aspects to a human, rather than a single entity similar to our concept of the soul. Each immortal aspect had a different destination after death if the person proved to have lived a worthy life. One of those immortal aspects was the *Shua* which became an immortal star in the heavens.

The number 5 has been associated with humanity from the earliest times [3=Deity, 4=the material world, 5=humanity], probably because of the five extremities (head arms and legs). The association of the human with the pentagram is also ancient.

The pentagram developed in early cultures, not as a symbol for a devil, but as a symbol of mankind. Also, because it is constructed using the "golden ratio"-the mathematical proportion which not only describes the relationship of each part of man's body 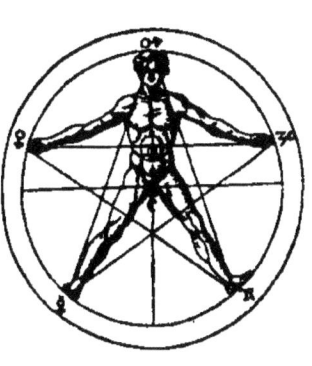 to the other parts but also the relationship involved in almost every aspect of creation to every other aspect-it symbolized the activity of the Deity. How then did it become associated (only in modern times) with satanic forces?

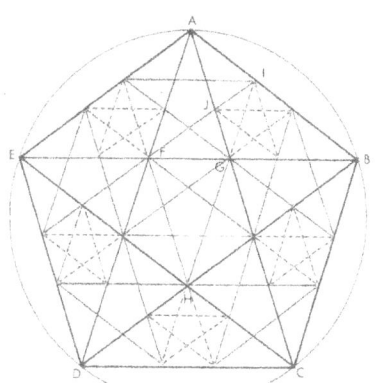

In texts and illustrations of sorcery, the magus was sometimes shown standing inside a pentagram while invoking a demon, or sometimes standing outside and invoking the demon to appear within the pentagram. Even if we assume that such illustrations were intended to be taken literally (which is not a safe assumption) the magus was not invoking a demon to worship it, he was invoking it to command it to obey his will. Early writing, including the Bible, had suggested that God gave dominion to man over all created things (see Hebrews 2:8 - "In putting everything under him, God left nothing that is not subject to him."), which would include spirits. The pentagram was "protection" against the demon because it was a symbol of man's sovereignty over the demon. It controlled and limited the evil spirit. Far from being intended as a symbol of the ascendency of evil, it was a symbol of the ascendency of humanity. There is more than a little irony in the fact that a symbol of mankind should be used by fanatics to attack an organization dedicated to human development.

The Eastern Star "reversed pentagram" probably derived from the early Renaissance symbol, "the star of the Incarnation" which was used to represent the moment at which Christ was incarnate in the Virgin Mary by the Holy Ghost. The downward-pointing ray represented the coming of the divine to earth—the entry of the spiritual into the material. The symbol may also be related to a five-pointed star of red, white, blue, green, and yellow used by the Druse as a symbol of Deity. It is worth repeating.

PRINCIPLE 2: SYMBOLS MEAN WHAT THE SYMBOL-USER USES THEM TO MEAN.

Imagine two boys.

Ted had a great tree-house in his back yard. He loved it, spent many hours of both play and rich fantasy there. When life got a little rough, he would go there and just sit, looking at the leaves and hearing the birds. Bill climbed a tree in his back yard, but he fell out, badly injuring himself. He spent weeks in the hospital in splints and a great deal of pain. It was more than a year before he had completely recovered. Both are now grown. Each will react very differently, now, if they see a tree or even an image of a tree, whether or not they are consciously aware of their reaction. Ted will probably want to have trees in his yard. When he sees a picture of a tree there are going to be warm associations in his mind. Bill probably doesn't have large trees in his yard, and when he sees a picture of a tree, he may be a little uncomfortable.

Both of them have an intellectual meaning for the picture, of course, they know what it is. Their knowledge may be extensive or cursory, but they can identify the symbol. Their intellectual responses may be nearly identical, but their emotional responses are going to be very different.

PRINCIPLE 3 - SYMBOLS TRIGGER BOTH INTELLECTUAL AND EMOTIONAL RESPONSES.

Under unusual circumstances, those emotional reactions may be profound (the reaction of parents of a small child to the sound of screeching brakes in the street, or of anyone to a photograph of their beloved). Usually, reactions are much less pronounced—a matter of mild pleasure, or dislike, or humor, or sorrow, or discomfort, or confusion. It may be a matter of "kind of like," or "don't care for." Almost unnoticed though these reactions may be, however, they do mean that different people will respond to the same symbol in slightly different ways. They just don't all "feel" the same. Artists and communicators make use of those differences in crafting images.

The most simple way to illustrate a change in the emotional content of a symbol while holding the intellectual contest constant is with type faces. Let's take a fairly intellectually-neutral statement—It is fifteen minutes before noon—and present the same statement in different type styles. The chances are that you will not "feel quite the same way" about each line.

It is fifteen minutes before noon

It is fifteen minutes before noon

It is fifteen minutes before noon

It is fifteen minutes before noon

IT IS FIFTEEN MINUTES BEFORE NOON

IT IS FIFTEEN MINUTES BEFORE NOON

It is fifteen minutes before noon

It is fifteen minutes before noon

The differences can be even more noticeable if we use a symbol which has some emotional loading to begin

with and see it presented in different ways. Masonry uses the image of a skull to represent death, to remind us that no man can truly begin to live until he has overcome the dread of death, and that "we leave our lives behind us for history to pass on when we step into the grave. There, the pontiff lays down his miter, the rich man his jewels, and the poor man his rags, and all stand together to be judged." Here are different representations of the symbol. Note that the way in which each is drawn changes our feelings and reactions.

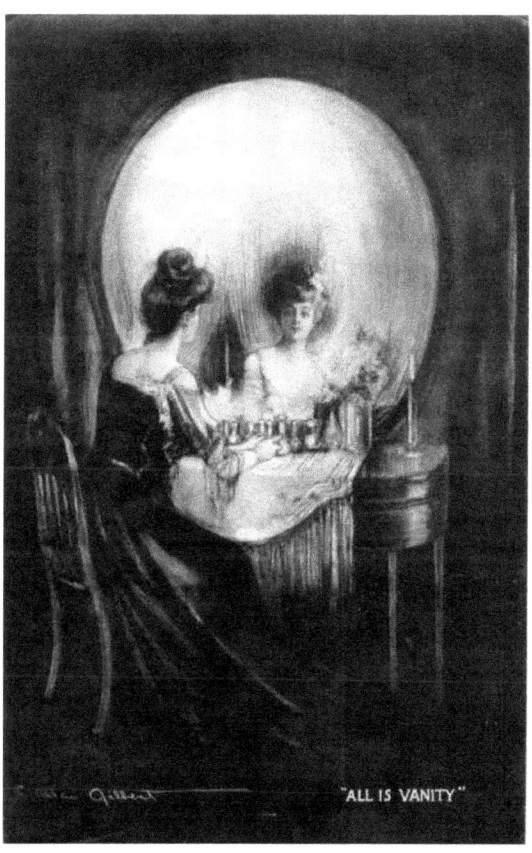

And in the drawing by Allen Gilbert entitled "All is Vanity" we can see a use of the symbol as a commentary.

Again Principle 3: SYMBOLS TRIGGER BOTH INTELLECTUAL AND EMOTIONAL RESPONSES.

> "Breathes there the man, with soul so dead,
> Who never to himself hath said,
> This is my own, my native land!"

In "The Lay of the Last Minstrel" Sir Walter Scott catches one of the moments typical of symbols. Symbols can, at times, short-circuit the intellectual process and present us with powerful and unexpected surges of emotion. Even the most cynical and jaded of us can suddenly catch a glimpse of the American flag floating high in the sky and find ourselves overwhelmed with emotion.

A piece of music often does the same thing.

Sometimes, in hindsight, we can deduce a chain of associations which led from the symbol to the emotional response—sometimes we can't. But even when we can figure it out afterward the reaction at the time is immediate and overpowering. Thus we have principle 4.

PRINCIPLE 4 - SYMBOLS CAN TRIGGER EMOTIONAL RESPONSES WITHOUT A CONSCIOUS THOUGHT PROCESS.

Even a skunk can believe in flowers.

PRINCIPLE 5 - SYMBOLS CAN BE CULTURAL OR PERSONAL. A cultural symbol is one whose primary associations are defined by a group to which we belong. That group may be a language group (e.g. past and present speakers of English, who have decided on the meanings of the words of our language), or a national group (e.g. people living in the United States), a professional group (doctors have special meanings for words or symbols as they are used in medicine), a religious group (members of your denomination), or other, including members of your Fraternity, your family, or your political party, to name just a few. By custom and often by law, groups will establish meaning for some symbols commonly used by the members of the group. American culture has established meanings for such things as stop signs, green traffic lights, solid lines next to the center stripe on a road, police badges, and drawings of a little red school house. A person from our culture will have meanings for those symbols, even if he never drove a car or attended school.

Often, culturally-determined symbols will not cross cultural lines. Even if their denomination does not use the crucifix as a symbol, almost anyone from our culture—Christian or not—will recognize it as a symbol of faith, compassion, and reverence. But we are told that many people from Asia and the South Seas, seeing a crucifix for the first time, regarded it with horror as a symbol representing unspeakable cruelty and agony. (Since the meanings of a symbol are in the mind of the person encountering the symbol, both were correct.)

Not that we can lay claim to being sympathetic respecters of others' religious concepts and images. For many Americans, the image of the great Egyptian creator god, Atum, sexually stimulating himself so that from his seed the lesser gods and all living things could be created gives rise to scorn, derision, and a feeling that the whole image is slightly "dirty." It is safe to assume that the ancient Egyptians saw it, instead, as sacred and holy, and representing the great creative act of the universe.

These are all examples of culturally-determined symbols. But, as we said, there are personally determined symbols as well. For me, and probably for no one else in the world, the best symbol of indomitable human spirit and courage is a small figurine of a skunk holding a rose. It was given to me decades ago by a very good friend, who was about to enter a program to treat drug addiction. He knew it was going to be a terribly long and painful process, and that there was a chance he would not survive, and a better than 50-50 chance that he would not succeed. (He did succeed, but only after living through a nightmare I cannot even imagine.) The day before he left, he gave me the figurine, with a note which said, "Even a skunk can believe in flowers." I honor his courage and determination each time I see the figurine.

This Principle—**SYMBOLS CAN BE CULTURAL OR PERSONAL**—is truly central to the study of the symbolism of Masonry because it describes the pattern we hope will occur. *We start by learning the associations of the symbols as taught by the Masonic culture, but then, with thought, with knowledge from other sources, and by intuition, we develop them into personal symbols. They take on associations which come from our own life experiences and values. That is when they truly become powerful and valuable.* Any musician can tell you there is a vast difference between "playing the notes," and "playing the music." There is a similar difference here.

read all instructions before beginning assembly

So read the first page of the assembly booklet which came with a swing set I once bought. At face value, that seems very strange. "Bring the vehicle you are driving to a complete halt, then proceed to read all the instructions before you try to put this thing together."?

Of course it doesn't mean that. Although the "real" meaning associated with a stop sign is "bring the vehicle to a halt," the writer of the instructions borrowed the symbol to strengthen the point of stopping the assembly until the notes had been read. It is an illustration of our final principle.

PRINCIPLE 6 - IF THE MEANING ASSOCIATED WITH A SYMBOL IS KNOWN, THE SYMBOL CAN BE CHANGED OR ASSOCIATED WITH OTHER SYMBOLS TO CREATE A "META-MEANING," A MEANING WHICH GOES BEYOND THE ORIGINAL.

A fine example is in a commercial by the Dow Chemical Company. The Periodic Table of Elements hangs in almost every science classroom in the United States. In classic form, it is a table of the elements composed of oblong boxes containing numbers indicating the element's atomic number and atomic weight, and other information. The most noticeable feature is a two letter abbreviation of the Latin name of the element. The box for iron looks like this.

The point of the commercial is that the "human element" is the most important. So, superimposed over some beautiful photography is this image which refers back to the chart of elements. This plays on the double meaning of "element" and reenforces the idea of the commercial.

A word of warning is needed here, however. Different versions of a symbol may be the result of changing artistic styles and tastes, or even changing political situations. In such a case, it is dangerous to infer a change in meaning without checking the background and history. Probably the most recognized symbol of the Scottish Rite of Freemasonry is the double-headed eagle. As it happens this is also an ancient symbol and one which appears in many cultures. In some cases, the drawing of the symbol may tell us more about the time and culture which produced it than the meaning it is intended to trigger in the mind. Note the following examples.

But I Digress...

I will admit that, to me, the 32° design bottom right looks as if someone had badly startled the bird. The large double eagle upper right is one of my great favorites. Designed by Brother Kris Dexter, that is an eagle with an attitude!

We have all seen a statue or drawing of the goddess Themis, (whom we sometimes call "Justice") calm, serene, holding the balance in one hand and resting the other on the hilt of a sword. It is one of the most familiar icons in our culture. It communicates that justice is deliberate, impartial, not given to favoritism or to rash actions. But we may not realize that there are two traditions in the portrayal of Themis. Consider these drawings from the 1800's, still in contemporary use.

She is not always shown as blindfolded, and the sword is sometimes shown raised. While all the images convey the same general meaning, there are certainly suggested shades of meaning as to whether justice is militant or passive, blind to anything but the case itself or aware of the larger world, etc. These are examples of modification.

As an experiment in the way modification effects the meaning of symbols, take a few seconds to imagine each of the following, and make a mental note of your reactions.

Imagine that Themis is shown holding not a sword but a machine gun.

Imagine that she is holding the sword, but it is dripping blood.

Imagine that she is peeking out from under the blindfold.

Imagine that she is shown wearing patched and tattered clothing.

Imagine that the sword is broken.

Imagine that in one pan of the balance is a dollar sign and in the other is a small child.

Imagine that she is shown with one foot on a fallen enemy.

Imagine she is shown, lounging in a chair, sword and balance discarded beside her, holding a drink.

Imagine the statue is broken.

Imagine that she is shown kneeling—having cast aside both sword and balance, cradling and weeping over the body of a child.

It is easy to see how the message changes from image to image. Some may seem sarcastic, some may seem heroic, some may seem to point out justice denied or perverted, some may suggest justice made stronger. In large measure, the response will be personal to you. Essentially, two different sets of thoughts/reactions are being triggered. They may be in conflict or discordant, or they may re-enforce each other.

These manipulated symbols, and the new symbols they form, can be extremely powerful. Most Americans react strongly to the sight of an American flag being burned disrespectfully. It is the attitude of the person burning the flag, not the burning itself, which arouses the emotion. After all, burning is the legally appropriate way of disposing of a flag which is soiled or damaged.

We can use symbol manipulation to suggest relationships between two concepts. Most people are touched by the Normal Rockwell painting of Santa Claus kneeling in prayer beside the crib. One of the most powerful images to emerge from the 1960's was the picture of a daisy in the muzzle of an M-16.

We can use symbol manipulation to suggest shades of meaning and richness. Music functions as a symbol (it can make us think of other things) as the American composer Charles Ives showed in his organ work "Variations on 'America'" in which he wrote the song "America" in a range of different ways to suggest religious faith, a 4th of July celebration, a country fair, and the quiet strength of the home.

An excellent example of symbol manipulation or alteration to convey a story is given by Rudolf Koch in *The Book of Signs*. He redraws this sequence of symbols engraved in a late medieval church.

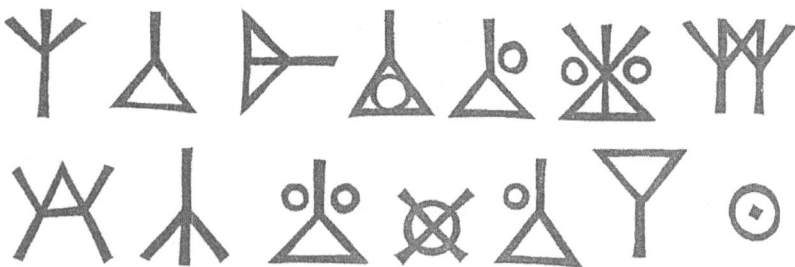

As an exercise (and with the hint that it is the story of life) try to decipher the sign sequence before you read the explanation. It is given in the back, before the Glossary.

Masonry frequently manipulates symbols,
in order to provide additional meanings to the same symbol. Often the purpose is to suggest movement and development. For example the relative movement of the compasses in regard to the square suggest movement from the material to the spiritual.

Other progressive symbol manipulations include:
- the circumambulation of the Lodge room once, twice, and thrice;
- the movement of the cable-tow in the three Degrees
- the movement of the bare foot in the three Degrees
- the described movement from a point to a line, to a superficies, to a solid
- the raising and lowering of Warden's columns in those jurisdictions which use them
- due form
- the three progressive burials
- lighting or extinguishing candles
- the number, colors, and positions of the candles in the Scottish Rite Degrees
- the colors of the Scottish Rite caps
- the worked stones presented in the York Rite

Once again: **PRINCIPLE 6 - IF THE MEANING ASSOCIATED WITH A SYMBOL IS KNOWN, THE SYMBOL CAN BE CHANGED OR ASSOCIATED WITH OTHER SYMBOLS TO CREATE A "METAMEANING," A MEANING WHICH GOES BEYOND THE ORIGINAL.**

A brief review of the six principles before leaping off into the human brain:

PRINCIPLE 1 — MEANINGS ARE IN PEOPLE, NOT IN SYMBOLS.

Symbols do not, in and of themselves, "mean" anything. A symbol is a stimulus which evokes a response.

PRINCIPLE 2 — SYMBOLS MEAN WHAT THE SYMBOL-USER USES THEM TO MEAN.

Since the meaning evoked by a symbol resides within the individual, he is the sole judge of the meaning he has for a symbol. It is intellectually sloppy, at best, to insist that a symbol only means one thing or that everyone who uses a symbol uses it in the same way.

PRINCIPLE 3 — SYMBOLS TRIGGER BOTH INTELLECTUAL AND EMOTIONAL RESPONSES

Number symbols setting forth a problem in arithmetic will probably trigger primarily intellectual responses. The sound of a frightened child crying will probably trigger a primarily emotional response, at least initially. A vast range is possible.

PRINCIPLE 4 - SYMBOLS CAN TRIGGER EMOTIONAL RESPONSES WITHOUT A CONSCIOUS THOUGHT PROCESS.

It is not uncommon for us to get "caught" by sudden emotions or sorrow, pride, joy, anger, compassion, laughter, love, and disgust, to name only a few. Setting aside mental illness, this happens because some symbol triggers a response which slips past the rational "censors" most people have. This fact is useful in designing symbols which are to have an emotional impact.

PRINCIPLE 5 — SYMBOLS CAN BE CULTURAL OR PERSONAL (USUALLY BOTH).

This is true because our thinking, value systems, and ideas are influenced by both. We all share some of the values of the groups to which we belong-family, church, region of the country, nation, western civilization, humanity. But we also have our own life experiences including things which have happened to us, books we have read, plays we have seen, music we have heard, friendships we have formed, and much more; and those experiences give definition to our intellectual and emotional responses. No symbol arouses exactly the same thoughts and feelings in two people.

PRINCIPLE 6 — IF THE MEANING ASSOCIATED WITH A SYMBOL IS KNOWN, THE SYMBOL CAN BE CHANGED OR ASSOCIATED WITH OTHER SYMBOLS TO CREATE A "META-MEANING," A MEANING WHICH GOES BEYOND THE ORIGINAL.

The same process is at work when we learn more about a symbol or its traditional associations. Part of interpreting a symbol is the process of understanding how these changes have been made and what they accomplished.

So, how does it work?

There is much we do not understand about the working of the mind, but we can chart the general steps.

1. We encounter something which the mind interprets as a symbol. As we know, this can be an image, a sound, a smell, something we touch.
2. With or without our conscious awareness, the symbol enters into our mind— which is to say that

our sense receptors send electric/chemical impulses to the brain,
3. If our knowledge or life experiences have given us any meaning which we associate with the symbol, that meaning is triggered in the mind.
   A. If we have no associated meanings at all, there is a very good chance we will not see the symbol, even if we are looking at it—that's essentially how camouflage works.
   B. If it is a symbol for which we have very few meanings and those are primarily cultural as opposed to personal (e.g. πr^2) only one meaning may be triggered.
   C. In most cases, however, a chain of meanings or associations is likely to be triggered. More about that in a moment.
   D. If the symbol is one we associate with pairs or opposites, its "partner" may be triggered.

   The **symbol** may trigger the **thought/ meaning**

salt	pepper
up	down
right	left
night	day
square	compasses
good	evil
black	white
mother	father
in	out

   to list just a few
   E. The context and situation in which we encounter a symbol usually determines the first meanings we associate with it. If Brother Jones hears the word "square" in Lodge, his first

associations are likely to be "compasses," "altar," etc. If he is also the supervisor of a construction project and hears the word "square" on the job, he probably will not think of "compasses" first.

It is almost as if we had a different brain, or at least mind, for each situation in which we often find ourselves. It has been said that if a person thinks the same way on a picnic, in church, and at a football game, he is thinking inappropriately in at least two of the three places. All of us have had the experience of being asked a question in a unexpected setting-being asked a question about Freemasonry at work, for example-and experiencing a sort of mental "bump" while we "shift gears."

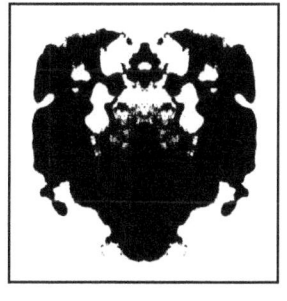

"Lie down on the couch, close your eyes, and tell me the first thing which comes into your mind"

It is this triggering effect of word symbols which forms the basis for the word association tests sometimes used by psychologists. Persons with some particular emotional disturbances tend to make the same or similar associations with words, and so the pattern of a patient's responses can give an indication as to underlying problems. Roughly the same thing is true of image symbols, which is the basis of the Rorschach ink blot test.

All this may seem complicated enough, but the real complexity has yet to start. When we encounter a symbol, we rarely think only of one thing, and the thought seldom stops with one or two associations. Again, most of us have had the experience of listening to a conversation or a lecture, and hearing something which starts a whole chain of thoughts and associations, usually leading us far away from the original, until we suddenly become aware of our surroundings again with a bump. Our minds work very quickly, and so we are not always completely aware of all the steps. We also usually operate on more than one level, and so symbols gain richness as we think about them and work with them.

To illustrate a simple trigger chain, consider the symbol "white;" either as a word symbol or as a paint chip. In this chart the symbol ⇨ will mean "triggers an associated meaning" (e.g. red ⇨ anger means "red" triggers the associated meaning "anger"). The symbol ⊃ will mean "triggers the other half of the pair" (e.g. day ⊃ night means "day" triggers the other half of the pair.

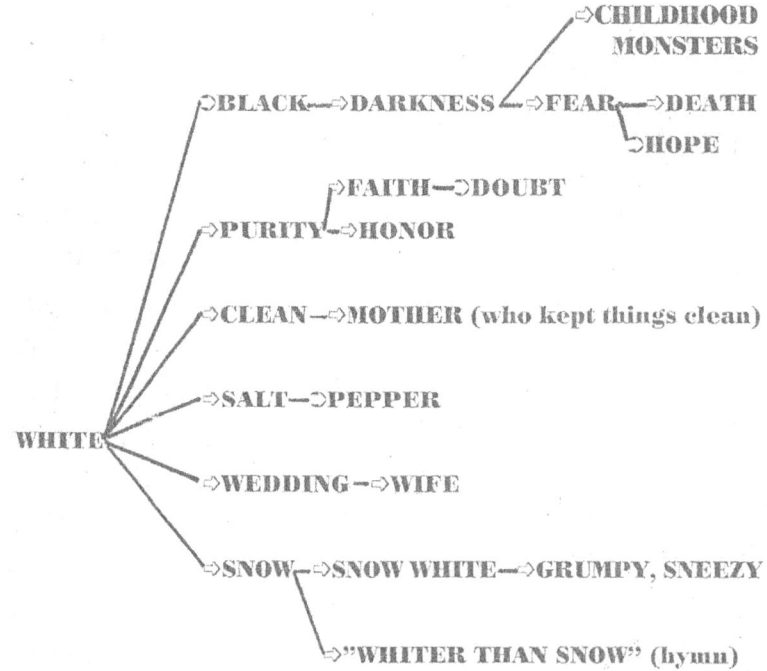

It may seem there is a great leap from "white" to "Grumpy," but most of us make even greater leaps when we free-associate.

This chain triggering of symbols, as was said, accounts for their richness. Obviously the degree of that richness is dependent upon our knowledge and experiences, including those things we have read, seen, and heard.

As an exercise in working with symbols, try to write down or chart out like the example above, your association chains with the following word symbols:

    candle   acacia
    rod   cloud
    bitter   surf

On removing the log from mine own eye before commenting on the mote in yours

We've repeatedly made the point that MEANINGS ARE IN PEOPLE, and A SYMBOL MEANS WHAT THE SYMBOL USER USES IT TO MEAN. I thought I was

unlikely to fall into the trap—until I saw this image on the Internet. Nothing of course is more fun or makes us feel better than moral indignation, and I indulged myself to the full. "It's those accursed anti-Masons," said I. "It's a dirty attack on Masonry, and it's blasphemy as well, to substitute a skull for the initial of the Deity! What else could it mean?!" I then read the accompanying note, in which the Brother (not an anti-Mason) who had designed it as a tattoo explained that it showed the Square and Compasses as triumphant over death—that it was a visual representation of the Masonic motto "Those whom virtue had joined, death shall not separate." Point taken.

Now, let's tackle one of the most fundamental and complex concepts in Freemasonry— one which is represented through several sets of symbols. *But remember this essential warning: no one speaks officially for Freemasonry, especially as far as the meanings of its symbols is are concerned. What follows is true to the best of my belief, but it is true only for me. You may or may not agree, and that is perfectly all right.* It is a speculative science, but that does not mean you are bound by anyone's speculation.

Background
From the time of ancient Egypt, probably from man's earliest awareness, we seem to have realized that there are two distinct character types, ways of thinking, "dispositions to respond," types of consciousness (they have been called all that and more) in the human experience. The interplay between these two "consciousnesses" has been a primary source of human conflict and is the very soul of tragedy. The Greeks dealt with these often, as did Shakespeare, but it was not until Friedrich Nietzsche wrote *The Birth of Tragedy* that they were codified and named.

One type of consciousness is named for the Greek god, Apollo, the sun god. The other is named for the Greek god Dionysus, the god of wine, and of the life force of nature. The character of each god is complex, as is the consciousness each represents, and it may be helpful to outline these characteristics briefly.

APOLLO

☆ god of the sun
☆ pictured as a beautiful youth, either nude or clothed
☆ attributes (identifying symbols) include sun, bow and arrows, and lyre
☆ god of lyric poetry, represented by lyre
☆ worship accentuated reason
☆ associated with mysticism and prophecy. The Oracle at Delphi was his priestess

DIONYSUS

✯ god of wine and life-force
✯ pictured as an infant, a youth, or an old man: sometimes shown as a vigorous bearded adult man dressed as a woman
✯ attributes include wine cup, grapes, grape vines, bread, and thrysus (white rod with pine cone on top)
✯ god of dramatic poetry, plays were written as part of his worship and the name of his temple, the *Theatron*, gives us the word "theatre."
✯ worshipers sometimes experienced "divine madness" running uncontrollably across the landscape singing and dancing wildly
✯ associated with reproduction and the life-drive, not just in sexuality but in the way life strives to continue, the awareness that life survives by consuming life, the interconnectedness of all living things

☆associated with the moon

The nature of the Apollonian and Dionysian consciousnesses derives from the characters of the two gods. But it is very important not to think of them as good and evil. I've used an open star to represent Apollo and a star with both black and white elements to indicate Dionysus, because there is much of the dark in the Dionysian consciousness. BUT IT IS NOT THE DARK OF EVIL. It is the dark shade of the forest and the cave, the dark of the abyss from which all life emerges. It is sexuality, but not limited to animal passion. It is the driving force of life to make itself felt. It is passion and feeling. It is life feeding on life, but knowing that there is no moral component to that because all life is connected. As Joseph Campbell was wont to remark: "The lion will lie down with the lamb, the lion will then eat the lamb, and both the lion and the lamb know that nothing evil is happening." Dionysus is living life in the midst of the brawl, the pain of both birth and death, the awareness of being alive. Let us compare the two types of consciousness.

APOLLONIAN CONSCIOUSNESS
☆also known as "solar consciousness"
☆values logic and rationality
☆male
☆seeks Light
☆aggressive in defense of life
☆detached, can be remote and uncaring
☆solves problems
☆selects experiences he wishes to have
☆does not easily compromise

☆distrusts emotions
☆wishes to think rather than feel
☆seeks to rise above the struggle of life
☆cool
☆aristocratic, with a strong sense of "us and them"
☆self-protective or ego-protective
☆ likes pattern and predictability
☆values idealism
☆distrusts instincts
☆slow to commit to others, commits to a cause more easily

DIONYSIAN CONSCIOUSNESS
✭also known as "lunar consciousness"
✭values feeling, emotion, "authenticity"
✭female
✭seeks fulfilment
✭creates and nourishes life
✭involved in life, values participation, "bring it on"
✭distrusts thinking which focuses exclusively on logic
✭is more curious about how others feel than what they think
✭dislikes impartiality
✭values practicality
✭trusts their instincts
✭commits to others as individuals not groups
✭distrusts authority, which is seen as cold and calculating

Throughout much of recorded history, humanity has struggled with combining and reconciling these two types of consciousness. Either, if too strong in an individual, leads to problems. There is evidence that a major purpose of the ancient mystery schools and initiation was the bringing of these two types of consciousness into balance within the person.

Freemasonry is replete with symbols which represent the resolution of these two types of consciousness.

The three lesser lights represent the sun (solar or Apollonian consciousness) the moon (lunar or Dionysian consciousness) and the Worshipful Master. The Worshipful Master serves as a symbol of the individual Mason, who is seeking mastery over his life. He represents the individual in whom the sun and moon are in balance.

Because it was originally passed on by word of mouth, we do not know the intended punctuation of the answer to the question, "What come you here to do?" but many think it was "To learn, to subdue my passions, and to improve myself, in Masonry." If so, then the meaning might be "to learn" (Apollonian consciousness), "to subdue my passions" (Dionysian consciousness) "and to improve myself" (find the balance).

In the Fellowcraft Degree, we deal with the pillars Jachin and Boaz. We do not know if they were bronze or brass (the ancient Hebrew word is the same for both). In either case, we are dealing with a sun metal and a moon metal-copper and tin (brass) or copper and zinc (bronze); the pillars themselves represent a combination or balance of the two types of consciousness. There is a long tradition in Freemasonry associating Jachin with male or solar attributes and Boaz with female or lunar attributes. The pillars are topped with the celestial and terrestrial spheres, which can be seen as symbolizing the sky-father and earth-mother associations. The candidate passes between them, again representing the middle point or equilibrium between the two. In his circumambulation, the candidate follows the path or the sun, symbolically moving between day and night and ending up at the altar or point of equilibrium. Solomon can also be a symbol of the balance between the solar and lunar consciousness or the Apollonian and Dionysian ways of being. In the Scottish Rite, of course, this equilibrium is represented by both of the great symbols of the Rite: the balance and the double-headed eagle.

Again, the warning is repeated: no one speaks for Masonry. This interpretation of the symbol works for me. That doesn't mean it is right for anyone else on the planet.

Your Turn

As an exercise, and using the principles and patterns we've discussed, work through

the symbolism of the pot of incense.

Background (cultural) information

✦Incense appears to have been a part of worship and celebration of all kinds from ancient times on.

✦Throughout most of history, it has been extremely costly.

✦One of the first great trade routes was the "incense road."

✦Entire nations rose and fell because of the economics of that road.

✦A golden altar for the burning of incense was a part of the furnishings of the temple built by Solomon.

✦Incense produces a pleasing smell.

✦A container of burning incense will be hot.

✦The smoke arising from the incense carries the smell.

✦Frankincense was one of the gifts of the Three Kings.

✦Incense is a natural product, usually the resin of a tree.

✦The great majority of the world's religions use incense.

✦Several Protestant denominations do not use incense, a few find the thought offensive.

✦There is a Biblical story in which some men, not of the priestly tribe, burned "strange incense" before God and were struck down.

✦While most American homes do not burn incense, a majority do use scented candles, scented sprays or air-fresheners, devices which hold either scented oils or wax tablets, some of which use electricity or a burning candle to heat the substance.

✦The 1960's saw an increase in interest in incense, echoes of which remain today.

✦Smoke rises.

Masonic Blue Lodge Ritual Reference

"The pot of incense is an emblem of a pure heart which is always an acceptable sacrifice to the Deity, and as this glows with fervent heat, so should our hearts continually glow with gratitude to the Great and Beneficent Author of our existence for the manifold blessings and comforts we enjoy."

Personal Experience and Knowledge

+- Does your religious background include the use of incense?
+- What are your feelings about the use of incense in a religious context?
+- What smells do you find enjoyable?
+- Do you associate incense with strength? weakness? the masculine? the feminine? worship only? home? a time period of your life? a cultural movement of which you approve? a cultural movement of which you disapprove?
+- What other feelings, thoughts, experiences do you have related to the concept of burning incense?

Using this, and any other information you have, think about the symbol of the pot of burning incense. What does the symbol tell you about Freemasonry? What does it tell you about yourself and your life? What does it tell you about good behavior? What does it tell you about relationships?

A final thought.

There is a continuing debate among Masonic writers as to the purpose and use of the symbols. One school of thought is that the Mason should not go beyond the meanings of the symbols given in the ritual. The other is that we are supposed to use the symbols of Freemasonry and the meanings given in the ritual as a springboard or point of departure for our own thoughts and speculations; that transforming the Masonic symbols from cultural to personal symbols and then using them to discover more about ourselves is the primary way in which "masonry takes good men and makes them better." It is not possible to prove which view is correct.

But there is no question as to which is the more fun.

The meaning of the symbol sequence given by Koch

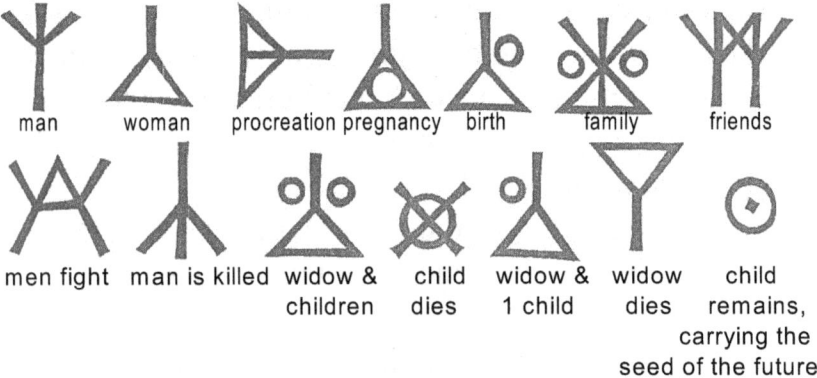

Glossary

attribute - a symbol used in art to identify a person, especially a saint, whose attribute is usually the means of their martyrdom-since no one knows what the people actually looked like. Thus a male figure with an attribute of an X-shaped cross (holding an X-shaped cross) is St. Andrew; a female figure with an attribute of a wheel is St. Cathryn, etc.

emblem - technically, an emblem is a image used to represent an idea, whereas a symbol is simply a substitution of a sign for a thing. In practice, the word symbol is generally used to mean both.

ensign - a flag or banner used to represent a nation, organization, or individual of power (king, president, pontiff, etc.)

icon - an image, traditionally flat as opposed to three-dimensional, used especially, but not exclusively, in reference to religious symbolism.

iconography - a collection of icons, symbols, signs, etc., which are associated with a given context. We can speak of the "iconography of the 4th of July," or of "Episcopal iconography," which is a division of "religious iconography," or of "Blue Lodge iconography," "Scottish Rite iconography," or "York Rite iconography," which are subsets of "Masonic iconography," etc.

insigne (plural, insignia) - a symbol or image used as a badge of identification.

logo (logotype) - originally, a cast metal slug, used in printing, which imprinted a design used to identify a business or store. Now the design itself.

referent - the real-world object or idea represented by a symbol

semiotics/semiology - the study of signs (symbols, etc.) and how they convey meaning {essentially, what we're concerned with in this booklet}

sign - an image, action, etc., which operates at a simple level and requires only limited knowledge to communicate (e.g. waving someone through an intersection). Compare with signal.

signal - a symbol operating at the most basic level, working by instinct and not requiring knowledge on the part of the observer (e.g. a deer signaling danger by flashing its white tail).

symbol - in the broadest sense, anything which triggers a meaning or makes us think of something else almost everything we encounter the symbol.

symbolism - the use of a sign or symbol to communicate a message symbology-the study of symbols or signs in their various manifestations.

symptom - the image of a thing which accompanies a second thing and is regarded as evidence of the second thing's presence (e.g. a flashing red light accompanies dangerous situations and is considered a warning that a dangerous situation is present).

signet - a seal, usually carved into a ring and impressed into sealing wax, hence, by extension, a mark used for the identification of property, etc., (now sometimes seen
in tattoos).

trophy - generally, any symbol or image which represents victory, either over an adversary or in some event of skill or ability. In religious iconography, an image which represents victory over death and the grave.

type - an image which is seen as representing the best or finest example of the thing symbolized

Resources

Many of these books are out of print and will have to be found on the Internet. On the other hand, many are being republished. Dover books tends to keep it's books in print for long periods of time, as does the Masonic Service

Association. If I know a book is available from those sources, it is so noted. Several dictionaries of symbols have been included. You may wonder why you would need more than one dictionary of symbols. There is no one work which contains all, or even most, of the symbols you will encounter. I have, and use, all of these.

Count Eugene Goblet d' Alvielle, *Symbols, Their Migration and Universality* (Dover) This is an early book, but still one of the best showing how symbols develop, change their meaning, and move from nation to nation.

Harold Bayley, *The Lost Language of Symbolism: The Origins of Symbols, Mythologies, and Folklore* Good background resource.

Hans Biedermann, *Dictionary of Symbolism: Cultural Icons and the Meanings Behind Them* A very useful, heavily illustrated reference book.

Daniel Beresniak, *Symbols of Freemasonry* a beautifully-illustrated book; not as helpful as some, but a nice addition to any Masonic library.

Joseph Campbell, *The Hero with a Thousand Faces*
   Historical Atlas of World Mythology
   The Inner Reaches of Outer Space: Metaphor and Myth As Religion The Masks of God (Vol. 1-4)
   The Mythic Image
   Myths to Live By
   Thou Art That: Transforming Religious Metaphor
      Transformations of Myth Through Time

(Note: much of Campbell's material is available on cassette tape, on video, and on DVD. I'd recommend any and all of it.)

J. E. Cirlot, *A Dictionary of Symbols* Written in Spanish, the English translation by Jack Sage has become one of the most important books for the study of symbolism.

R. T. Rundle Clark, *Myth and Symbol in Ancient Egypt* Many of the symbols we use both in Freemasonry and in our daily lives came from or were influenced by Egypt. This book gives a good overview.

George Ferguson, *Signs and Symbols in Christian Art* A beautiful book, with many illustrations and 16 tipped-in full color plates. Good discussions of such things as attributes.

Robert Fulghum, *From Beginning to End: The Rituals of Our Lives* As the title suggests, the book deals primarily with the rituals which accompany the activities of daily life. The mention of symbols is only occasional, but there are clear implications of the ways in which symbols evolve from daily activity.

Clare Gibson, *Sacred Symbols: A Guide to the Timeless Icons of Faith and Worship* Not as extensive as the title would suggest, but the book contains some excellent illustrations.

Vincent Foster Hopper, *Medieval Number Symbolism: Its Sources, Meaning, and Influence on Thought and Expression* (Dover) Originally published in 1938, this is still one of the best resources on the symbolism of numbers. Very useful.

Nadia Julien, *The Mammoth Dictionary of Symbols: Understanding the Hidden Language of Symbols* Very helpful book.

Carl G. Jung, *et al., Man and His Symbols* Jung probably influenced the study of symbols more than any other single person. His discovery of archetypical images opened a new era of understanding human culture and tradition.

Rudolf Koch, *The Book of Signs* (Dover) Good source book for many symbols historically used primarily in Europe. Koch also has a brief but interesting section on the stonemason's marks.

Robert Lawlor, *Sacred Geometry: Philosophy and Practice* A good introduction to this specialized area of symbolism which is so important in Masonry.

William Leaf & Sally Purcell, *Heraldic Symbols: Islamic Insignia and Western Heraldry* A useful book in the study of the history and development of symbols.

Ernst Lehner, *Symbols, Signs and Signets* (Dover) The book illustrates over 1,300 symbols from all periods of history and all geographic areas. There is little text, but the illustrations give you a chance to study and compare symbolic presentation of ideas. Very useful.
W. Kirk MacNulty, *Freemasonry: A Journey Through Ritual and Symbol* One of the most important books on

Masonic Symbolism of the late 1900's. I give a copy of this book to anyone I know is starting a serious study of Masonic symbolism.

Friedrich Nietzsche, *The Birth of Tragedy* Important generally, but especially important because of Nietzsche's discussion of the Apollonian and Dionysian character styles which play an important part in Masonic symbolism.

Shirley Plessner, *Symbolism of the Eastern Star* One of the very few books on the subject.

Alexander Roob, *The Hermetic Museum: Alchemy and Mysticism* This book is not easy to find, but well worth the trouble. It is a paperback, very thick, with hundreds of full-color illustrations on high quality paper. One of the most beautiful collections of symbols ever produced.

Oliver Day Street, *Symbolism of the Three Degrees* A useful overview, and an excellent insight into the understanding of the Degrees in the early 1900's.

Robert Wang, *The Jungian Tarot and Its Archetypal Imagery* A good course in the interpretation of archetypal images in a different context. Not easy reading, but very interesting.

Author not given, *Pocket Encyclopedia of Masonic Symbols* (Masonic Service Association of North America) There is a surprising amount of information in this little booklet, more than enough for most purposes. It is possible to go into greater depth on almost all the symbols mentioned, but it is a very good starting point for the study of Masonic symbolism.

SHORT TALK BULLETINS
from the Masonic Service Association of North America

\#   Title
10-30 "The 47th Problem"
6-55 "Astronomy and Freemasonry"
9-51 "Beehive"
7-54 "Behind the Symbol"
3-65 "The Blazing Star"
3-25 "The Cable-Tow"
5-24 "The Compasses"
9-50 "Cord, Rope, and Cable-Tow"
8-30 "Corn, Wine and Oil"
4-96 "The Five Noble Orders of Architecture"
4-53 "'From a Point to a Line. . .'"
11-46 "Hands in Freemasonry"
1 0-89 "The Hiramic Legend"
11-66 "Horizontals"
5-28 "The Legend of the Lost Word"
12-27 "Lesser Lights" 6-33 "The Letter 'G'" 5-34 "Masonic Geometry"
12-34 "Passages of the Jordan"
8-98 "The Plants and Animals of Freemasonry"
8-31 "Point Within a Circle"
5-35 "Pot of Incense"
11-23 "The Rite of Destitution"
4-33 "The Rite of Discalceation"
9-27 "The Ruffians"
9-56 "The Significant Numbers"
8-37 "Signs"

11-32 "Sprig of Acacia"
11-62 "A Stairway and a Ladder"
12-57 "Symbol of Industry"
3-25 "Symbolism"
2-62 "Symbolism: The Circle"
12-00 "Symbolism in Ritual"
7 -95 "The Symbolism of Stone"
7 -93 "The Symbolism of the Winding Staircase" 2-52 "Tool Symbolism"
11-74 "Veiled in Allegory and Illustrated by Symbols"

This material was originally prepared as a lecture for the "Beyond the Ritual" Masonic study and discussion group which meets in Guthrie, Oklahoma.

Speeches

The Symbolism of the Fellow Craft Degree

Brethren, let me start by apologizing for not being with you in person. I was greatly flattered to be asked to address you, and very sorry that a health problem made it impossible for me to do so in person. So my thanks to your Worshipful Master for extending the invitation, and my apologies to him, personally, for fulfilling it in so impersonal a fashion.

I especially regret not being with you, because the Fellow Craft Degree is one of my great loves. To me, it is one of the richest and most complex of all the Degrees of all the Bodies in the vast family of Freemasonry.

Because of the amount of material, I will be confining myself primarily to the second section of the Degree, known as the Middle Chamber lecture or the Winding Stair lecture. Of necessity, I will be using the Oklahoma Work for the discussion. There are significant differences in the Degree from jurisdiction to jurisdiction, but I think it fair to say that the major themes remain the same.

Also, before I begin, the usual caveats. Most importantly, when it comes to the meanings and the symbols of Masonry, no one speaks or can speak "officially" for the Fraternity. What you will hear is the truth as I see it, but you have every right to take a bucket of what follows and go to the relief of the nearest dirty hog.

Secondly, any language from the Degree which I quote is monitorial in Oklahoma. If it is esoteric in your jurisdictions, I offer my apologies.

Thirdly, I admit up front that I have been reading about Masonry and the Degrees for more than half a century, with the result that I am no longer certain at all which ideas are mine and which I have purloined from the work of others. Some ideas have evolved in conversations, and may well have been the ideas of others in the conversation. It may be as well to imagine a large set of quotation marks before the first word and after the last. There are, however, three works to which I would especially draw your attention. One is W. Kirk MacNulty's excellent book *Freemasonry: A Journey through Ritual and Symbol*. The section on the Fellow Craft Degree is both enlightening and challenging. The second is a paper by Brother Thomas D. Worrel, "The Seven Liberal Arts," presented to the Northern California Research Lodge on March 20, 1997. The paper can be down-loaded from the Internet. The third is *The Alchemical Keys to Masonic Ritual* by Timothy Hogan. While I will be suggesting some different interpretations than can be found in these three sources, they are extremely valuable in understanding the Degree.

On, then, to the Fellow Craft Degree.

The ritual tells us that the theme of the Fellow Craft Degree is knowledge. Specifically it says:

"If the object of the first degree is to symbolize the struggles of a candidate groping in darkness for intellectual light, that of the second degree represents the same candidate laboring amid all the difficulties that encumber the young beginner in the attainment of learning and science. The Entered Apprentice

is to emerge from darkness to light; the Fellow Craft is to come out of ignorance into knowledge"

I would take it a little further and say that I see the theme of the Degree as the movement from knowledge to gnosis, and therefore, also, of transition. While we will be focusing on the second section of the Degree, there is a very important foreshadowing in the penalty of the obligation of the first section.

To digress for a moment: the penalties of the Degrees contain some of the most important, condensed, symbolism in all Freemasonry, which is why it is so important that the candidate both hear and understand them. Each of the Degrees of the Blue Lodge is organized around a unifying theme or set of themes as lessons. The penalty of the Degree involves the destruction of the part of the body associated with that lesson, as well as two of the four (or five) alchemical or classic elements: earth, air, fire, water, and spirit. There are significant astrological associations as well, but that is beyond out present purpose. Thus the primary theme of the Entered Apprentice Degree is the importance of secrecy and the ability to control one's tongue. The penalty involves the destruction of the organs of speech, and the elements earth and water (sand and sea).

At the time the Fellow Craft Degree was being created, it was commonly believed that knowledge resided in the heart—no one was quite sure what the brains were for. That is why we have such expressions as "to learn it by heart," and "he knew in his heart." The penalty involves the destruction of that which has been abused if the person violated the lesson of the Degree (heart - knowledge) and the elements of air and earth.

It is, I think, generally accepted that Masonry takes many of its symbols from the twin sources of alchemy or hermeticism and the kabbalah. As we will see, both these and the concept of the portal will be important in the symbolism of the Fellow Craft.

Because the symbolism of the portal is so important in this Degree, it is worth taking just a few moments to think about portal symbolism. While portals can symbolize many things at once, they virtually always symbolize the movement from one state of being to another, or from one reality to another. The most fundamental of all portals is the opening to the birth canal and womb, and the bringing forth of life. In medieval iconography, this was usually represented by the *vesica piscis*, which looks much like an oval with a pointed top and bottom. It was used as a frame in much religious sculpting, and is frequently shown enclosing the Mother and Child. Folk lore abounds in stories in which a mortal enters a portal—often the space between two trees or two standing stones, sometimes a mirror or pool—and finds himself in the fairy world. Again, the symbolism is of leaving one condition and entering another.

Thus the second section of the Fellow Craft begins when the Brother leaves the preparation room (a symbol of one's condition before some transforming experience) and enters the Lodge. It is important to remember that he does not enter the Middle Chamber. Rather, he must create the Middle Chamber—or perhaps the path to the Middle Chamber—by his own acquisition of knowledge and understanding.

The Oklahoma work contains unique material at this point. To the best of my knowledge, it has been adopted for optional use in Georgia, but is not found elsewhere. I have reproduced it here, and if there is time, the Worshipful Master may want it read. If not, I will simply remark that it is known as the Eulogy to Mother. A simplified version appears in the DeMolay ritual as the Flower Talk. It may be coincidence, of course, but the major emphasis of the material is on the mother's role in birth and her connection to the world of the spirit, which seems to me to be a reenforcement of the portal theme.

> *After the Almighty Creator had thus made man and provided for his wants, He saw that it was not good for man to be alone, so as His last and best gift to him, He created woman. She was so lovely and so winsome that what before had seemed to him most fair now seemed to him but mean; in ministry so soft and tender, in loyalty so kind and true, she has ever fulfilled her mission and helped to mend his faults and mould him into virtue. My brother, Masonry teaches many beautiful lessons, but none of more importance than true respect for womanhood.*
>
> *As we stand here, were I to draw for you a picture of love divine, it would not be that of a stately angel with a form that is full of grace, but a bent and toilworn woman with a grave and tender face; no golden rings would enfold her, nor rosy her cheeks nor fair, but the face of a angel of pity framed in snow white hair; her hands are not white and slender, but roughened with work and woe, by bearing other's burdens and soothing the tears that flow; no halo of light surrounds her, no wondrous power she hath, but many and many a blessing is spoken along her path; others may paint their angels with white-robed forms of grace, but my sweet angel of pity has my mother's careworn face.*
>
> *But why endeavor to convey to you an ideal which is already enshrined within your heart, for deep down, safely locked within that secret chamber, you keep that cherished ideal, sacred and holy; it is your mother. It*

> was she alone, all alone, who went down into the valley of the shadow of death to receive your trembling soul at the gates of life; it was she who pillowed your baby head within the elbow of her bended arm; it was from her tender breast you drew with life giving fluid that sustained you in your helpless years.
>
> It was she who first taught your lisping tongue to frame that God-given prayer, "Our Father who are in heaven," in which all races, sects and kind may join. There is no man so vile, so base, so low, but who in his sin-stained soul, keeps pure and apart a little place for his mother's memory. And when, in the silent watches of the night his mind turns back to pure and happy childhood hours, he remembers that mother and is drawn closer to God.

Having entered through the portal of the preparation room, he is almost immediately confronted with a second one, marked by the portal guardians, the pillars Jachin and Boaz. There simply isn't time in this paper to go into the symbolism of portal guardians, but much has been written about it and I invite your attention to it. Jachin and Boaz are, of course, the pillars from the front of Solomon's Temple. The ritual of some jurisdictions includes the information that they were hollow, and the written archives of Israel were stored inside. This can be seen as saying that the young Fellow Craft can also deposit within them his own past, that he need not take with him any farther any of the failures, shortcomings, or errors of the past.

This is important because of the being sometimes known as "the dweller on the threshold," a personalization of all the fears, limitations, and frustrations we have accumulated through living, and who actively opposes our growth and liberation.

Through a series of associations, Jachin and Boaz symbolize wisdom and strength. The Young Fellow Craft pauses as he passes between them, and thus becomes, himself, the pillar of beauty or pillar of harmony. He completes the three supports of the Lodge (wisdom, strength, and beauty) and the three pillars of the Tree of Life from the kabbalah. He is the one in whom the attributes are in balance. It is therefore exactly the same symbolism as in the lesser lights, the sun, moon, and Master of the Lodge or the one in whom the solar (Apollonian) and lunar (Dionysian) attributes are in balance.

That symbolism is re-enforced in another way as well. We are not certain whether the original Jachin and Boaz were bronze or brass (the ancient word being the same) but in either case, they are a mixture of a solar metal (copper) and a lunar metal (either zinc or tin).

The pillars represent another portal, of course, but there are two more associated with them which may not be so apparent. They are topped by the celestial and terrestrial spheres. One obvious meaning is the ancient duality of skyfather and earthmother. But marked on the celestial sphere are two points known to astronomy since ancient Mesopotamia—the crossing of the celestial equator and the plane of the ecliptic. The celestial equator is a line formed in the sky by projecting the line of the earth's equator into space. The plane of the ecliptic is the plane in which the earth orbits the sun. If earth were not tilted on its axis, the celestial equator and the plane of the ecliptic would be identical. Because it is tilted, the two lie at an angle to each other. They thus form a large X in the sky on each side of the sun. From ancient times, those points (which also mark the solstices) had been considered portals. Ancient thought suggested that it was the point at which the universe came into being, and also portals by which souls entered the universe to travel to earth by the seven planets, and the point by which souls returned to heaven after ascending through the planetary spheres.

The X shape has long been a symbol of change and transition, and was used from the earliest times. That is probably why X is used to represent the unknown in math. If you look at medieval book illuminations or renaissance paintings, you will often find an X shape when change or transformation is being pictured. So, for example, look at the positions of arms or wings in many paintings of the Annunciation as in this by Fra Angelico.

So the celestial sphere is marked with these two portals, or symbols of transformation.

The young Fellow Craft then passes the pillars and enters the area of the winding stair.

The Senior Deacon next leads the young Fellow Craft up the stairs. In most Lodge rooms this is represented by a painted ground cloth, often quite beautiful. But I have been in Lodge rooms in which the stairs are a literal part of the architecture of the room, sometimes leading to a space above the Senior Warden's station.

The stairs are in sets of three, five, and seven. Much here is esoteric in several jurisdictions, so let me generalize by saying that the first three deal with preparation for learning. They represent the three principal officers of the Lodge, and therefore, by extension, the concept of body, mind, and spirit; all of much must be properly focused or "in tune" if the education/transformation is to be successful.

The symbolism of the next five is more complex. At the surface level they represent the five senses: hearing, seeing, feeling, smelling, and tasting. Those are the traditional ways in which information about the outside world comes into us. We hear something or see something; we touch it, smell it, or taste it, and we are aware of a thing or condition outside our bodies.

The steps also represent the five classical orders of architecture. But the ritual also tells us that two, the Tuscan and the Composite, are creations of the Romans and are of less significance. It also tells us "To the Greeks, therefore, and not to the Romans, we are indebted for what is great, judicious and distinct in architecture." It is pure speculation, of course, but I have always suspected that, since we are talking about knowledge, the coded message here may be that it is the Greek, not the Roman approach, to education which is important. Writers from the period suggest that the Romans were pragmatists about education; if they did not see an immediate use for something they were not interested in learning it. The Greeks valued knowledge of and for itself.

There is another important aspect to the section on the forms of architecture, which, in Oklahoma, has been made optional language and is seldom given (understandably, I suppose, because the Senior Deacon's lecture in the Oklahoma work, when done in full and at less than a machine gun pace requires between 50 minutes and an hour to deliver). In discussing the proportions and inspiration for the three Greek orders, the optional lecture tells us that the Doric was formed after the model of a strong robust man, the Ionic was formed after the model of an agreeable young woman of elegant shape, and the Corinthian was inspired by the tomb of a child. That means, of course, that we have referenced man, woman, and child, and that is a classical allusion to the Pythagorean Theorem.

So, climbing the five steps, we have reviewed the means by which information traditionally enters the mind through the five senses, we have been reminded that knowledge is important for its own sake, we have seen beauty described by numbers in the forms of architecture, and we have been reminded of the work of Pythagoras.

Then we start up the seven liberal arts.

The medieval world placed great importance on the seven liberal arts. They were composed of the *trivium* or three-fold path (grammar, logic, and rhetoric) and the *quadrivium* or four-fold path (arithmetic, music, geometry, and astronomy). The seven arts, represented by the figures of seven women, adorn the *Portail Royal* or royal porch at the Cathedral of Chartres. As one writer puts it,

"It can be read as indications for the steps to be followed on a path of spiritual development. For

the Chartres masters, the seven liberal arts were crucial. Studying them was a way to inner discipline and the training of one's spiritual faculties. For the masters and their pupils, the seven liberal arts were more than disciplines; they were beings."

The seven liberal arts were not only a tour through the accumulated knowledge of mankind, they were a tour through the universe as well. Each of the arts was associated with one of the planets known to the ancients. Dante, in the *Convivio*, gives the correspondences as:

  Grammar. . . . . Moon
  Logic. . . . . Mercury
  Rhetoric. . . . . Venus
  Arithmetic. Sun
  Music. . . . . Mars
  Geometry. . . . . Jupiter
  Astronomy. Saturn

There are many different ways of viewing the *trivium* and *quadrivium*. One which I find useful is to think of the first three as ways of testing or verifying information and the last four as ways of applying or discovering information. Grammar is far more than a third grade teacher explaining that one should not say "I ain't got no books." The structure of a language determines the things which can be thought in that language. And since language is only a specific example of a symbol system, the rules by which any symbol system works determine the thoughts which can be expressed in that symbol system. Logic is a means both of testing and discovery, rhetoric is both a means of testing and of communication.

With both the *trivium* and the *quadrivium*, it is important to understand that the process of thinking about the subject matter was as important as the subject matter itself. This was a truism in education during my early years in school, although it seems largely to have been lost in more recent years. We were told repeatedly that the important thing was to learn how to think, and that the various subjects we studied should teach us different ways of thinking.

The process can also be read in terms of the Kabbalah. We start with the young Fellow Craft as the middle pillar of the Tree of Life (Jachin and Boaz being the other pillars). Several Masonic writers have suggested correspondences between the Liberal Arts and the Sefirot. I would like to suggest a somewhat different relationship.

The mystic ladder is a very ancient symbol, and one which is not limited to the Judeo-Christian tradition. The ladder may be thought of as a special instance of the portal, since its obvious purpose is to go from one place or condition to another. There are obvious associations with Jacob's Ladder, but also with Native American myths of the people entering the world by climbing a latter from the underworld. A ladder or set of steps forms a significant symbol in many folk traditions—the rainbow serving as a ladder in some and rays of sunlight serving as a ladder in others. But the great theme is that of ascension or advancement to a higher state of being. Obviously, the Tree of Life can be visualized as a ladder as well.

If we think of everything which has transpired in the second section of the Fellow Craft Degree before we encounter the seven liberal arts as representing the world or daily existence, it is possible to see the remainder of the Degree with this correspondence to the Tree of Life of the kabbalah. Using the Sephirotic order given by Rabbi Moses ben Jacob Cordovero:

	Planetary Association	Sephirah
Before the 7 steps.........	Earth......	*Malkuth* {physical reality}
Grammar.......	Moon......	*Yesod* {coherent knowledge}
Logic..........	Mercury....	*Hod* {observational power}
Rhetoric........	Venus.....	*Netzach* {contemplation}
Arithmetic.......	Sun........	*Tipheret* {creative power}
Music..........	Mars.......	*Gevurah* {judgement, intention}
Geometry.......	Jupiter.....	*Chesed* {grace, power of vision}
Astronomy......	Saturn.....	*Binah* {understanding, reason, power of love}

That, of course, leaves two Sephiroth, *Chokmah* and *Keter*, to which we will return in a moment.

MacNulty provides a correspondence between the liberal arts and the officers of the Lodge as shown on the next page.

	Planetary Association	Sephirah	MacNulty
Before the 7 steps	Earth	Malkuth	
Grammar	Moon	Yesod	Tyler
Logic	Mercury	Hod	Inner Guard
Rhetoric	Venus	Netzach	Junior Deacon
Arithmetic	Sun	Tipheret	Senior Deacon
Music	Mars	Gevurah	Senior Warden
Geometry	Jupiter	Chesed	Junior Warden
Astronomy	Saturn	Binah	Worshipful Master

If, as I think, a major dynamic of the Degree is transformation, it can be interesting to add the seven stages of alchemical transformation to the chart.

Planetary Association	Sephirah	MacNulty	Alchemical Transformation
Before the 7 steps .... Earth	Malkuth	Tyler	
Grammar ... Moon	Yesod	Inner Guard	Calcination
Logic ..... Mercury	Hod	Junior Deacon	Dissolution
Rhetoric ... Venus	Netzach	Senior Deacon	Separation
Arithmetic .. Sun	Tiphereth	Senior Warden	Fermentation
Music ..... Mars	Gevurah	Junior Warden	Conjunction
Geometry . Jupiter	Chesed	W. Master	Distillation
Astronomy . Saturn	Binah		Coagulation

And, while it is certainly open to argument, I would suggest the possibility of correspondences with the Major Arcana of the tarot as well. (It does not follow the traditional numbering of the cards, but could be thought of as a spread.)

	Planetary Association	Sephirah	MacNulty	Alchemical Transformation	Tarot
Before the 7 steps	Earth	Malkuth			the Fool {questing Candidate}
Grammar	Moon	Yesod	Tyler	Calcination	the Magician {transformation through use of Will}
Logic	Mercury	Hod	Inner Guard	Dissolution	the Emperor {the structured World}
Rhetoric	Venus	Netzach	Junior Deacon	Separation	the Hierophant {the holder of Hidden knowledge}
Arithmetic	Sun	Tipheret	Senior Deacon	Fermentation	the Strength card {clarity of Action; directness}
Music	Mars	Gevurah	Senior Warden	Conjunction	the Chariot {emotions under regulation and control}
Geometry	Jupiter	Chesed	Junior Warden	Distillation	the Hermit {wisdom, observation}
Astronomy	Saturn	Binah	W. Master	Coagulation	the World

When the Senior Deacon and the young Fellow Craft reach the top of the stairs, the ritual includes what I consider one of the most astonishing, powerful statements ever made in the English language. In the Oklahoma work, it reads:

> *You have this evening, my brother, pressed beneath your feet, transmounted and transcended all the powers and passions, the senses and sciences of man. Now remember, that while many have made the ascent of that flight of winding stairs, not one, by Masonic consent, has ever passed downward.*

WOW!

Think through that sentence with me. You have pressed beneath your feet, gone above and gone beyond, everything you can experience through your senses, everything man has ever learned, everything mankind has ever felt.

Pretty heady stuff!

At the top of the stairs, we find yet another portal. The portal guardian this time in the Junior Warden. He is guarding the outer door of the Middle Chamber. That space, the anteroom to the Middle Chamber, can be associated with the Sephirah *Chokmah* {Divine reality, revelation, power of wisdom}.

It is here that he learns the word "shibboleth," a word which now designates any means of identification. In the Oklahoma work, he is reminded of the Biblical citation of the word, and then he is told that it means "a sheaf of corn suspended near a waterfall." I am aware that not all jurisdictions define it that way, but it is common enough that most of the glass magic lantern slides used to illustrate the lectures in 1800's show it.

Now it is true that "shibboleth" can be translated as a sheaf of corn (grain) or as running water. But the element which has been added in the ritual is the concept of suspension. The grain is "suspended near a waterfall;" and a waterfall is water "in suspension." What is symbolized by this addition?

There are two important symbolic systems we simply have not had time to discuss in this paper, but which I believe can be shown to be important sources from which some of the symbols of the Degree may have been taken. One is Dante's *Divine Comedy*, and the other is the tarot. Dr. Robert O'Neal has traced many important correspondences between the two systems of symbols, and there is no question that the work of Dante was very popular in England at the time the ritual of the Fellow Craft Degree must have been created. I suspect the purpose of adding the element of suspension to the definition of shibboleth is an allusion to the tarot card of the hanged man. As you know, the card most often shows a man, hanging upside down by one foot, with one leg crossed in front or behind the other, thus forming an X. One traditional interpretation of the card is that of a traitor, but another is of "life in suspension," or life about to undergo change and transformation. That would seem to fit with the identification of the anteroom of the Middle Chamber with *Chokmah*.

The young Fellow Craft then encounters the final portal guardian in the Senior Warden. Passing him, we arrive at the Middle Chamber, where we find the Worshipful Master.

It is important to remember that, as one symbolic meaning of the Lodge is the idealized life of the individual Mason, so the Worshipful Master symbolizes the idealized Mason, the one in whom all things are in balance and harmony, and who has awakened to his true nature and potential. We have successfully passed through the portals. And here the name of the young Fellow Craft is enrolled among the workmen, entitling him to payment in corn, wine, and oil—the ethereal foods which sustain the spiritual life. He is instructed in the mysteries of the letter "G" which include geometry, which was believed to be a means of discovering and partially understanding the nature of Deity. He is no longer entirely human, at least not the same human he was, because he has begun to comprehend something of the Deity within himself. He begins to understand 1 Corinthians 3:16 "Know ye not that ye are the temple of God, and that the spirit of God dwelleth in you?"

So where have we arrived? I think the movement in the Degree, as I indicated before, is from knowledge to gnosis. We are now in the realm of intuition—of knowing without knowing how we know—revelation—inspiration—direct, non-verbal connection with Deity. At least symbolically, we have left behind not only the traditional or mundane means of acquiring knowledge, but also the means of testing knowledge. In alchemical terms we have completed the great work. In terms of the kabbalah we are identified with *Keter*. In Dante's terms we have reached the realm of paradise, as nearly as one can while still alive.

We have, in fact, pressed beneath our feet, transmounted and transcended all the powers and passions, the senses and sciences of man

---

Speech prepared for Washington Alexandria Lodge, Alexandria, Virginia, 2008

Privacy, Peace, & Harmony

By tradition, the minutes of each Lodge meeting end with the sentence: "The Lodge was closed in ancient form, peace and harmony prevailing." Many people do not realize that is not just a matter of tradition—it used to be a matter of Masonic law. In many places, it still is.

It is worth remembering why Freemasonry has a tradition of secrecy. In the Middle Ages, secrecy was an economic necessity. Qualified stone masons were well paid for the time. The great Gothic building boom of the 1200's was in full swing, and the demand for new buildings was great. That meant that the demand for qualified builders was great. But how was someone to know, when a man showed up at a work site, claiming to be skilled in masonry, that he was qualified?

It was literally a matter of life and death. Unqualified builders were much more likely to cause accidents on the job, and most of those accidents were fatal. Poor work in construction might not show up immediately, but after a short time buildings fell. And paper certificates assuring others that a man was a qualified builder did little good in a time when few people could read and write,

The masons solved the problem by giving passwords and signs to men when they became qualified as builders, and by keeping those passwords and signs strictly secret.

Another tradition which developed at the same time was that nothing discussed inside the Lodge was ever discussed outside. That point was so important that it is found in the oldest Masonic document which exists—the Regius Poem, written about the year 1380. The poem lists several essential points for the conduct of Masons. The third point, translated into modern English, reads:

> The third point must be strictly observed.
> ... The privities (that is to say, those things which happen) in the Lodge room, must never be told; nor shall you ever tell others of the Lodge business. Keep all such information to yourself, lest you bring shame upon yourself as a teller of tales or a violator of confidences.

It remains true today that it is a serious offense against Masonic ethics, if not Masonic law, to argue about the business of the Lodge when not in Lodge. The original reasons are obvious—the Lodge was the business office of the guild. It is never wise to discuss business strategy and matters in public. Today, it is not a matter of trade secrets; but it is a strong tradition that our business is our business. It is private, not public, and should no more be discussed in public than should sensitive family matters. There is a powerful additional reason, of course. Non-Masons will not want to join a fraternity which openly disagrees in public. They have enough squabbling in their own lives without seeking out more.

A third tradition which developed in the Middle Ages was that no conflict between members is to remain unresolved. Again, it was originally a matter of survival. On a medieval construction job, accidental death was a very frequent reality. If two members of the Lodge had an argument--if there were, in the words of the ritual, "private piques and quarrels," you could not completely trust the man working next to you. It would be easy for him to arrange an "accident," or just not extend the little extra effort which might keep you from falling.

That is probably the reason the Regius Poem lists several things a Mason must do and must not do. If we paraphrase them into modern English, you can see that they center on things which can cause conflict.

Do not take work away from another Mason.

Do not criticize another man or his work or find fault with him: if you see him doing something you think is wrong, advise him, but never discuss it with another person.

Especially when dealing with a Brother, keep all promises and pay all obligations quickly.

Never violate the chastity of the female relative of a Mason (and the Regius Poem adds that you must leave his mistress alone as well.

You are not required to *like* another Mason, but you *are* required to *love* him and to treat him as a Brother.

There had to be complete trust, and that meant there had to be complete harmony.

For that reason, a Lodge could not be closed if two or more members had an unresolved conflict. The tradition of a Lodge not being open on Sunday is a modern innovation from the late 1800's. Originally a Lodge could not be *closed* unless there was true peace, and if that meant that the Lodge stayed open five or six days—or five or six weeks, so it was. Eventually, pressure from other members would force the quarreling parties to work out a compromise.

Our language today contains many references to those traditions.

> *"Masons being brethren, there exist no invidious distinctions among them," and that they "love each other mightily."*

> *"We, as Free and Accepted Masons, are taught to make use of it for the more noble and glorious purpose of spreading the cement of brotherly love and affection; that cement which unites us into one sacred band, or society, or friends and brothers, among whom no contention should ever exist, but that noble contention, or rather emulation, of who best can work and best agree."*

> *". . . dependence is one of the strongest bonds of society: men were made dependent on each other for protection and security, thereby enjoying better opportunities for fulfilling the duties of reciprocal love and friendship."*

Since preserving the peace and harmony and privacy of the Lodge was his most important duty, a series of significant powers surrounded and still surrounds the Worshipful Master.

He alone decides what matters come before the Lodge for discussion. The simple fact that a Brother makes a motion in Lodge does not mean that the Worshipful Master must entertain that motion or even acknowledge that it was made.

He alone decides how long discussion will continue on any topic.

He alone decides who will be allowed to speak on any topic, and how long they may speak, The Worshipful Master, not *Robert's Rules of Order*, governs the discussions of a Lodge.

He has the right to exclude any member who is causing dissension in the Lodge, and there is no appeal from that decision.

And the person with all that power cannot campaign for that office, cannot twist arms, cannot be nominated by a friend--thus creating the appearance of favoritism. He is selected by a process in which each member of the Lodge, alone in the depths of his conscience, asks himself— "Apart from all other considerations, which member of this Lodge is the best suited, by wisdom and temperament, to be Master, even if I disagree with almost everything he says."

The proof of each man's worthiness to be a Master Mason and a member of this Fraternity is his ability to ask himself that question.

And thus it has been time out of mind.

So the foundations of privacy, peace and harmony were laid early in our history. But they have been reenforced since.

In many countries in the past 300 years, just being a Mason could get you killed. Whether we are speaking of the persecutions of the church, of Hitler's concentration camps, the Russian gulag, or some countries in South America, being a Freemason was literally punishable by death. Brothers had to rely on others with complete trust. And the tradition that you did not leave a Lodge room with an unresolved conflict was even more powerful.

So powerful, in fact, that during the Cherokee Civil War, fought in Oklahoma at the time of the War Between the States, it is said that the beginning of the end of the war happened when men from both sides, men who had sworn to kill each other and who had killed many on the opposing side, met at a Masonic altar and knew they could not honorably leave until they had found a resolution to their conflict.

These three principles—

Privacy - the rule that what happens in Lodge stays in Lodge.

Peace - Masons are not allowed to become angry with each other, nor criticize each other, nor speak ill of each other

Harmony - the peace and tranquility of the Lodge must be preserved at all times, and that it is unMasonic to bring about division or distension within a Lodge

—have served us well for nearly a thousand years. May it always be true of this Lodge that the secretary can honestly write that the meeting was closed in ancient form, Peace and Harmony prevailing.

Speech written for the Oklahoma Lodge Leadership Conference, 2005

Obstacles and Outside Influences: Willie Wonka and the Lodge

Perhaps, unless you took a grandchild to see it, you have not seen the movie "Willie Wonka and the Chocolate Factory." If you have not, I'd recommend you rent the video and watch it at home—there are some fine performances and some telling points.

To give a brief overview of the plot, Willie Wonka, the nearly legendary owner of the best candy and chocolate factory in the world, holds a contest in which a few children, each accompanied by a parent, are invited to tour the factory and have all the candy they want. It is even rumored that he may give the entire factory to one of the children. The factory is a wonderful, almost magical place. But as the tour continues, child after child shows serious personality flaws, and it becomes apparent that the parents not only tolerate but encourage those flaws. One child is simply a complete glutton, another is a spoiled brat demanding everything in sight, no matter how unreasonable it may be, and throwing tantrums when she does not get her way at once. Another child is completely impulsive and unthinking. One by one, they eliminate themselves.

Finely, only Charlie and his Grandfather are left. Things happen to tempt Charlie, but he resists the temptations. He has honor and he has integrity, and those are the qualities for which Mr. Wonka is searching—the qualities he must find in the person to whom he gives his factory.

You could easily substitute the Lodge for the chocolate factory, and candidates for the children. Each of us is concerned about those who will carry on after us. (Well, almost all of us. I admit I have heard a few Masons say that they don't care if Masonry dies when they do, as long as it doesn't make any changes.)

But most of us want the Fraternity to survive. And most of us know that the Fraternity has always changed. Change IS the universal law of nature. It's important to realize that Masonry, as we know and love it, is the product of constant change. We all know that men like George Washington and Benjamin Franklin were members of the Fraternity, and we are proud of that, and rightly. But we should also remember that, were they to visit a Lodge today, they would find very little—other than the titles of the officers— which was familiar to them. As we know from the diaries of the time, men were made Masons in a single day. There was no process of taking a Degree, learning lectures, and coming back in a month to take the next.

And it isn't just the ritual. Masonic Lodges in the time of Washington were hotbeds of political activity. The Lodge took a stand on almost every public issue. Discussions of religion were also common. We have become so used, today, to saying that politics and religion are not discussed in Lodge, that we have forgotten the actual words are that PARTISAN politics and SECTARIAN religion are not to be discussed.

And while Lodges did some charitable work from time to time, it was not a major activity of the Lodge. Most of those changes took place in the early part of the 20th Century. And, since it met the needs of the men at that time, Freemasonry grew and flourished. Any organization will grow if it provides something that people want. When those wants change, if the institution does not change also, it dies. How many manufacturers of buggy whips are left in the United States?

Even though we often lose sight of it ourselves, the purpose of Freemasonry is made clear in the words of the ritual.

> *"Masonry is a speculative and moral science and philosophy founded on an operative art."*

"Grant that the sublime principles of Freemasonry may subdue every discordant passion within us."

"Let us then, Brethren, apply ourselves with becoming zeal to the practice of the excellent principles inculcated by our Fraternity. Let us ever remember that the great objects of our Fraternity are the restraint of our desires and passions, the cultivation of an active benevolence, and the promotion of a correct knowledge of the duties we owe to God, our neighbors and ourselves. . . . Let us cultivate the great moral virtues which are laid down on our Masonic Trestle Board, and improve in everything that is good, amiable and useful."

"I come to learn, to subdue my passions, and to improve myself in Masonry."

". . . but we, as Free and Accepted Masons, are taught to make use of it for the more noble and glorious purpose of divesting our minds and consciences of all the vices and superfluities of life . . ."

"By the rough ashlar we are reminded of our rude and imperfect state by nature; by the Perfect Ashlar, that state of perfection at which we hope to arrive, by a virtuous education, our own endeavors, and the blessing of God..."

"The Plumb admonishes us to walk uprightly in our several stations before God and man, squaring our actions with the square of virtue and morality . . ."

"By Speculative Masonry we learn to subdue the passions, act upon the square, keep a tongue of good report, maintain secrecy and practice charity."

"The study of the Liberal Arts, that valuable branch of education which tends so effectively to polish and adorn the mind, is earnestly recommended to your consideration. . ."

> *"To the man whose mind has thus been molded to virtue and science, Nature presents one more great and useful lesson—the knowledge of himself. She leads him by contemplation to the closing hours of his existence and when, by means of that contemplation, she has conducted him through the various windings of this mortal life, she finally instructs him how to die. She leads him to reflect upon the inevitable destiny, and prompts the inward monitor to say that death has no string equal to the stain of falsehood and that the certainty of death at any time is preferable to the possibility of dishonor."*

And, while not a part of the ritual, there is a phrase which we say and hear so often we usually don't pay any attention to the meanings. "Masonry takes a good man and makes him better."

It is hard to doubt that the real purpose of Masonry is the development and self-development of the individual.

It is that, I believe, more than movies or television, more than the Vietnam War, more than the rebellion of the '60's, which has underlain the decrease in membership. Which seems, I know, a very strange thing to say.

In the Victorian era, and the Edwardian era which followed it, an individual's character was considered the most important thing about him. It was understood that the primary responsibility of parents—at least as important as providing food and shelter—was to look after the development of the character of the child. There was not universal agreement on how best to do that, but there was universal agreement that "as the twig is bent, so grows the tree," and that if you brought up a child in the way he should go, he would not depart from it in later life.

And, when you became an adult, you took over the responsibility for the development of your own character, but it was assumed to be a life-long process. Literally thousands of books were written on the topic. "Improving books," they were commonly called. It was understood that, by reading the stories of the lives of great men and women, one learned by example. Such examples were also used in school and in church.

Perhaps the ultimate expression of this cultural attitude came in the poem by Longfellow which a professor of mine once remarked was "A good sermon, but questionable poetry:"

> *Lives of great men all remind us*
>   *We can make our lives sublime,*
> *And, departing, leave behind us*
>   *Footprints on the sands of time;*
>
> *Footprints, that perhaps another,*
>   *Sailing o'er life's solemn main,*
> *A forlorn and shipwrecked brother,*
>   *Seeing, shall take heart again.*
>
> *Let us, then, be up and doing,*
>   *With a heart for any fate;*
> *Still achieving, still pursuing,*
>   *Learn to labor and to wait.*

Again, it would be hard to overstate the importance of the continuing development of a person's character in the 1800's and early to mid 1900's. In both high and popular culture, the theme was everywhere. In theatre, it gave rise to the melodrama as a popular form, while also giving rise to such powerful and classic theatre as "Ghosts," "The Cherry Orchard," "Tosca," "Death of a Salesman," and much more. It gave rise to the original radio "soap opera," radio programs some 15 minutes in length which presented episodes each day from a continuing life story.

In general, the cultural view of the character in North America, England, and Canada might be summarized like this:

✠ The character of an individual must be carefully developed—it does not happen by chance. It is as surely the result of planned training as is the body of an athlete or the mind of a scholar.

✠ The character of an individual is influenced by his bloodline, but depends upon the examples, training, and instruction provided by the family and also by friends, books, and other inputs.

✠ The formation of the character begins in infancy, and is never completely finished.

✠ The person must continually be aware of the state of his own character, must take steps to strengthen it, and must carefully avoid those things which can weaken or damage it.

✠ It is strengthened and developed by education, by the consideration of examples, by support of others who are on the same quest, by inspirational music or literature, by the acceptance and performance of duty, by the memories of our Mothers, and by the influence of a good woman.

There is one more element to point out before bringing all this together. That is the question of equality.

In the 1800's and early to mid 1900's equality was a concept confined to law. However widely or narrowly it might be applied, and whatever groups might be included or excluded, it still referred to a person's legal standing and legal rights. It did not apply to the character, quality, or personality of individuals, and a Victorian or Edwardian would have looked at you in amused incredulity if you had suggested it.

That is to say, all people were equal in a court of law, but they were not equal as individuals. It was nonsense to say that no one was better or worse than anyone else.

In the 1960's, due largely perhaps to the civil rights movement and also to a hold-over effect from the Second World War which had made us suspicious of claims of superiority, we became very uncomfortable in suggesting that one person was better than another. (It would have made sense to become uncomfortable in saying that one race was better than another, but the culture applied the same discomfort on an individual basis.) A Victorian (setting aside the time difference) considering Mother Theresa and a dope dealer selling to children in the schoolyard, would have had no hesitation at all is saying that there was a qualitative difference between them, and that the one was a remarkably good person and the other a two-legged animal.

No Victorian would have any trouble saying that Dr. Martin Luther King, Jr., was a fine and upstanding man and his assassin was a piece of trash. But our culture has become very uncomfortable in making such judgements. It is as if we fear to make any distinctions at all. It is as if what people become by accident and without guidance is "good enough," and to suggest otherwise—to suggest that Mother

Theresa is "better" than the dope dealer—is to be a racist, an elitist, or some other kind of "ist."

This phenomenon, which has been growing for some time, was brought home to me recently by an ad on television, encouraging parents to talk to their children about drugs as a way of preventing their usage—a worthy goal if ever there were one. But in this ad, a mother stops her son on the way out the door in the evening. The kid appears to be about 14 years old. He has multiple piercings about the face, with several gold rings in his ears and eyebrows. His hair is dyed in several colors, and his clothing is—unusual. She asks him where he will be and who will be there, and then sends him on his way. The announcer says, "Let your kids be who they are, but talk to them about drugs."

"Let your kids be who they are?" What happened to "bending the twig?" What happened to the responsibility of a parent to mold the development of the child? Since when did the development of character become a game of random chance?

And should we be surprised that a Fraternity whose main purpose is the development of the character of its members, rather than being popular, should be regarded as quaint and old fashioned and irrelevant?

If the story ended there, I would see little hope for the fraternity. But, in fact, the story does not end there.

We are seeing strange stirrings in society. Many of our Lodges are getting an increased number of candidates. And they are younger. And many of them are both disillusioned and hungry.

They are disillusioned with materialism. Many of them have built economically successful lives at an early age—and it isn't enough. They have most of the toys, and have discovered that it is no fun to play by yourself. And they see men in politics and in business and in leadership positions in large churches getting into trouble which arises from greed or a lust for power, and they start to wonder if anyone is left who is honest. And they start to look for a group of people who still believe in honor and integrity. And to that man, we are NOT quaint, old fashioned, and irrelevant—we are the thing he most needs and wants.

There are an increasing number of these men who have come to believe that character does count. That there is a difference in people, not in their potential, but in what they choose to become. That all cats may be grey at night, but the night is only half the day. He will come, and he will bring his spiritual brothers, **as long as we fulfill our part of the bargain, and provide the character strengthening and development we have traditionally promised**.

There is another trend in society which has started to move in our direction, if we are wise enough to take advantage of it. Any of us who get large numbers of e-mail from young Masons can tell you that there has been an interesting shift in the last two or three years. The great majority of the questions used to deal with Masonic history, or protocol, or a question about a symbol. Now, the majority are about spirituality and the spiritual side of Masonry. It isn't that they are confusing the Fraternity with a church. They know and understand the difference. But they are searching for a more universal spiritual experience. They want to experience their connection to the universe. Many of the Masonic chat groups on the Internet are devoted almost exclusively to these questions. They come to Masonry because we say we teach these things. And they then wonder where the teacher is and where the teachings are. They form groups to talk about these issued, but they still hope to discover how the rituals of Masonry "work" spiritually. They are sincere and dedicated. But they are waiting for the promise to be fulfilled.

So there, as I see it, are the opportunities. We have young men who are seeking character development and growth, and are coming to Freemasonry in the expectation that it will fulfill its historic role of taking them and making them into better men. We have other young men who are seeking a spiritual experience which will give meaning to their lives. They want to explore the symbols of Masonry and delve deeply behind those symbols. They are seeking light and truth. They are standing at the door of Mr. Wonka's chocolate factory, ready to prove themselves worthy inheritors and guardians of the riches within.
Freemasonry is their natural home. If we are just wise enough to do what we have promised.

Speech to York Rite Southwest Conference, September 11, 2003

Pedal Vulneration

I know it is the tradition that a speaker at a breakfast should pick a topic of a humorous and light nature. But we are faced with a situation so grave and portentous I must ask your indulgence to be serious this morning.

Masonry, the grand Masonic tradition which stretches back to antiquity—at least as far as the 1950's—is in jeopardy. The Masonry of the meeting in which we pay bills, correct each other on some point of ritual, and then adjourn to the lobby to settle into ancient chairs, conformed to our bodies over the decades, to drink coffee and play dominoes—the Masonry which gives us so much comfort in the knowledge that we will see no new faces and face no new issues—is at risk!

Grand Lodges, often abetted by other Masonic Bodies, have been making efforts to destroy the Masonry we love—to make the general public aware of us, to get us recognized on television and in print.

Some—and I shame to tell you this—have even gone so far as to encourage Masons to talk with their friends about Masonry!

Brothers, we must awaken before it is too late.

We have been complacent. Far too many of us, when we have heard of these programs, have said, "Ah well, it is only a Grand Master's Program. We have been here before. It will take four months to implement, have a four month life, and be ignored for the remaining four months as we begin to wonder what the next Grand Master will do."

I must tell you, and I would not expect you to believe me if I did not tell you this is true on my Masonic honor, in many Grand Jurisdictions Grand Master after Grand Master has continued this program called "Masonic Renewal," and even strengthened it and added to it. Men are beginning to speak of a Masonic Renaissance.

Nay, it is even worse! Those three mighty phrases which have served us as a bulwark against change: "We've never done that before;" "We tried it, it didn't work;" and "It's against Masonic tradition"—are beginning to fail in instance after instance. Even our mighty, impregnable barrier "There can be no innovations in Masonry" has been weakened as men have questioned if there is a difference between "innovation" and "development."

I have even seen it suggested that Masonry is becoming relevant to the world!!

Clearly, we must act to prevent this.

Fortunately, there is help. I wish to read to you from a recently-published pamphlet, reproduced below:

The Masonic Art of Pedal Vulneration

or

HOW TO SHOOT YOURSELF IN YOUR OWN FOOT!

by
Brother Theodoric Coot

Many Lodges have a serious problem. Masonry is gaining more attention that it has had in decades. Far too many people are applying for membership in the Fraternity. For those dedicated to letting Masonry die, this is a situation which must be dealt with, and quickly.

Fortunately, help is available.

The Masonic Self-Destruction Committee has come to the rescue. They have studied the Lodges which do the best job of discouraging new members and driving away the few who apply for membership anyhow. The principles they discovered are offered here in booklet form. **Follow these simple rules, and you can help your Lodge and all of Masonry enjoy a comfortable and peaceful decline into the grave!**

1. IF SOME FRIEND ASKS YOU ABOUT MASONRY, SAY "I CAN'T TALK TO YOU ABOUT THAT, IT'S ALL SECRET!"

We all know, of course, that very little is secret about the Fraternity, BUT THEY DON'T KNOW THAT. Refusing to tell people anything is a good way to create a reputation for stealth and secrecy, and to make people suspect we're up to something. Almost no one would want to join an organization like that.

2. IF THEY WANT A PETITION IN SPITE OF THAT, MAKE SURE YOU DON'T HAVE ONE WITH YOU

Tell them that you'll get them one later, then forget about it. If they ask you again, give them one, but make sure you wait a few weeks before remembering to give it to the Lodge. Nothing drives people away like feeling ignored.

3. TRY TO GET PUT ON THE INVESTIGATING COMMITTEE. THAT COMMITTEE CAN DO MORE THAN ANYONE ELSE TO DRIVE A POTENTIAL CANDIDATE AWAY!

First of all, ONLY ONE OF THE THREE members of the committee should actually call on the petitioner. If all three go, it might appear that we were showing him some respect.

Then, as soon as you get there, order his wife and children out of the room. There is no reason, of course, why his wife should not be present, and many reasons why she should. But we need to communicate at once that she isn't welcome anywhere near a Masonic Lodge. Some misguided Lodges, starting programs to involve the whole family, have actually shown an alarming UPTURN in membership and member activity.

Approach your conversation with the Petitioner in the spirit of the Master Inquisitor putting DeMolay on the rack. Make clear in your tone of voice and your questions that you suspect he stopped by a public clinic for the treatment of sexually-transmitted diseases on his way home after having been released from prison.

If he lights up a cigarette, look at him and say, in a cold voice, "Is that Marijuana?" If he asks you a question about Masonry, say "You'll know about that when you need to--right now we're finding out about you."

Remember, he may not know that he isn't worth as much as the dirt under your feet--you may need to remind him of that by your attitude.

4. IF, IN SPITE OF YOUR BEST EFFORTS, THE LODGE VOTES TO ADMIT HIM, HOLD OFF LETTING HIM KNOW UNTIL THE LAST POSSIBLE DAY BEFORE THE E.A. IS SET. *DURING ALL THAT TIME, LIE TO HIM ABOUT THE NATURE OF THE INITIATION!*
This is good time to bring up the story about riding the goat. Make him feel that the Initiation is designed to embarrass him and humiliate him. **Under no circumstances let him know that it is a beautiful and meaningful ritual, centuries old, which is designed to teach great truths of ethics and morality!**

Instead, build on memories of the sillier junior high and high school initiations, suggesting that this is even worse. If you work at it, you can convince him that Masons are nothing but high school adolescents who never grew up. You can make us seen revoltingly childish, with just a little effort.

Sure, it's a grave Masonic offense to do these things, and you can get hauled up before a Masonic Tribunal, but it's worth some risk to make sure your Lodge dies with the others.

5. MAKE SURE NO ONE OFFERS TO GO TO HIS HOUSE, PICK HIM UP, AND BRING HIM TO THE LODGE ON THE NIGHT OF HIS FIRST DEGREE.

6. IF HE SHOWS UP ANYHOW, MAKE SURE EVERYONE IGNORES HIM.

Remind the Brothers who signed his Petition NOT to come to his Initiation. He might see a friendly face he knows. Tell the Brethren present to remember that they are to form small groups in the lobby and talk to each other, not to him. The only exception might be an old Brother who can feed him more lies about how scary the initiation is.

EVEN WHEN HE ENTERS THE LODGE ROOM FOR THE E.A. DEGREE, IT IS STILL NOT TOO LATE TO DRIVE HIM AWAY IF YOU REALLY WORK AT IT. WITH DILIGENT EFFORT, YOU CAN KEEP HIM FROM ADVANCING TO THE OTHER TWO DEGREES!

7. CAREFULLY AVOID THE COURTESY OF BEING SILENT DURING THE DEGREE.

Whisper loudly, and be sure to laugh from time to time. If you are lucky, he will think you are laughing at him and be offended. *Remember, if you treat the initiation as a beautiful and serious ceremony, he may, too!* It is critical, therefore, that you loudly correct others if they make a mistake in the ritual work. If the man sitting next to you is wearing a hearing aid, ask him to turn it off, then shout at him about the weather, crops, anything at all to be distracting. If you can tell jokes involving animal sound effects, so much the better.

8. IF THE LODGE GATHERS FOR REFRESHMENTS AFTER THE DEGREE, IGNORE HIM COMPLETELY AND DO NOT SPEAK TO HIM, OR (BETTER BUT MORE DIFFICULT) SPEAK TO HIM IN SUCH A WAY THAT HE REALLY FEELS OUT OF PLACE.

Remember he's still feeling a little uncertain— he's new at this. It's a good time to put him in his place, whatever that may be. Let him know that since you served on the Table Decoration Committee of the High Poo-Bah's party in 1908, you are far too exalted a personage to have any interest in him.

Dragging in all the Masonic jargon you possibly can is a good way to do this. You know that he has not had a chance to learn all the buzz-words, so use them, as many as possible in a sentence. This will not only allow you to show off, but it may discourage him enough that he will never return.

9. ABOVE ALL, NOW AND AT ALL TIMES, NEVER ANSWER A QUESTION!
If he asks you something you know, mumble a response, with an expression which says that he's an idiot for asking. If you don't know the answer, NEVER, NEVER BE HONEST AND SAY, "I DON'T KNOW, BUT I'LL FIND OUT." Or, "I DON'T KNOW, BUT LET'S GO ASK BROTHER SMITH." Instead, look down on him and say, "You're not supposed to ask questions!"

We live in dangerous times. If we are not careful, Masonry will become again the driving, exciting, vital force it once was. We can protect ourselves from that danger—continue our soft and comfortable glide to the grave—only by being constantly vigilant! EVERY BROTHER MUST WORK, AND WORK HARD, AT TURNING OFF PETITIONERS, DESTROYING RESPECT, AND CREATING AT ATMOSPHERE OF SUSPICION, SECRECY, AND CHILDISH DELAYED ADOLESCENCE.

It will not be easy!

But, working against each other, WE CAN DO IT!!!

Speech delivered at a breakfast meeting at the Conference of Grand Masters of North America, Spring, 1997

A Work in Progress

I feel a little diffident, standing up to speak in front of a group which contains some of the best Masonic speakers in America. There is Jimmy Dean Hartzell, who does what has to be the best Middle Chamber Lecture in Oklahoma. There is Bob Davis, who is one of the finest Masonic speakers around. Over there is Ill. Joe Jennings, Jr., who is not only a fine speaker, but those who have been lucky enough to see his one-man show about a Colonial Mason know that he is a fine actor as well. There is M∴W∴ Richard Fletcher, who has given more speeches on more Masonic topics to more audiences that Bob Davis and I added together. I am reminded of Brother Mark Twain's line about being the center of attention at a hanging—if it weren't for the honor of the thing he thought he'd just pass.

I was telling my good buddy Brother Damon Devereaux, Guthrie Chief of Police, that I was going to be speaking this evening. He said, "Well, just remember the law even limits how long we can interrogate a prisoner, so don't be afraid to be brief."

Actually, he didn't need to worry. I learned that important lesson many years ago, one Sunday at St. John's Episcopal Church in Norman. It happened that the Bishop of Hawaii was visiting, and had been invited to address the congregation as a courtesy. Now communion was being served, and on such days there is seldom a sermon in the Episcopal church, certainly not a lengthy one.

Nevertheless, the good Bishop was determined to give value for money, as it were, and preached at length— —at great length. Wives were envisioning roasts which had been left in ovens filling homes with smoke. Fathers had stopped encouraging their young not to squirm. Almost everyone had developed an increased understanding of eternity.

Finally, he concluded, and the rest of the service went as rapidly as possible. Then came the closing hymn, and I think the music director must have had a warning in a dream when she selected the music. Choir and congregation roared into that fine old hymn, "How Firm a Foundation." And then we came to the third line—"What more can he say than to you he hath said?"—there was a strange sound, rather like a cross between a gargle and a hiccup, which ran through choir and congregation.

And then it broke. In spite of all our efforts and determination. Everyone simply sat down and started laughing hysterically at once. The organ died in a series of strangled wheezes as the organist, unable to see through the tears of laughter, simply slapped at the keys and gave it up as a bad job. "What more can he say than to you he hath said?" Nothing! He said it all!!

I was highly honored when the Grand Master asked me to speak at his banquet. It is a privilege to do so before so many distinguished Masons and Ladies from so large a geographic area.

For many years I have been intrigued by a question: What is it that makes Masons different from other men? There is a difference. If you have ever visited a Masonic meeting being held in a hotel somewhere, you know that you can sit in the lobby and spot the Masons as they come in the door (even if they are not loaded down with lapel pins, Masonic neckties or name badges). There is something about the way they speak, and move. And it isn't exclusive to Masons—I have known many men who are not members of the fraternity who exhibit the same characteristic. Almost all Masons have it, but not all who have it are Masons. It is very hard to pin down.

The wife of one Brother said to me, "Masons are easy to spot, they always treat women the same way a favorite uncle does." I can't testify to the question from a woman's point of view, but I do know there is something——something is different.

Masons come from all parts of the world, so it isn't a geographic distinction.

I know Masons with advanced degrees and post-doctoral studies, and I know Masons who dropped out of high school—it isn't an educational difference.

There are Masons of every race on the planet. It isn't a matter of ethnicity.

I know Masons who are Presidents of vast, multi-national business concerns and others who work, when they can, for minimum wage. It isn't an economic difference.

Some Masons are among the most brilliant and intellectually gifted men I have ever known—and I have Masonic friends who, while among the best-hearted and kindest of men, are somewhat intellectually limited. It isn't a matter of smarts.

I know Masons who represent the best of the "old money" in their communities, and those who live on what would be the wrong side of the tracks, if they had any tracks. It isn't a matter of social status.

I know Brothers who are Roman Catholics, Orthodox Catholics, fundamentalist Protestants, liberal Protestants, Jews, and followers of Islam, as well as three Buddhists, one Zoroastrian, two Hindus, and at least two Wiccans. It isn't a matter of religious persuasion.

So what is it? As best I can tell, it is an attitude, a very subtle attitude. I was having a lot of trouble putting it into words, until I saw a wall plaque which captured the difference in 6 words:

I'm not finished with me yet

One of the most disastrous lies the social engineers have foisted upon our society is that "everyone and everything is good as it is."

One person I know who has little to recommend him used to have a sign on his desk which said, "I'm OK, God doesn't make junk." Neither does Rolls-Royce, but that doesn't mean someone can't wreck one of their cars.

Some schools have done away with grades, because if you grade students, some will make higher grades than others, and that means some may not feel good about themselves.

One recent study insists that reform is needed in the prison system—not because we have a recidivism rate which is the shame of the first world—not because there is evidence that the system isn't working——no, reform is needed because rapists leaving prison have a negative self-image.

As a society, we have decided that feeling good about yourself, feeling that you are complete and fine just as you are, is some kind of human right. Our parents understood that those feelings were a *privilege* which you earned through hard work, study, character development, self-criticism, and determination.

And that, I think, is the difference. Almost every Mason I have talked to understands, at some deep level, that a life and a character have to be built; they don't just happen.

A Mason says that he has come to the Fraternity to learn, to subdue his passions, and to improve himself. That very statement says "I know I'm not finished with me yet—I have more work left to do on me." That is the lesson of the working tools, the lesson of virtually all of Masonry. We know we are works in progress, not finished yet. And we know we have an obligation to work on ourselves every day.

The great philosopher, Martin Buber, suggested that there were three basic orientations a person could take—me, we, and thee. A sort of negative version of that can be found in the famous I-You-He comparisons. You know:

I am financially responsible; you are thrifty, he is a miser.

I am firm in my convictions; you are stubborn; he is pig-headed.

I am open to new information; you are indecisive; he flip-flops.

Or, as my father was fond of remarking, The difference between a great leader and a damned tyrant is whether or not you get caught at it.

But, to use Buber's terms, all infants start out thinking in terms of "me." I want what I want when I want it. If I'm hungry, I want my bottle right now! If I'm wet, I want to be changed now! Sadly, some people never grow out of that. They remain the center of the universe—of a very small universe.

But, if we are fortunate, we grow out of the "me" phase, and enter into the "we" phase. Here we are willing to include one or more other people in the list of those who are important. It's all right if you are successful, as long as I am at least as successful.

A few then move to the "thee" (in the sense of "thou" or "You") phase, in which we put other's interests and welfare ahead of our own.

Masonry teaches the importance of that. Reminds us again and again that the ego must die before any growth is possible.

And growth is the goal of Masonry, as it is the goal of any mature and reasonable person. The importance is not in who we are, but in what we are becoming.

So the special thing about Masons, at least those for whom the Degrees "took," is the knowledge that we aren't finished.

We are not as kind as we should be.
We are not as considerate as we should be.
We are not as inclined to thought as we should be.
We are not as charitable as we should be.
We are not as non-judgmental as we should be.
We are not as knowledgeable as we should be.
We are more self-important than we should be.
We are more self-indulgent than we should be.
We are more impatient than we should be.

    That's the bad news.

The good news is that we know all that. In the words of the old prayer book, "We acknowledge and bewail our manifold sins and wickednessess." As Masons, we know that building a life takes a lifetime of work and thought and self-awareness.

We know we're not finished with us yet———but we've still got the tools in our hands.

And we have a great advantage, in that every other Mason in the world is obligated to whisper good council in our ear when he sees us starting to do anything questionable.

As some of you know, my favorite example of good council was the Christian Church in a small Oklahoma town in the 1950's which was in need of a new minister. Now as you may know, in the Christian Church, when we need a new minister, we form a committee to go steal one. The elders had heard of a young minister—a Reverend Donnelley—in Ireland who really wanted to come to the United States.

So they corresponded, and it sounded very good, and they invited him to bring his family and become their minister. It was great, there was just one problem—no matter what he chose as his text, he always ended up preaching against the British.

So finally the elders called upon him, and they said,

"Now Rev. Donnelley, we are as happy as we can be with you and your family. You are a fine preacher and great in the pastoral role. Everyone in town loves you and your family. There's just one little thing. It seems no matter the text, you end up preaching against the British. Now there are no British here, and anyway the feelings here just aren't that strong. So we would appreciate it if you could focus a bit more on those things which touch our lives."

"Well now, Brethren, I appreciate your words. Sure and I wasn't even aware of the habit. I'll amend it."

Next Sunday, the congregation waited in some curiosity, but sure enough he was as good as his word. He has selected The Last Supper as his topic, and he was clearly approaching the climax of the sermon, with nary a word about the British.

"Ah, picture it, Brothers and Sisters. There they were in that pleasant upper room, in the quiet, away from the noise and bustle of the street. And they had had a good meal, and shared wine together. And then, suddenly, our Lord looked sad enough to pierce the heart of the heathen. And he looked around at the 12, and he said 'This night, this very night, one of ye will betray me.'

"Well there was great consternation and uproar, and Peter looked at Him and said, 'Lord, is it I?' And James, called the Beloved, looked at Him and said, 'Lord, is it I?' And Thomas, Thomas who doubted and whose faith was stronger because he doubted, Thomas looked at Him and said, 'Lord, is it I?'

"And then Judas—ach Judas! Judas the traitor! Judas the foul one! Judas the black-hearted betrayer of his Lord, looked at him, and he said 'I say, governer, ya don't mean me, do ya.'"

Well, there it is. All of us have a life to live, and, if we are thoughtful, a life to build. I can only hope that your life brings you as much joy, as much love, as much happiness, as much richness, and as much fulfillment as has mine.

Speech delivered to the Annual Communication of the Grand Lodge of the State of Oklahoma, 2007

The 23 Lives of Albert Pike

Albert Pike has become something of an obsession with me. I am fascinated that one man could have done so much—could have been so much—in one lifetime. One result of this fixation was my book *Albert Pike, The Man Beyond the Monument,* an anecdotal biography.

A second result is a work in progress, an annotated chronology of Pike's life. When I started this project, I gave it the working title of "The Eight Lives of Albert Pike" because I thought Pike had eight distinctly different and impressive careers. The working title is now "The 23 Lives of Albert Pike:" and the number is still rising as I continue my research. Let me quickly sketch those careers for you.

TEACHER— Pike started as a teacher and would return to teaching several times in his life. When he no longer taught in a classroom, he used the pages of newspapers and the Scottish Rite to inform and educate people.

POET— He started writing poems at a very early age. Edgar Allan Poe praised him as America's greatest classic poet, and Pike's poems were printed in the major literary magazines of the day.

ESSAYIST— Pike's essays covered an immense amount of ground. Some, such as the essays on the transcontinental railroad, the economic future of the South, and the importance of infrastructure improvements in Arkansas, were essentially economic. Many were political, satiric, or biographical. Others were philosophic, such as the essays which comprise *Morals and Dogma.*

TRAPPER/EXPLORER— His trek through what is now Oklahoma, Texas, and New Mexico was the source of several short stories and poems.

HISTORIAN— Pike's records give us the earliest description we have of several areas of New Mexico. Also, he contributed to histories written by others, most notably John Hallum's *Biographical and Pictorial History of Arkansas* and Ben LaBree's *The Confederate Soldier in the Civil War,* 1861-1865.

REVOLUTIONARY— As a young man, Pike was a revolutionary, and he never lost that fire. Support for revolutions occurs in his poems "The Struggle for Freedom," "France," "The Fall of Poland," "When Shall the Nations All Be Free?" and "Yes, Call Us Rebels!" Again and again, he wrote into the ritual of the Scottish Rite the absolute right of men to self-determination, the wrongness of tyranny in any form, and the right of an oppressed people to retake their liberty by any means necessary, including violence.

SHORT STORY WRITER— He wrote short stories which appeared in *The Pearl, The Literary Gazette, The American Monthly Magazine,* and in his book titled *Prose Sketches and Poems, Written in the Western Country.*

NEWSPAPER EDITOR— He edited *The Arkansas Advocate, The Memphis Appeal,* and *The Patriot.*

BON VIVANT— Typically today, we simply order the entree we want and take whatever comes with it. But a meal in the 19th Century was a very different thing. One selected the first course from many alternatives, prepared in many different ways, and a wine to accompany it. One specified what vegetables were to accompany that course, how the salad was to be prepared, etc. The same was true for each course of the meal. Five courses were considered minimal, and seven were not uncommon. Pike was so knowledgeable in the area that many people in restaurants would simply tell their waiters to duplicate whatever Pike was ordering.

LAWYER— Pike became one of the best-known lawyers in the South. He had a very large practice and was admitted to practice before the United States Supreme Court.

LEGAL SCHOLAR— In addition to practicing law, Pike developed a reputation as a legal scholar. He recodified the laws of Arkansas and created an index for them; he wrote and published *The Arkansas Form Book,* which contained not only digests of the law but a complete set of legal forms (wills, mortgages, etc.); he was the reporter for the Arkansas Supreme Court; and he became a recognized authority in the field of comparative law.

EDUCATIONAL REFORMER— Pike's interest in education and its reform never weakened. He advocated a system of free, publicly supported education in Arkansas. His theories about the learning patterns of children and the importance of self learning anticipated Montessori.

POLITICAL ACTIVIST— Until the outbreak of the Civil War, Pike was deeply involved in the political life of Arkansas and the South. He served as chairman of numerous political parties and committees, wrote extensively in the area, and worked tirelessly in campaigns.

HUMORIST— Pike's humorous writing takes several forms. In prose, we have his mock essays such as those on the "philosophy" of walking, bowling, and smoking a cigar. We also have his amusing "Anecdotes of the Arkansas Bar" and, in poetry, comic or satiric works such as "A Fine Arkansas Gentleman," "O Jamie Brewed a Bowl O' Punch," "A Dollar, or Two," "Spree at Johnnie Coyle's" and "To a Friend He Could Never Say No."

PUBLISHER— In addition to working as editor, Pike was owner or part owner of several newspapers and one-short-lived literary magazine.

APOLOGIST— The term "apologist," meaning one who. writes or speaks in defense of some person, cause or action, has largely vanished from contemporary English. Yet in his eloquence, passion and zeal, Pike deserves to rank with the great American apologists Benjamin Franklin, Thomas Jefferson, Thomas Paine, and Henry David Thoreau. Perhaps his best known apologia is his defense of both the Masonic Fraternity and the American value system against the attack by Pope Leo XIII in the Papal Bull *Humanum Genus*. But his powerful portrayals of the lot of women in the 19th Century, his defense of the poor and his support of the Bill of Rights, show that his concerns for justice and toleration were universal.

MILITARY COMMANDER— Pike served as Captain of the Little Rock Artillery, as a Captain in the War with Mexico, and as a General in the Civil War. Controversy still swirls around Pike as soldier, but scholars, like his principal biographer, Professor Walter Lee Brown in the new, definitive biography *A Life of Albert Pike* published by the University of Arkansas Press, point out his strategic decisions and general martial competence.

ORATOR— He was the best-known orator in Arkansas and one of the best-known in the South. He was in constant demand at debate societies, for political conventions, and for patriotic events.

CHIEF JUSTICE— Pike served as a Chief Justice of the Supreme Court of Arkansas under the Confederacy.

SOCIAL REFORMER— He became convinced that social reform was essential and advocated reforms which were highly radical for his time, including the rights. and equality of women, the legal protection of children, economic reform to keep too much wealth from concentrating in too few hands, improved working conditions for laborers and economic actions to insulate them against the cycles of business, and the reform of both jails and the treatment of criminals.

INDIAN ADVOCATE— Pike was deeply concerned about the treatment of American Indians by the government and white society. He had several good friends among the tribes and used to spend a great deal of time. hunting and camping with them. He became their advocate in Congress, pressing for the payment of the claims due to them from the federal government.

PHILOSOPHER— Philosophy was, perhaps, Pike's truest love. He read it constantly and wrote widely on the topic. In *Morals and Dogma,* he attempted one of the first general courses in philosophy and comparative religion ever written.

MASON— He was, in many ways, the quintessential Mason of the 1800s. He held offices in virtually every Masonic Body, but his work and tenure as Sovereign Grand Commander of the Scottish Rite, including his revision of the Rite's Ritual, laid the foundation for the organization as it exists today.

Clearly, as this brief review of his many careers underlines, Pike had a busy life of multiple accomplishments. Today, our image of Pike comes from the photographs and busts made of him in his later years. We have wrapped him with so much plaster, marble, and bronze that we have lost sight of the vital man himself. Read Pike and discover him as he really was.

You won't be disappointed!

Paper given to the Minnesota Masonic Education Seminar meeting at the Masonic Exposition held in Minneapolis, Minnesota, October 4-5, 1996.

"...The Greatest Work of Alchemy"
Albert Pike and the Question of Race

Admittedly, this is a controversial topic. Race has become a taboo issue in our society—although many of our greatest thinkers have warned us that by pretending the issue does not exist, we are "setting ourselves up" for problems in the future.

But it is an important topic, especially because so many critics of Masonry point to Albert Pike as some sort of quintessential racist, and then claim that the entire fraternity is tainted with his image.

That is grossly unfair to Pike, as we shall see.

Pike wrote much on the issues of race, equality, and Brotherhood. What he wrote is profound.

In order to understand it, however, we must know something of the way the question of race was viewed in Pike's time. More than one hundred and fifty years have passed since he first wrote on the topic, and the world has changed much. And Pike's remarks and ideas must be judged in the context of his own time, not our own. As is true of all of us, he was a creature of his time, even though he was often far in advance. It would be as utterly unreasonable and unfair to judge Pike's comments on race by the standards of today's liberals as it would be to judge a typewriter patented in the 1860's by today's computer word processors. Walter Lee Brown, in his doctoral dissertation *Albert Pike, 1809-1891* points out that Pike was extremely liberal for his time and geographic area, but Pike was a Southern liberal of the 1840's, not a Northern liberal of the 1990's.

That background is important for another reason as well. During Pike's life, the entire concept of race was undergoing a radical revision. It was an interesting and popular topic of conversation during much of the 1800's. Lectures on race were a standard part of the Lyceum circuit. And it all happened because of the study of language.

Both the commonly and scientifically accepted definition of race at the beginning of the 1800's was vastly different than now. There was no essential difference between race and nationality. It was firmly believed that the Irish, the English, the Germans and the French, were all separate races, for example. Instead of the few racial classifications we use today, the people of the time just before Pike used dozens if not hundreds.

But then students of language began to seriously study languages—not just to learn to speak them, but to see how languages changed and developed over time. It was soon shown that one could trace the migrations of a people over thousands of years, could show incursions, cultural conflicts, dominance and subjection by the changes which had occurred in a language. And as they traced them further and further back, languages began to merge and combine. And, as a result, it was shown that many modern languages arose in a tribe from the Caucasus, known as the Aryans, who had migrated across much of the world and had left clear linguistic markers. These discoveries were reported in newspapers. They became the subject of sermons in church and conversation over Sunday dinner. Those who were so inclined, of course, found opportunity in this to "prove" that their own racial group was inherently superior in some fashion. But still it resulted in a broadening of outlook. The British and French might still insist that their own nationality had somehow managed to evolve a little further than the other—such insistings are a part of the history of scientific discourse of the time—but they could no longer claim to be *racially* superior, when they clearly belonged to the same race.

Humans being humans, racial tensions actually increased with the knowledge. It was almost as if a Frenchman (for example) had said: "If I cannot assert a slight racial superiority over the Englishman, I can assert an even stronger superiority of the English and French over the Hispanic." And I do not mean to imply that only the white races engaged in that sort of thinking. It was more wide-spread than that. It was as if, having discovered that there were only a few large racial groups, many people of the time felt compelled to assert that the differences were even greater.

That culminated, of course, with the racial hatred of Hitler, and the "final solution" he imposed upon so much of the world.

That background makes Pike's positions even more remarkable.

For purposes of this paper, I wish to discuss Pike's positions on slavery, on the American Indian, and on women. I will agree at once with anyone who points out that women are not a race; but in today's terms, women are frequently classified as a "minority" and issues of gender are often blended with those of race.

Pike's views on these issues were greatly influenced by, and arose from, the great passion of his life, which he wrote so often into the rituals of the Scottish Rite and adverted to so frequently in his other writings--a profound belief in Liberty, Fraternity, and Equality.

As he wrote in *Morals and Dogma*:

From the political point of view there is but a single principle,--the sovereignty of man over himself. The sovereignty of one's self over one's self is called **Liberty.** *Where two or several of these sovereignties associate, the State begins. But in this association there is no abdication. Each sovereignty parts with a certain portion of itself to form the common right. That portion is the same of all. There is equal contribution by all to the joint sovereignty.*

This identity of concession which each makes to all, is **Equality.** *The common right is nothing more or less than the protection of all, pouring its rays on each. This protection of each by all, is* **Fraternity.** *Liberty is the summit, Equality the base. Equality is not all vegetation on a level, a society of big spears of grass and stunted oaks, a neighborhood of jealousies, emasculating each other. It is, civilly, all aptitudes having equal opportunity; politically, all votes having equal weight; religiously, all consciences having equal rights.*[1]

Pike saw Masonry as the natural supporter of the rights of all men and women.

The great distinguishing characteristic of a Mason is sympathy with his kind. He recognizes in the human race one great family, all connected with himself by those invisible links, and the mighty net-work of circumstance, forged and woven by God.[2]

And he warned against the easy non-thinking of bigotry, and intolerance, whether that intolerance was racial, moral, economic, regional, or gender-based. He pointed out that the Mason must do more than "not harm," he must make a positive difference.

In *The Book of the Lodge*, he wrote:

Custom and Prejudice are the blind guides of the blind.[3]

In his rituals for Adoptive Masonry for the Apprentice Degree, he said:

Masonry endeavors, by its charities, to relieve want and distress, comfort the afflicted and heal the wounds of the broken-hearted. But it aims at more than this; it is the Apostle of Liberty, Equality and Fraternity, and requires of its initiates devotedness and patriotism. These duties of life are more than life.[4]

And again, in *Morals and Dogma*:

Masonry is a march and a struggle toward the Light. For the individual as well as the nation, Light is Virtue, Manliness, Intelligence, Liberty. Tyranny over the soul or body, is darkness.[5]

THE ISSUE OF SLAVERY

"Tyranny over the soul or body is darkness." That view was to cost Pike almost everything he held dear. For tyranny over the body is slavery. Pike did not deceive himself about its evils.

In an article cited by Allsopp, Pike wrote:

[Slavery is] a disease, whose spectral shadow lies always upon America's threshold, originating in the avarice and cruelty of the slave trade . . . .[6]

Reading many of the sermons and articles of the time is a revelation in human psychology, and makes Pike's words, as a Southerner, even more remarkable. It was argued that the slave trade was actually a work of God, a benefit conferred upon the African who was thereby brought to a great and enlightened land where he could leave his savagery behind, improve his moral condition from the examples around him, and have hope of salvation. Brown, in his doctoral dissertation on Pike, summarizes the pro-slavery position taken on the stump and in the pulpit in these words. ". . . slavery was good, . . . slavery was perfect, it was the builder of the noble character and leadership qualities of the slaveholder; slavery was the only sound and permanent basis for republican government; it was the only truly beneficial relationship between capital and labor ever devised; and, finally, the South, like ancient Greece, was a perfect society because it was based on the institution of slavery."[7] Pike saw things a little more coldly.

In a series of articles published primarily in The Arkansas Advocate shortly before the outbreak of the War Between the States under the general title of "Letters to the People of the Northern States," Pike wrote:

I am not one of those who believe slavery a blessing. I know it is an evil, as great cities are an evil; as the concentration of capital is a few hands, oppressing labor, is an evil; as the utter annihilation of free-will and individuality in the army and navy, is an evil; as in the world everything is mixed of evil and good. Such is the rule of God's providence, and the mode by which He has chosen so to arrange the affairs of the world. Nor do I deny the abuses of slavery. . . . Necessarily it gives power that may be abused. Nor will I under-rate its abuses. It involves frequent separation of families. . . . It gives occasion to prostitution. The slave toils all his life for mere clothing, shelter, and food; and lash is heard sometime upon the plantations, and in rare cases, cruelties punishable by the law are practiced.[8]

And in *Morals and Dogma* he wrote:

Commercial greed values the lives of men no more than it values the lives of ants. The slave-trade is as acceptable to a people enthralled by that greed, as the trade in ivory or spices, if the profits are as large.[9]

Pike was deeply committed to the economic growth of the South. He thought that only by growth could the South break its complete dependence on agriculture and thus on slavery. He was realist enough to know that slavery would not end voluntarily as long as it was economically viable. But if the South could become a center of manufacturing and shipping, growth would follow. He was one of the first men, if not the first, to envision and publicly advocate a trans-continental railroad. If the eastern terminus could be located in the South, it could bring quick and sustained economic stimulation.[10]

He became enormously frustrated from time to time with the slowness of others to see the obvious needs for such improvements. As he wrote to John Coyle:

I am weary of Arkansas---weary and worn out, and must get out into the world, somewhere. I am sick of the constant squabbling and snarling that goes on around me, and of the antediluvian notions of Boobydom. The government of the State is in the fullest sense of the word a Boobyocracy, and itself lies supine like a lean sow in a gutter, "with meditative grunts of much content," waiting for the good time to come when railroads, school houses and other public improvements will build themselves, and nobody have it to pay for. That's their idea of the millennium.[11]

But he worked hard politically and in editorials to bring about a sort of economic summit of the South, at which plans could be made for regional development. But the meeting soon turned away from its original purpose and instead started agitation to extend the slave trade. That was too much for Pike.

At the latter meeting [a Convention of Southern states, held at Savannah] *I opposed a resolution offered in favor of the renewal of the slave trade, and afterwards declined to attend the meeting at Knoxville, because that subject had been agitated and the resolution was likely to be offered again.*[12]

No, for Pike, the considerations of the brotherhood of man were more important than the interests of any region. He BELIEVED in the great principles of Liberty, Equality and Fraternity. And, years after the Civil War, Pike wrote:

The horrors and atrocities, the grievous losses and calamitous consequences of a great civil war have proven to us that the wrongs done to the negro race by the slave-trade were to bear their inevitable fruit of death, disaster and distress, in our homes and households, when the perpetrators of the wrongs had long since gone to their last account.

All wrongs and cruelties, of individuals or nations, must bear their accursed fruit of evil consequences, simply because God is just; and if the consequences fall upon those who had no part in the wrongs, then the guilt of their doer is double, for he does a double wrong; and if upon his children, it is increased many fold; because his highest duty is to see to it that no harm should come to them through his misdeeds.[13]

THE STRENGTH AND EQUALITY OF WOMEN

The world has changed much on the issue of women since Pike's day. It was still a common belief at the time that woman *could not* be educated, except in those pursuits "suitable" for women. In the deep South, there was so powerful a prejudice against the education of women that two different languages nearly developed, one for use by men in talking to men and one for the use of women. Men spoke to women in what amounted nearly to baby talk. On many plantations, the speech of the women was far more nearly like that of the slaves then of the men. The suggestion that a woman could be the equal of a man was, to most of Pike's contemporaries, utter nonsense.

Pike saw it differently.

He created a ritual for a branch of Masonry to include both men and women, and the emphasis was clearly upon the women. His ritual never became popular--the Order of the Eastern Star took its place. But it's easy to see how Pike felt about the equality of women. Listen to a few examples from that ritual.

The progress of society and civilization being perhaps more certainly indicated by the ascent of woman in the social scale, than by any other one circumstance or symptom, the coöperation of your sex is indispensable to Freemasonry in carrying into execution its plans, and aiding the onward progress of the human race.[14]

In seeking to infuse new life into the Ancient and Accepted Scottish Rite of Freemasonry, we could not but feel how important it was to have the coöperation of women. Not only have Grace Darling, risking her life again and again amid the hungry breakers, to rescue the crew of a wrecked vessel, and Florence Nightingale and her Sister Angels of Mercy and Beneficence, nursing the sick and wounded in Crimean hospitals, shown us to what sublime heights of heroism and devotedness woman can ascend, strong in Love and Faith; but we have such examples round us everywhere, to-day, among the matrons and the daughters of our own land.

Superior to us in this field of glorious and sublime exertion, your sex have not proved less clearly their equality in the domains of intellect and science. With all the modest dignity of a true woman, Elizabeth Barret Browning stands by the side of the chief masters of song. To women we owe many of those most powerful fictions, creations of intellect and the imagination, which are but the drama of life and character and events in another form. In the sciences, there are female names that stand among the highest. A woman ranks as a geologist with Mantell and Miller and Murchison. A woman is the efficient co-laborer of Herschel in astronomy. A woman teaches political economy to men; and everywhere it is found that the keen, clear, quick intellect of woman wins unexpected triumphs.[15]

The Masonry Pike envisioned for women was fully-fledged Masonry, not some sort of auxiliary order.

The first condition of any institution intended for your sex, and bearing the name of Masonry, is, in order for it not to be a fraud upon you, that it should offer you the opportunity of working with Freemasonry toward a common end. . . . It is only by becoming one of our co-workers, and by meeting in your Lodges for the same purposes for which we meet in ours, by encouraging, cheering, inciting, and if need be shaming us, you can feel that you are not mocked with an unreality, when what is conferred upon you is called Masonry.[16]

But Pike was at his most radical on the topic of women when he wrote about sex. Again, the attitudes of the time are a little hard for us to recapture now. First, women were not supposed to enjoy sex at all. Sex, the writers of the time tell us, was a husband's right and a woman's duty. The books on "Mental Hygiene"—the nearest thing that century produced to texts on psychology until the work of Freud and his contemporaries—insisted that for a women to enjoy sex, especially to enjoy it to the point that she physically responded to is, was a sign of mental illness. And, of course, for a woman to have sex outside of marriage was to condemn her, literally, to the gutter or to an institution for depraved women, for life.

Pike, on the other hand, regarded women's enjoyment of sex as natural and normal. He wrote:

The laws of society as well as the world's ways, sadly need mending. It is the fashion, now, to say that the worst use to which you can put a man is to hang him. I am not so sure of that; but I am sure, that the worst use to which you can put a woman is to condemn her to a life of shame, because she has once done amiss, not by the act, which is natural and innocent, but by the absence of the law's sanction for it. Nothing is so heartlessly cruel as to interpose an insurmountable barrier, to make her return to respectability impossible.[17]

Finally, I would like to spend a few moments examining what Pike had to say about the rights of Indians. (With a quick side note. I know the "politically correct" term among some, currently, is "Native American" rather than Indian. But that term is more popular outside the Indian community than inside it. I am going to rely on my own Creek heritage and preference, as well as those of my Indian friends, and use the terms "Indian," and "American Indian.")

THE RIGHTS OF INDIANS

Again, Pike was far ahead of his time in his attitudes toward Indians. It was not uncommon at the time for the government to adopt policies and actions which amounted to sheer genocide. The phrase, "The only good Indian is a dead Indian," is not just a line sometimes heard in an old western, it was, often, the policy of the army. And sympathetic writers were few and far between. As Pike remarked of the Creeks:

They have no Froissart to chronicle their deeds or chivalry, and to recount their unnumbered wrongs. Over the graves of their forefathers the white man builds, and plants and runs his plough; it is fortunate for our national reputation that their history cannot be written in full; it would be fortunate for that reputation, if even what had been allowed upon our records was obliterated.[18]

And of the tribes in general, he wrote:

God would not be just, if the manifold injustices of crimes of the great American republic toward the Indian tribes, to say nothing of other wrongs, did not make inevitable the swift and complete ruin of the commonwealth.[19]

Pike had long association with the Indian tribes of the West. During the Confederacy, he was sent as representative to the tribes west of Arkansas and dealt extensively with them, especially with the Cherokee. The treaties he negotiated for the Confederacy with the tribes are remarkable documents.

They granted economic rights, political rights, and autonomy which far exceeded anything the Union have been willing to concede.

The points included the right to determine tribal membership, the right to expel unwanted whites from their lands, the legal standing to sue and to be witnesses, a delegate to the Confederate House of Representatives, and the right to control their own trade.[20]

He was fascinated by the Indian culture, and had been for many years. In the early part of his life he had several encounters with the tribes during his explorations through what would become the states of Oklahoma and New Mexico. Told with a touch of the typical Pike humor, he wrote accounts of those encounters.

It was past noon when we reached [the Indian village], for it was at least thirteen miles from the river. As we approached, the inhabitants of the village, who had been warned of our approach, not only by various strange shouts, but also by messengers, came out to meet us in great numbers; and after crossing a branch of the river, we entered the camp with our arms nearly shaken off at the elbows, by the rough, but friendly greetings of our new friends. Entering the village, which consisted of about thirty lodges, we were conducted to the chief's tent, where we found a young Frenchman, who could speak very good English. He informed us that this was the tent of the principal chief, and that our property would be very safe in it. We entered and shook hands with the chief and his subordinates, who occupied the interior. We bestowed ourselves in various positions upon the buffalo robes which were laid about the fire, and maintained a true Indian gravity, until they should see fit to address us. The young Frenchman then asked us where we were from. We told him, and he interpreted it to our hosts. . . . We gave them some details of our route, to which the listened with surprise, and perhaps with incredulity. If so, they were too polite to show it. . . After the conference was over, I produced my pipe and began to fill it. A half dozen pipes were immediately shown, and requests were made for tobacco, to which I was, of course, bound to respond, and we had a general smoke. We passed the remainder of this day and the next with them, and were called upon, every hour in the day, to go to some lodge and eat. In the course of the second day and evening, we ate fifteen times, and were obliged to do so, or affront them.

The Osages are generally fine, large, noble-looking men . . . and fed us bountifully on the meat of the buffalo, bear, deer and pole-cat; of the latter of which, however, we partook merely out of compliment.[21]

He formed relationships with the tribes which were to last the rest of his life. He became an advocate for them (today we would call him a "lobbyist") before Congress, trying to help settle the claims the Indians had and to enforce the treaty provisions which the government generally forgot before the ink of the signatures had dried.

Throughout his life, until advancing age made it impossible, he would leave Arkansas or Washington for weeks at a time and go camping and buffalo hunting with his Indian friends.

Allsopp writes: *". . .he would sometimes join an Indian hunting party and spend weeks in search of game, when his legal practice would admit of his absence. It was in this way that he formed lasting friendships with the Indians, who finally employed him as counsel to represent their interest at the National Capital. His legal work of this character assumed huge proportions. He took a genuine interest in trying to right the wrongs which he said the Red man has suffered at the hands of the White race. He learned to talk to some of the tribes in their own language, and it is stated on good authority that he had actually been recognized as a chief by one tribe of Indians, which is somewhat remarkable."*[22]

He became especially irate with the typical habit, both in and out of Congress, of referring to the Indians as "savages." In a biting satire, which reminds the reader strongly of Swift's "A Modest Proposal," Pike attacked the critics of the Indians, pointing out that it was just possible that Indians, too, were human and had souls, and suggesting that, when it came to savagery, the Whites would do well to look to their own glass house before throwing too many stones.

I do not know what these red men might have become in war. But knowing what savages war makes of men of our own kith and kin, what horrors followed the taking of San Sebastian, what devilish deeds were done on both sides in our late horrible civil war; and that if Indians scalp even the living and torture and burn their prisoners, there have been the Inquisition and the auto-de-fay, *and ten thousand murders of Christians of one sect by Christians of another, roastings of Jews in England and of the feet of women in our civil war to force disclosure of the hiding places of money and valuables, and a thousand cruel crimes, done where the shadows of Christian churches reached, when law and religions were supposed to reign hand in hand over all the country, I can pity rather than hate the "wild red Indian," and hope that Christ died for him also, as well as for us; and that even in him human nature is not all evil, and can remember with grateful affection my Indian friends.*[23]

THE FUTURE OF RACE RELATIONS

There are times when Pike can simply astound the reader with ideas which were far in advance of his time. His concept of the future of race relations is a case in point. Before the term "melting pot" had been coined to describe the process of American immigration and naturalization, Pike used much the same image, calling it an "immense crucible" in which the nature of the American character was being forged.

That would have been remarkable enough, but the truly remarkable point is that Pike arrived at a conclusion which has only been popularly espoused in the last few years. For he did not believe that racial differences would disappear in the process. Rather, he believed that each race would keep its own special heritage—its roots—with its individual strengths, and that the American character which finally emerged would not be the result of the loss of the cultural traditions and characters but rather a combination of strengths, each retaining its original vigor but cooperating and interacting with all the others.

It was a formidable insight.

This latest of republics, this great country, in which, fortunately, there is ample scope and verge enough for the experiment, is, as it were, an immense crucible, wherein is now being carried onward to successful or unsuccessful issue, the grandest work of alchemy that a wondering world has ever fixed its gaze upon.

For here are flung together thirty-one millions of people, native and foreign-born, of many races, and speaking many tongues, of every creed and faith, of every phase of opinion, of many habits of thought, total strangers to each other; a vast mass of apparently discordant elements, hostile, heterogeneous, incongruous; to be, if possible by any chemistry, made in process of time to combine into one homogeneous whole.

The antipathies that inflame and exasperate, and make our sky moody and threatening, are those of race and its instincts, and of opinions growing unconsciously out of ancient faiths and unfaiths. . . .

The differences of race will never cease to produce their habitual effects. Opinions and faiths will never be moulded into one monotonous sameness. But a wise Providence will use and is using these differences as the very means of producing true unity and real harmony, by causing them to become like the instrumental divisions of an orchestra, which balance each other, and completely accord, without assimilation. It is some grand law of Heaven's enacting, that the universal harmony should flow grandly forth, from the clashing elements in all the worlds.

. . Differences of opinion and apparent antipathies, often offensively expressed and embodied in aggressive political action, and even culminating in war, are yet

manifestly seen to be, in God's providence, blessings, if wisely availed of and profited by, and the means which it suits His wisdom to use, in order finally to establish a new, distinct and grand nationality, a unit of force, power and action, ruled by the same great ideas of popular liberty and order, of brotherhood, and equality, in the eye of the law, with a national character, one, original, with no prototype; in which nationality and character all the varying shades of race, temperament and peculiarity are not to be obliterated or tamed down into one monotonous sameness, but blended, mingled and combined into one admirable harmonious whole.[24]

And so, in the end, Pike was an optimist as he viewed the future of humanity and the relations between the races. That optimism is remarkable for one who fought in the Civil War and was so badly scarred, emotionally and financially, by Reconstruction. But his faith was stronger than his fear, and determination triumphed over despair.

He summed up his faith in the future in the ritual of the 33°, the culminating Degree of the Ancient and Accepted Scottish Rite of Freemasonry:

But still, the world does move, and we must not despair, though little come of our labours in our own time, Surely the Earth will at last become God's true Temple, the habitation of Truth and Love, when all men will constitute one people, living as the children of a common Father should, in obedience to His eternal laws of Equity and Charity.

When, all over the world, Truth shall have taken the place of Error, Liberty of Despotism, Justice of Inequity, and Toleration of Persecution, the Holy Empire of Scottish

Masonry will be established, the Holy Land reconquered, and the Holy House of the Temple rebuilt.[25]

NOTES

[1] Albert Pike, *Morals and Dogma*, pp. 43-44

[2] *Ibid*. P.176

[3] Albert Pike, *The Book of the Lodge*, p. 101

[4] Albert Pike, "Ritual of the Apprentice Degree," *The Masonry of Adoption: Masonic Rituals for Women*, p. 34

[5] *Morals and Dogma*, p. 32

[6] Albert Pike, quoted in Fred W. Allsop, *Albert Pike: A Biography*, Little Rock: Parke-Harper Company, 1928 p. 177

[7] Walter Lee Brown, *Albert Pike, 1809-1891: Dissertation Presented to the Faculty of the Graduate School of the University of Texas in Partial Fulfillment of the Requirements for the Degree of Doctor of Philosophy* Austin, Texas: unpublished. January, 1955, pp. 215-216

[8] Albert Pike, "Letters to the People of the Northern States," quoted in Fred W. Allsop, *Albert Pike: A Biography*, (Q.V.) P. 181

[9] *Morals and Dogma*, p. 70

[10] Albert Pike, "Plain Talk, Starvation, Migration or Railroads," *Little Rock Whig*, December 25, 1851.

[11] Albert Pike, Letter to John Coyle, personal friend and editor of *National Intelligencer*, dated Little Rock, April 20, 1855

[12] Pike, quoted in Allsopp, p. 104

[13] Albert Pike, "Essay X - Of Indian Nature and Wrongs" *Essays to Vinnie*, Autograph manuscript of essays

written to Vinnie Ream, preserved in the archives of the House of the Temple, Washington, D.C., p. 183

This speech was the 1995 Pires Lecture, delivered at the Dallas Scottish Rite Temple

Fundamentalism is not Faith

Fundamentalism is not faith!

The Ancient and Accepted Scottish Rite has always held to the truth that an individual's faith is entirely a matter of individual conscience. It would be unthinkable for Masonry in any of its branches to oppose faith in any denominational or religious expression.

But Fundamentalism is not faith, it is a form of emotional illness or inadequacy which sometimes expresses itself in the belief system of the individual.

Fundamentalism is a deep emotional insecurity, which cannot tolerate opinions or values which do not conform, in exact detail, to those of the afflicted individual.

The same emotional illness may express itself by making a father a demanding tyrant, who refuses to allow his wife to have her own personality and demands unquestioning obedience of his children, at the expense of their own emotional growth. In many cases, the individual becomes a wife beater and child abuser.

It may express itself as an aggressive personality, always looking for a fight.

It may express itself by turning the afflicted person into a self-appointed public censor, demanding the removal of books from public libraries, or subject matter from school curricula, when those violate the beliefs of the fundamentalist.

It may express itself as an attempt to interfere with the rights of parents, for there are fundamentalists of social theory as surely as there are fundamentalists of religion. These individuals, convinced that they know how children should be raised and tolerating no deviation from their pet theories, have often tried to pass legislation forcing parents to rear children by their preferred methods.

It may express itself as bigotry, intolerance, racism, persecution, or physical violence. Throughout history it has often expressed itself as a sort of super-patriotism which converts into chauvinism.

Sadly, there are also Masonic fundamentalists, insisting that "Masonry is only the ritual," or that "Masonry is only charity," or "Masonry is only Blue Lodge," and becoming as rigid and as irrational in their beliefs as Caligula himself.

It is, in all places and at all times, a threat, and it represents those things to which Masonry has always been opposed. And to oppose it is not to oppose religion or individual conscience, it is to oppose the illness which created Caligula, Torquemada, and Hitler.

Fundamentalism always damages those about it. Whether the victim is the child of a fundamentalist father, beaten and broken in spirit until it becomes "conformable unto the ways of the Lord," a wife, battered because she does not instantly obey every command and gratify every wish, the occupants of a vast building, bombed by Islamic fundamentalists because of imagined grievances, an author, under threat of death because his writings offend a fundamentalist "religious" leader, a fraternity, because fundamentalists fear its practice of allowing all good men to be members, regardless of their individual faiths, or

Christians, burned as torches and fed to lions to satiate the megalomania of a fundamentalist, garbed as a Roman emperor, who has conceived of himself as a god.

No, opposition to fundamentalism is not opposition to faith or denomination. It is opposition to the perversion of faith by madness.

Masonry—and more especially, perhaps, the Ancient and Accepted Scottish Rite—is a child of the Enlightenment. The Enlightenment, so throughly and understandably hated by fundamentalists, taught that unthinking piousness was the equivalent of ignorance. Albert Pike expressed the Enlightenment ideal well when he said "true religion consists of a balance between the two greatest gifts of God—faith and reason."

Fundamentalism sees reason as dangerous—as likely to lead toward error and away from "true faith." Fundamentalists build rigid structures, whether in their daily lives, the job, the families or their places of worship. Being rigid, they are vulnerable to attack by even incidental pressures. Every datum the fundamentalist encounters is instantly evaluated against the already-held conceptions, values, ideas and beliefs. Any variance from those already-held conceptions, values, ideas and beliefs is seen, not as an interesting idea, not as a spur to thought, and not even as an unfortunate error on the part of the other. It is seen as a threat and an attack, against which an immediate defense must be raised. As Dr. Gary Leazer points out, the fundamentalist sees ideas which do not conform exactly to his own—and those who hold such ideas—as enemies to be utterly destroyed. In that way, only, can they defend their version of truth and keep it intact.

Thus fundamentalism makes itself the enemy of education (as opposed to indoctrination) and builds private schools in which it can make certain that children are not exposed to "foreign and godless ideas."

It makes itself the enemy of the arts (save, as in the case of Soviet fundamentalism, arts which carries a message of which it approves—arts and artists of which it disapproves are eliminated or exiled, or, as in the case of the American experience with political fundamentalism known as McCarthyism, blacklisted).

It makes itself the enemy of other faiths and denominations, denying that others can be "real" Christians, Moslems, Jews, etc., since they do not subscribe to the fundamentalist's own views.

It sees toleration and compromise as vices, not as virtues, because "all compromise is a pact with the devil."

The fundamentalist mind-set is essentially authoritarian in nature. It yields, instantly and without reservation, to authority which it perceives as being higher than itself. It is for that reason that fundamentalism in a hierarchy—whether that be the hierarch of the medieval church or the hierarchy of the military in Nazi Germany—is so inherently dangerous. Fundamentalists carry out orders from those perceived to be in authority, without thought or evaluation—whether that order be to torture someone suspected of heresy or to fill a gas chamber with people considered less than human.

The attacks against Freemasonry have not ended—if anything they have intensified. The intensity is probably because the attacks have largely fallen upon deaf ears. Some Masons have withdrawn from the fraternity because of pressure from their church, but a more typical attitude is: "If my Lodge tells me I can't be a member of my Church, I will leave my Lodge—if my Church tells me I can't be a member of my Lodge, I will find another Church."

The Scottish Rite in the United States has been fighting fundamentalist attacks against the fraternity through information, and especially by support of the Masonic Renewal Committee of North America and the Masonic Information Service, established by a grant from John Robinson and administered through the Masonic Service Association of North America. Robinson was a tireless crusader against the anti-Masonic fundamentalists, although he was not, at the time. a Freemason. Even knowing that he was dying of cancer, and even when travel was painful and exhausting, he traveled the country, engaging in radio and television debates with anti-Masonic fundamentalists with telling results. Proceeds from his last book, *A Pilgrim's Path*, were dedicated to establishing the Masonic Information Service which he had envisioned. His work is now being carried on by donations from Grand Lodges and from the Scottish Rite.

The Masonic Information Service has produced and printed several pamphlets for Lodges and individual Masons to use in explaining Masonry to non-Masons. Among others, "What's A Mason?" "There is No Sin in Symbols," and "Get a Life," have proven to be very popular, and hundreds of thousand of copies have been distributed.

Much as been done.

Much more must be done.

Freemasonry must fight fundamentalism wherever it appears. We must support patriotism, but oppose chauvinism. We must teach—in fact we must insist upon—toleration. We must do so not only within the tiled recesses of our Lodge Rooms and auditoria but in the world as well. We must make information available to our own members and to the public. If necessary, we must join in legal actions to stop fundamentalist attacks on the basic freedoms and rights of human beings. We must continue to be, as we have historically been, the apostles of liberty and freedom of thought. We must not be co-conspirators, by silence, in the emergence of a new Dark Age.

We can do these things, The Scottish Rite can and must continue its tradition of championing individualism and individual freedom.

Two hundred years ago, Masonry and the Scottish Rite helped in the spread of the great ideals of the Enlightenment across the world. We must do no less today.

Speech delivered at a Scottish Rite Reunion, 1998

The Annoying Prospect of Living

Brother Mark Twain, in his book *A Tramp Abroad*, writes this description of a sunrise in the Alps, a famous spectacle many tourists came to see.

"One could see the grand Alpine masses dimly outlined against the black firmament, and one or two faint stars blinking through rifts in the night. Fully clothed and wrapped in blankets, we huddled ourselves up, by the window, with lighted pipes, and fell into chat while we waited, in exceeding comfort, to see how an Alpine sunrise was going to look by candlelight. By and by a delicate, spiritual sort of effulgence spread itself by imperceptible degrees over the loftiest altitudes of the

snowy waste—but there the effort seemed to stop. I said, presently, 'There is a hitch about this sunrise somewhere. It doesn't seem to go. What do you reckon is the matter with it?'

"'I don't know. It appears to hang fire somewhere. I never saw a sunrise act like that before.'

"Harris jumped up and said 'I've got it. I know what's the matter with it. We've been looking at the place where the sun set last night.'

"It was perfectly true. We had arisen in the middle of the night, with little sleep, to sit staring west, waiting for the sunrise."

Brethren, in some ways, that is true of many of us. Whether we like to admit it or not, we have become accustomed to the prospect of the death of Masonry. We've tried to hold it off, but many have suspected that we were fighting a losing battle. We have settled into what one of my friends calls "the comfortable and gentle warmth of decay." Oh, we put on a brave face; we try things, but most of our conversation is about how we can downsize our programs, our buildings, our charities and our budgets. Consciously or not, many of us have prepared for a dignified death—prepared to go gently into that good-night.

Meanwhile, behind our backs, the sun has been rising.

I'm afraid we are facing the annoying prospect of living.

I tell you honestly, in all the decades I have been watching Masonry, I have never seen as much potential, or interest, as there is today. And it is a culture-wide phenomenon.

In the last few years, the academic community has discovered the Fraternity. In most of the 1900's you will search in vain for any mention of Freemasonry in histories of the United States. Then, suddenly, we are everywhere as historians have discovered that we are one of the major unexplored factors of history. Let me give you just a few current examples.

Margaret Jacob, Professor of History at UCLA wrote *Living the Enlightenment: Freemasonry and Politics in Eighteenth Century Europe* in 1991, in which she showed how Freemasonry was largely responsible for the spread of democracy in Europe. In 2003, she published *The Radical Enlightenment: Pantheists, Freemasons, and Republicans*, and in 2005, she wrote *The Origins of Freemasonry: Facts and Fictions*.

James Stevens Curl is Emeritus Professor of Architectural History of Leicester Polytechnic in England and author of books on architecture which are considered standard in the profession. In 2002 he brought out a revised edition of his academically acclaimed book *The Art and Architecture of Freemasonry*.

Steven Bullock, professor at Worchester Polytechnic Institute and one of the most respected American historians, wrote *Revolutionary Brotherhood: Freemasonry and the Transformation of the American Social Order, 1730 - 1840*. In the book he clearly shows the importance of Freemasonry in forming the national character and values of the United States.

Douglas Smith, who has a Ph.D. in Russian History from UCLA, published *Working the Rough Stone: Freemasonry and Society in Eighteenth-Century Russia*, in 1999. In the book he shows how the Czar imported Freemasonry into Russia as a part of his attempt to move Russia into the modern world.

But in the last two or three years, even books which are not "about" Masonry have contained references, either brief or extensive about the role Masonry played in the subject. That includes books about Benjamin Franklin; Lewis and Clark; Elias Ashmole; Sir Christopher Wren and the rebuilding of London after the great fire; the founding of the Royal Society for the Advancement of Science; to list just a few topics,

All these books, and many others, are published by academic presses. They are less concerned than the popular press with making money (although all these books have done well) But the popular press, the ones which fill the book stores and best-sellers list, don't publish books unless they think they will sell. So it is important that the last few months have seen three major popular-press books: *The Complete Idiot's Guide to Freemasonry*, by Dr. S. Brent Morris; *Freemasons for Dummies*, by Christopher Hodapp, and *The Everything Freemasons Book* by John Young and Barb Karg.

But Masonry's sudden star status isn't limited to the academic world. Consider novels like *Angels and Demons* and *The DaVinci Code*, or the science fiction classic *The Artifact* by W. Michael Gear in which the Brotherhood works out moral dilemmas of the future, Or the film *National Treasure.* Or the series of novels known as *The Adept* by Kathryn Kurtz, in which esoteric Masonry appears as a powerful force for good in the battles with evil on the astral plane.

This year marks the 250th Anniversary of the birth of Mozart. It is hardly surprising that a large number of recordings of his music are being made and released this year. But what I find interesting is that three previously issued recordings of Mozart's Masonic music have been re-released, three new collections of his Masonic Music have been recorded and released.

And then there is the album "Mozart the Mason" The cover shows a version of Blake's famous painting of Newton drawing the map of the world with the compasses, only Newton's head has been replaced with Mozart's and the map of the world has been replaced with a score. There is some very nice art work inside as well. But the interesting thing is that none of the music on the CD—the Preludes and Fugues K-404 and the Divertimento in E♭ K563 are usually considered as among his Masonic music. Again, record producers generally release that which they think will sell to some market. It is interesting that so much of Mozart's music is being identified with Masonic content.

But it doesn't end there. Among many other examples, Paul Bessel's web site lists the following:

> In the television series "In the Heat of the Night" sheriff Bill Gillespie is often clearly shown wearing a Masonic ring.
>
> Rapper DMX starts out a hit song with "I've been through mad different phases like Masons to find my way and now I know that happy days are not far away."
>
> The Irish-American rap group House of Pain has a song with contains the lyrics "Do you know about the Masons about their nation?" and later says "To the 33rd Degree you know that's me."
>
> In the video "It's Tricky" by RUN DMC, a young woman is wearing a 32 Degree Scottish Rite cap.

More and more, Masonic jewelry, Masonic symbols, and Masonic reference are appearing in popular culture. It's almost spooky.

So that is the first point. Someone knows we're here. That's the first hint of the sunrise behind us.

The second is in the nature of the men who are joining the fraternity.

Last year in Oklahoma we started a project which finished this year, and which is one of the most interesting projects I've even been involved with. It came out of a series of membership brain-storming sessions. We had been trying to figure out what the young men of today wanted from Freemasonry, what might motivate them to join the Fraternity. Did we have anything to offer which was relevant to their lives. We had been at it for several hours over a couple of days, when someone said "Just as a thought, instead of a group of men with more than 40 years each in Masonry trying to guess what young Masons want, why don't we ask them?"

This, of course, was so unreasonable that we immediately formed a sub-committee to burn the offending brother at the stake. But a week later, when it could no longer be considered a new idea (and the ashes had cooled) we all agreed that there might be something to be said for it.

Ultimately, we produced two surveys. One was for men who had been raised as Master Masons between January 1st, 2001, and March 26, 2005 (when the records were isolated in the computer) and who were 40 years of age or less at the time of their raising. The second was a survey of men who had taken either the Entered Apprentice of the Fellowcraft degree during that same period but who had not progressed to the Master Mason Degree, and who were also 40 years of age of less when they took the Degree.

We worked for a long time on the questions for the survey, and we have a copy for each Grand Lodge here.

Soon after the beginning of 2006, we finalized the questions and had the surveys printed. We than mailed them to the selected brethren with a letter from the Grand Master asking their cooperation and a postage-paid return envelope.

We sent 1,189 surveys to Master Masons and 1,368 to Entered Apprentices and Fellow Crafts who had not advanced.

Ultimately, 10.8% of the Master Masons and an astonishing 17% of the EAS and Fellowcrafts completed and returned the survey forms. This was followed by a long period of tabulation and analysis. I will not take your time by going over all the results—again, they are in the material we have brought to give you, But there are some things I should point out.

Just what sort of critter is the young man who is joining Freemasonry today? How is he like we were? In what ways is he different?

For one thing, he is well educated. 80% have some college work, have a college degree, or are still in college.

For another, he IS young. The average age of those returning the survey was 30.6 years.

He rarely has more then two children, more often has only one.

He is often in a second marriage.

He is more jealous of his time than he is of his money. He believes that he has almost no free time at all. Robert Putnam, in his very important book *Bowling Alone: The Collapse and Revival of American Community*, demonstrates very clearly that, in fact, he has far more free time than his father or grandfather had (and his father and grandfather were probably much more involved in organizations such as Freemasonry, the church, and a civic club than he is). But we must not forget that "perception IS reality." His father defined free time or leisure time in the same way a sociologist does—time not occupied by eating sleeping, or earning an income. HE defines free time as the time left over after eating, sleeping, earning an income, helping with the household chores, taking his kids to soccer and ballet, and working in the yard.

He is willing to find time for activities such as Freemasonry, but they have to repay the time he invests. Going to meetings, reading minutes and paying bills just doesn't cut it.

He is actively seeking time with men. When Masonic Renewal first began, a survey was done of American males in the age target group. In very large numbers, something like 70%, they told us that an organization to which they belong had to have activities for the entire family.

We now know that was a public attitude—that is, a thing people say because it is the politically correct thing to say, or because they think it is the expected attitude. In point of fact, most of the young men don't want their families anywhere near the Lodge, except for some special event. They want and need time with men, both men of their own age and men somewhat older.

They are motivated to join Masonry by the traditional motivations—they want to learn to be better men, they want to make a difference in the community, they are looking for real friendships, they want to be part of something bigger than they are. This is real. Listen to some of the things they wrote, in addition to just answering the questions on the survey.

Self-improvement was a motivation. I had promised myself that I would petition long ago. I knew if I didn't my time would be more taken by other things, and the time was right. Wish I had done it sooner.
I wanted to follow in the footsteps of my father and grandfather.
I knew there had to be something special about an organization so many respected men belong to.

So far, this has been the best decision of my young life.

Wanted to learn to be a good man and husband.

Wanted to be a part of a Fraternity that helps other people as well as one with a great history. I had a desire to be a part of something greater than I am that actually helps my fellow man.

My Grandfather was a Mason and my Father and Brother are Masons. I respect them a great deal. My Grandfather was the kind of man I strive to be, and I believe Masonry played a large part in the character of my Grandfather.

Some ideas and attitudes are easier to identify in conversation than in a survey. For about seven years now, I've been talking to young Master Masons every chance I get. Since I am the Director of the Work at the Guthrie Scottish Rite Temple, I get a chance twice a year to talk with between 50 and 60 during Reunions, and I have co-conspirators who also talk with them and report to me. One thing which is reflected in the survey and even more in the conversations is that these young men are on a real spiritual quest. I think that is sometimes hard for us to really believe.

In the 2000 national census, the designers of the census had to add a new category to those listed in "Religion," — "believers but not belongers." This is the most rapidly growing religious demographic in the United States. It is composed of men and women who say that they have a strong faith in God but do not belong to any organized religious denomination.

I believe it. Ties are unknown at a Scottish Rite Reunion in Oklahoma anymore, at least among the candidates, except when the class picture is being taken. Almost everyone wears an open-necked shirt. And around many of those necks is hanging a little Thor's Hammer. It's fun to watch their faces when they realize that I recognize the symbol—it's a little as if they expected me to publicly denounce them as heretics and tear up their Blue Lodge membership card.

The point is they are on a spiritual quest. They truly are. I end up in conversations with many of them until the early morning hours at a Reunion, and then in e-mail exchanges for long after that. I know that Bob Davis has the same experience. They are looking for spiritual growth, and they make it clear that they are NOT going to look for that in church.

In some ways, there is no surprise in that. Many churches will tell you that their purpose is not the spiritual growth of their parishioners; their purpose is to teach and enforce the doctrine of their faith, because that is the path to salvation.

So, where do you go if you have become aware of what theologians call the "God-shaped hole" in your heart or soul, but you are, for some reason, repelled by organized religion? For many young men, the answer is Freemasonry.

It is VERY important to note that Freemasonry does not offer, and they are not seeking, a path to salvation. That is an entirely different issue. They fully understand that we are a fraternity, not a religion. What they are seeking is spiritual growth and fulfillment, and they know, either by instinct or by reading, that the path to that growth has always been initiation.

Is there anything else we can say about the young Masons? Yes, they are intellectually curious and they are highly skilled users of the Internet. Most of them petition the fraternity only after study. You and I had no idea what was going to happen. For the most part, they do. Many have even read the full ritual on the Internet. They come with questions---and they do expect answers.

I'm interested in many aspects of Freemasonry that seem to be disbursed rarely and in secret. For the most part, I've been told such things as "I don't know who could answer that for you," or "That's interesting, hmmmm."

I want to learn more. I want to learn the history of the Masons, what the symbols mean, why we do the things we do. Is there someplace this is all pulled together?

I enjoy doing the ritual, but I want to know more than just the words. Why is there an opening and closing ceremony? Why are there sometimes 3 and sometimes 4 knocks on the door? I know they say it "locks" it, but what is the meaning behind it? Why do the lesser lights represent the sun, moon, and Master? Does that mean the Master is a representative of Mercury? Why are there celestial and terrestrial spheres on top of the pillars when there were no such spheres on the columns of Solomon's Temple? Why does the Junior Deacon sit facing the East while the Senior Deacon sits facing the south rather than the West? Every time I ask, I'm told it isn't important!

There is a point here which can't be made strongly enough. Most of the Masonic leaders with whom I grew up simply have it ingrained in their thinking as an article of faith that the one thing Masons don't want to know anything about is Freemasonry. For many of us, Masonic education meant learning the ritual—unless you were one of those weirdos who belonged to a Lodge of Research. These guys WANT TO LEARN ABOUT MASONRY as well as the ritual, and they do not confuse the two. They understand that the ritual is the path and Masonry is the destination. In the survey 54% were interested in belonging to or helping to form a study club, 56% wanted more Masonic education in Lodge, and 23% said they regarded Masonic Education in Lodge as extremely critical.

There are many other elements, but there are two in particular I want to touch on.

First of all, they have, in abundant measure, something which many of us may have lost. They have PRIDE.

I must admit that for many Masons of my age, myself, I fear, included, Masonic pride is rather like Marat's description of some luke-warm participants in the French Revolution. "They wear the people's cap on their heads, but their underwear's embroidered with crowns." There are probably a lot of reasons for that, not the least was the anti-Masonic movement of the 1990's. We are happy that we are Masons, but if it means confrontation, We'd just as soon the world didn't know.

Not so our younger brethren. If you want a real insight into their thinking, go to this web site—masonicink,com It is one of many web sites about Masonic tattoos. Talk about an utterly tabu topic in my youth! Tattoos were a class thing, and simply not to be done. You may be old enough to remember a Saturday Evening Post cover by Normal Rockwell, showing a young sailor just returned from the war with his mother weeping inconsolably over the fact that he has gotten a small tattoo.

Changed has the world.

Their Masonic "tatts" are a source of pride for many of our younger members. This particular web site (which does not sell or advertize tattoos, incidentally, just chronicles them) will show you a photo of the Brother, close up photographs of his tattoos, and a biographical sketch written by the brother. There are doctors, lawyers, ministers and others, proudly showing their tattoos (some of which cover the entire back). Interestingly, almost all of them have designed their own, using combinations of Masonic symbols, and they explain what those symbols mean to them and why they used them in that combination. To a lover of

Masonic symbolism, this is a rich field of study, and one I am just beginning to explore.

There are rooms in which I would like to be a little mouse in the corner. One of them is the Lodge room of a brother on the site who had just been installed as Chaplain in his Lodge, and celebrated the event be getting a very large York Rite emblem tattooed on his shoulder. I'd love to have been there when he showed the Brethren.

But think about what all this says. Think how strongly you have to believe in something to have it permanently displayed on your body. Whatever you may think of it, brothers, that is commitment!

So, frankly, I think the future of Masonry is very bright, we are appealing to a whole new generation of men, the ages of our candidates is getting younger and younger (the Worshipful Master of my Lodge in Guthrie is 36, and that makes him ten years older than any other officer except the Secretary). They are excited and committed. Yes, they will drop out for a while as they build careers and families-- that's nothing new. But they love Masonry, they are proud of being Masons, and they want to share it with their friends.

There is another exciting thing happening in Masonry—for the first time in my life, there are Masonic movements. I mean, people are coming up with a new idea, getting excited about it, and implementing it. One of the ideas is called "traditional observance."

While this is an oversimplification, these things are true of most Traditional Observance Lodges. The dues and initiation fees are higher than most Lodges. A typical year's dues would be $200. But they give value for money. The Lodge focus is on the initiation and personal growth of members. Charity may or may not be a part of the Lodge activity, but if it is, it is a minor part. They guard well the ballot box. Distinctions are laid aside. In Guildhall, a traditional observance Lodge in Oklahoma, while several Past Grand Masters are members, no one wears a PGM apron in the Lodge. The Lodge has a special apron made for each member, and those are the only aprons worn. There is a brief educational paper presented at each meeting. The Lodge officers enter in procession, to music. There is a period of silent meditation on some topic. The room is lighted by candles. Each quarter, the Lodge has a feast and festive board and brings in a noted Masonic scholar from out of state to give a paper. They do not do community projects. And most, if not all of the members belong to other Lodges as well.

Yes, there are exciting things happening in both the Masonic world and the world outside. Masonry will survive and thrive. That's the good news.

The not so good news is that I am not certain the fraternity is going to make it.

You see, that's another thing about these young guys—they very clearly separate Freemasonry from the Fraternity.

Freemasonry is the teaching, the lessons, the insights, the symbols the development provided by the ritual and the fellowship. Freemasonry is the classic hero's quest; the classic initiation which marks the division between being a grown-up boy and being an autonomous and complete man.

The fraternity is the framework.

Now, I must say a couple of things which you will find painful and annoying, and for which I apologize, but they are important.

Freemasonry will survive. But it is far less certain that Grand Lodges will survive.

First of all, a very important social dynamic is changing, and none of us really understand it.

One of the major psychological and sociological differences between men and women is what is sometimes call the extension of position power. That simply means this: for men, the leader of a group to which they belong is the leader even when they are not in the group context.

Another way to say that is the Worshipful Master of the Lodge is the Worshipful Master whether his Lodge brothers are with him in Lodge, or on the golf course, or just happen to meet at McDonald's. Even in settings which have nothing to do with the Lodge, Lodge members think of him as the Worshipful Master and treat him somewhat differently. Men have what we thought was an inborn deference to authority.

Women don't have that. If a woman meets the President of her P.E.O. Chapter "on the outside" so to speak, she meets her on the same basis that she always has and always will. While the Chapter is meeting, she will treat the President as the President, but that ends with the end of the meeting.

Very recently, sociologists have discovered that men are leaving their response to the extension of position power, and reacting much more like women would. You may have noticed certain stories in the press over the last two or three years, complaining that people don't treat judges, ministers, senators or representatives with the courtesy they used to. It is possible this is caused by the 24-hour news channels and the fact that we see and hear far too much about these people; we are not certain what the cause is, but if the trend continues, it will mean that organizations which depend on a sense of positional authority in their members may be in serious trouble.

Many of the young Masons today consider Grand Lodges completely irrelevant to their lives and Masonic experience. Especially, those issues which Grand Lodges have held dear, such things as jurisdiction and recognition, are seen as pointless at best and obstructionist at worst. As one young Mason said to me recently, "What makes somebody think they can get away with telling me who I can and can't talk to about anything I want?"

When I mentioned that the Grand Lodge of Oklahoma used to forbid an Oklahoma Mason to have a cipher key to the Oklahoma work, the response, slightly cleaned up, was "I'd like to see some stuck up so and so try to tell me what I can and can't read. There is a First Amendment, after all."

When, in response to a question, I tried to explain the concept of clandestine Masons, the reaction from another Brother was that no one was going to tell him what organizations he could or could not belong to, and if they tried, he'd see them in court.

I should stress that these were not radical people by their own standards—they don't mind at all being held to a higher ethical or moral standard—they see that as part of Masonry. But being told who they can and can't talk to or what they can or can't read they see as part of the fraternity structure, having nothing at all to do with Masonry, and they simply reject it out of hand.

I've heard many of them say, "It's too bad the Grand Lodge doesn't want to help, because there's a lot they could do, but I'm not going to let them get in my way."

I don't mean to suggest that there is a great deal of open rebellion. There isn't. I am saying that there is a risk that Grand Lodges will simply come to be viewed—rather as many people view the electoral college—as an interesting if sometimes frustrating relic of a necessity which no longer exists.

There is another issue that some young Masons have with Grand Lodges, at least as they perceive them. That problem is ego.

If we are going to be painfully honest with ourselves, we would have to admit that a visitor from Mars would probably think that Masonry exists only as a forum for men to praise each other, on the understanding that they will be praised in turn. (A good friend of mine, not a Mason but a clinical psychologist of some standing, after attending an open meeting of the Grand Lodge, was unkind enough to point out the large number of similarities between what he had seen that evening and the dominance grooming and defleaing rituals of a pack of chimpanzees. I told him to bug off.)

And, meaning no disrespect but simply observing reality—bad as we are about that, it is as nothing compared to the Eastern Star, and we are a distant third compared to Amaranth.

The young ones have no interest in massaging the egos of their elders, especially if the elder's only claim to fame is that he is a Grand Lodge officer. Now frankly, we've all known and felt that. Every state has had Grand Masters who were simply disasters. But you and I and the Brethren before us have always said, and truly meant, "It is the Office which is due the respect, even if the man holding that office for the moment is a loon." I was making that point in a discussion with some of the younger ones not too long ago.

"No, Jim" they said, "You are missing the point. We're not going to respect his office unless HE respects his office. But his office is that of the chief servant of the Craft, not

Caesar. If any man is so self-important that he expects someone to open doors for him, he needs to have them slammed in his face. Respect is earned; it doesn't come with the job. Did he ever take the Entered Apprentice Degree? Did he never learn the first lesson of Masonry; that the ego must die if the person is to live?"

Finally, there is one more point at which the young Mason and those of us who have occupied space for a longer time may have a misunderstanding.

He doesn't think Masonry is dying.

My Father was very involved in Masonry, especially the Scottish Rite. We talked about it many times, because he was greatly concerned about the future of the Craft. He thought it would probably end in suicide.

"Remember Jim," he said, "dying organizations love rules. Living organizations, growing organizations have neither time not patience with rules; they are too busy doing things and making things happen. They usually ignore what few rules there are, and they certainly don't let rules get in the way of the task. But when an organization loses its energy, when it starts to die, all it wants is ease and comfort, and it starts making rules. Its people have too much time on their hands, and so they sit around telling each other how terrible something is, and they say 'By Gadfry, we'll make sure no one can ever do THAT again.' Here's a copy of the Oklahoma Masonic Constitution and Laws I got in 1941—the year you were born. Compare that to today's."

The 1941 version was about 3 inches by 7 inches and about a quarter inch thick. It would easily fit in and inside coat pocket. Today's, as he knew, comes in a thick 3-ring binder.

But our young ones don't know we're dying, so the only attention they are likely to pay to the rules is how to get around them.

Yes, I have to admit that the prospect of living rather than dying is annoying. It means we leave that comfortable warmth of decay. It means we look at the world as it is, not as we think it ought to be. It means that we put our egos on the back burner, or, better, in the trash.

So, from the perspective of the young Masons (and we better listen, our average age in Oklahoma is about 68, and these twenty and thirty year-olds are going to be around a lot longer than we are) what does a Grand Lodge do to be relevant and meaningful?

First of all, do everything we can at the state level to create PRIDE in the Fraternity. Quit being afraid of being called "elitist." We may or may not be elitist, but we certainly better be elite. Take out ads in the newspapers and on television which simply say "Look how significant we are," We don't have to be arrogant, but it is time to take our light out from under the bushel.

Grand Lodges can coordinate public awareness campaigns better than anyone else.

Produce materials which help to tell the story of Masonry. We brought a couple of things to share with you. One is a booklet we give to everyone who comes a cornerstone laying (and we do a lot of them). It's purpose is just to tell people a little about the tradition and about Masonry, but it has proven very popular. The other is a think we call the Pathway Packet. It is a folder containing a petition, and information about Masonry. We sell these to the Lodges for $1 each, which just about covers the cost of printing. Willie Fudge who is with me, came up with both these ideas, and they have proven excellent.

But you can come up with plenty of ideas on your own. The task is to think in terms of ways in which the Grand Lodge can be of service to the Lodges and to the Brethren.

Information is another area. Most Lodges do a very poor job of teaching their people about Masonry, and yet we know from the surveys and other data that there is a great hunger to know that material. The Grand Lodge can develop educational programs, can develop teams which go sit down the Lodge officers and say "Ok, how can we help? What problems are you facing? We are not here to force you to do anything, but we are here to put the resources of the Grand Lodge behind you to make sure you have a success.

If you choose life, you can find a hundred ways to help Masonry live. I'm convinced it is going to.

Inconvenient as it may be.

Speech to The Midwest Conference of Masonic Grand Lodges
August 18 - 20, 2006

Something Fishy in the Lodge

All of us have those little, niggling questions about the ritual and the symbols of Masonry—those things we keep promising ourselves that we'll look up or try to figure out someday. One of mine has always been: although the moon is mentioned, almost all the symbolism inside the Lodge is solar—the Master's and Warden's stations are identified by sun position—labor and refreshment are identified by sun position——all daylight imagery. Why, then, is the covering of the Lodge the starry canopy? Why the shift to night imagery?

A light (so to speak) came on a few days ago in conversation with some well-informed Brethren. There's something important about the stars in relationship to the general imagery of the Lodge. And that important relationship is signaled to the Candidate before he enters the Lodge Room. Consider these words: "Even this ceremony of your gaining admission into this Lodge is emblematical of an event which sooner or later must overtake all mankind. It is emblematical, at least to some small degree, of nothing less than your last great change—your transition from Time to Eternity."

That's worth a moment of thought. We are not, as is often said, dealing with birth imagery in the Lodge, nor even with death imagery, we are dealing with transcendence. It brings us face to face with some of the oldest symbols known to man, and with some of the most profound of the mysteries.

The Gate of the Souls

The ancient belief was that all souls existed prior to birth. Standard Jewish theology was and is that all souls were created during the 7 time periods or days of creation, before the creation of Adam. The same belief was held in early Christianity and was taught by both Clement of Alexandria and by Origin, generally considered the first Christian theologian. About 300 years later, at one of the great Councils, it was decided that this was heresy and that souls were created either at birth or at conception. I would point out, however, that it was a council decision. We know something of the great Councils from contemporary descriptions and they can best be described as a combination of a meeting of the Democrat National Committee and a conference of mafia dons.

At any rate, the belief, both Christian and non-Christian, was that souls entered through a gate or portal in the constellation of Cancer and proceeded by all the planets to earth. After death, the soul again passed all the planets, and left the solar system through a gate in the constellation Capricorn.

If we draw that out as a schema, we have the classic symbol of a circle with two parallel lines. In Masonry, we say the two lines represent St. John the Baptist and St. John the Evangelist. They also, of course, mark the summer and winter solstices which was their original significance. And, guess what, the Summer Solstice is in Cancer and the Winter Solstice is in Capricorn.

Another way of saying the same thing is that we have images of the spirit of man moving from time to transcendence and back again. This movement to transcendence is also of course symbolized by the middle chamber in the Fellowcraft Degree.

We need to consider, for a moment, the circle. Being endless, complete, it is the earliest known symbol of Deity it also symbolizes the world.

Two circles symbolize the two worlds—the spiritual world and the physical world. If the two circles are drawn so that the circumference of one touches the center of the other, this space in between, this common area, is known as a vesica piscis. It literally translates as "fish bladder" merely as a description of the shape.

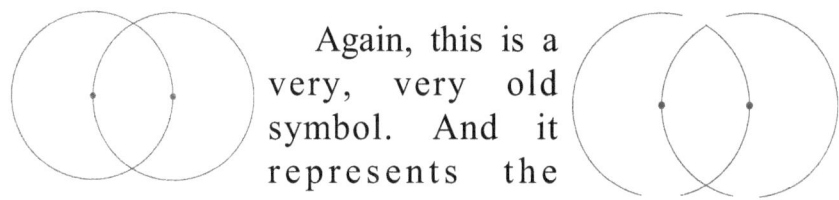

Again, this is a very, very old symbol. And it represents the opening or bridge or portal between the two worlds—the spiritual world and the physical world. If we blot out a little of the circles, you can see the origin of another important symbol—the fish associated with Christianity.

To the early Christians, Christ was the bridge point, He stood at the opening of the other world, and so the fish became a powerful symbol. They created a memory aid to help them identify each other. The first letters of the words which translate Jesus Christ, Son of God, Savior spell the Greek word for fish Ikthos.

In the Middle Ages and the Renaissance, the vesica was used as a frame continually in church art. Saints appeared in the vesica, as well as images the Virgin Mary and Christ. Always the symbolic meaning was the same, this person had found transcendence—they had passed from one world or condition to the other.

So where would the vesica be in a lodge room? If we draw a circle whose center is in Cancer and another whose center is in Capricorn — or, to say it another way, if we draw one circle centered on the summer solstice and another centered on the winter solstice — or to say it a third way, if we draw a circle whose center is St. john the Baptist and another circle whose center is St. John the Evangelist—then the vesica, the gateway to the two worlds, the entrance point which allows one to move into and out of transcendence, is the altar of the Lodge, and above it would shine Libra, the Scales, the symbol of equilibrium and balance.

In every possible way they could, the brethren who devised the ritual and the symbol system of Masonry signaled to us that the purpose of the Fraternity was transformation. It was our task to help men find their true personality, develop genuine ego-strength as opposed to mere bluff and selfishness, and become autonomous, independent, spiritually alert and active men.

They told us in simple English that the purpose of Masonry is to take good men and make them better. They told us, in the highly coded and encrypted language of the rituals and the even more deeply encoded language of the symbols, how it is done.

Speech for Phillalethes Luncheon, Guthrie, Oklahoma, December 2004

Rebirth

Most Worshipful Grand Master, Distinguished Brethren in the East, and Brothers of the Mystic Tie.

I sometimes wonder what it would have been like to be a Mason in the late 1500's in Scotland, when the rebirth of Masonry as a Speculative Craft from the Operative Craft was happening.

The Scots, to their credit, are known as very conservative of fundamental values. What must a craggy old warden of a Lodge thought when he saw men joining the Lodge who had never set one stone atop another in their entire lives; men who worked with pen and parchment, not their hands; and spent their time talking about ideas and theory. It must have offended his practical soul.

M∴W∴ Richard Fletcher, P∴G∴M∴ of Vermont, was not actually born in the state, although he moved there at a very early age. He is fond of explaining that when he called himself a Vermonter, an old Past Master of the Lodge said,

"Richard, if a cat jumps into an oven to have her litter, ye don't call her kittens 'biscuits.'"

It is in much the same spirit that an old Scots gamekeeper saw two business-suited tourists start across a old and weak bridge toward a rural church. He shouted to them to get off the bridge. They thought he was upset at their being on church property, and shouted back that it was all right because they were Presbyterians--the same as the national kirk of Scotland. "Ye dinna ken what I mean," the Scotsman shouted back. "Take about three more steps on yon bridge and ye'll be Baptists."

Yes, it must have been hard on that Operative Masonic Warden. It must have seemed to him that the whole world was turning upside down. How could a man call himself a Mason and not work stone? How could he claim to be a member of a Lodge and not live in a Lodge?

"I dinna ken what it is," he might have said, "but it's nay the Masonry."

And yet, of course, it was. It was Masonry about to emerge with renewed strength and life; Masonry about to change the emotional and cultural world as surely as operative Masonry had changed and shaped the physical world by building cathedrals, fortifications, and castles. The operative Masons had dreamed dreams of faith and security and safety, and worked with skill and sweat to bring those dreams to reality. The Speculative Masons would dream dreams of humanity, liberty, fairness, and intellectual liberty, and they would labor with skill, and often with sweat and blood and tears to bring those dreams to reality.

The operative Mason had only a little ritual---enough to define the few officers of the Lodge, set basic rules of conduct, and instruct in the practical work-place rules which kept people from getting hurt. The Speculative

Masons seized upon ritual as a means of instruction and thought, and expanded it to meet their needs.

In some ways, the two Masonrys were very different—but in all the important ways, they were the same. They were the means by which dream-driven men could accomplish those dreams.

As those dreams have changed over the centuries, Masonry has changed. Freemasonry has always been a living, breathing, dynamic thing. The Light Masonry celebrates is the light that shines in the eyes of dedicated and thoughtful men, engaged with life; not the chilled glint of light reflected from the dusty glass of a museum display case.

And so Masonry changed again, after the battles and revolutions which reshaped society. It became, essentially, a charity. We found new philanthropic causes, and devoted time and energy to them. We solved problems for the society and the culture. Philosophy became less important, and ritual became more so. Masons, perhaps, became less distinguished by what we thought than by how we thought. It was very comfortable, and very rewarding. And we hardly noticed that the comfort was that of a well-made coffin. That is the Masonry into which I was initiated, passed and raised.

And so I have a certain fellow-feeling with that old Scots operative Warden, because Masonry is changing again. I rejoice in that—because I know the alternative is death, and I love Masonry too much to watch it die, or to know that it will die shortly after I do. And I know that any organization which does not reflect the needs of its living members is not long with us. When was the last convention of the National Association of Buggy Whip Makers?

We have been given a second chance at life, and only the profoundly ungrateful would turn their backs on it. Social and cultural changes have resulted in young men looking for a source of spiritual and ethical values in venues other than religion.

The age of candidates seeking admission into Masonry is growing lower and lower. Only a few years ago, the typical candidate was in his mid-forties. Now he is in his early 30s.

He comes having researched Masonry on the Internet. Often he comes after having read the rituals. He comes knowing much about what he is doing, and he often comes with many questions. And he comes expecting answers.

As some of our Lodges have discovered, statements such as "you don't need to worry about that," "don't ask questions until you have learned the cat lectures," "the ritual has everything you need to know," don't fall on deaf ears--- they are heard--- and treated with the contempt they deserve.

It's important to understand that these young Masons do not come looking for a fight—that's the last thing they want. They want brotherhood. They want intellectual stimulation. They want to have someone at their back in the battles of life. They want to be with men dedicated to making a difference. They want to be with those who have subdued the ego and focus on that is real and not on "petty piques and quarrels." They want to be in an association with older men who have promised to mentor and to share wisdom and experience.

In other words, and rather embarrassingly, they come looking for exactly what we have telling the world we have to offer. In some ways, Brothers, we are in the position of a automobile dealership which advertized luxury cars for sale because we used to have them, and now have buyers on the sales floor wanting to purchase—and some Lodges are having to say, "wouldn't you rather have a nice golf cart instead." Monty Python fans may be reminded of the cheese shop sketch.

There is no question that Masonry is supposed to be all the things they are looking for. Our ritual says it. Our Masonic heroes have written about it. We have all knelt at the altar and promised to make it real. So we can hardly blame them for expecting to find it.

They are willing to cut us quite a bit of slack. They understand that no one knows everything. I have not yet found one who became angry when I said, "I don't know the answer, but I'll find out." or even better, "I don't know the answer, but let's find out together."

What they don't like is "Go away, kid, ya bother me!" And what happens, far too often, is that they do go away. And they tell their friends, don't take the trouble to look at Masonry, it doesn't have what we want."

Really, they are not asking for much. They are only asking for what we should be able to give in civility, let alone fraternity. "Don't ignore me, share with me, treat my questions and concerns as important, help me learn, let me help with the Lodge." And, perhaps most important, "Understand that I am dream-driven, too. And my dreams are important just as yours are."

And it is true. Just as the old operative Masons were driven by dreams, as the first speculative Masons were driven by dreams, as the Masons who created the great charities were driven by dreams, as we are driven by dreams, so are the young Masons. And they are dreams, not the nightmares they may seem to those of us who are long in the Masonic tooth. And they are our future.

For years, in speaking to Masonic groups, I told the audience that I was certain Masonry would survive—that something that "right" and that ancient simply could not die.

I can admit to myself, now, that I was whistling past the grave-yard. I wanted it to be true, I thought that if I told myself often and strongly enough, it would be true.

And now I know it IS true. Dream-driven organizations can never die. . .

. . . unless they kill the dream.

You see, my Brothers, in the life of every organization there comes a point of choice—a point at which circumstances, fate, even the dreams themselves culminate in a moment of decision. When that point is reached each person must make a choice. It isn't possible to avoid it; for not choosing is a choice. One choice leads on to new growth, strength, vigor, power and relevancy, with all of the effort and even pain that growth always entails. The other choice leads to the ease of death and the comfortable warmth of decay.

The fraternity is at the point, and each of us must choose.

You may choose life; or you may choose death; but you must choose.

Grand Oration, delivered to the Grand Lodge of the State of Oklahoma at the 2009 Annual Communication.

Scripts

Myth: The Footpath Within

Script for CD on Mythology

The College of the Consistory

Track 1 - Truth ≠ Fact
Track 2 - Tender Feet and Green Thumbs
Track 3 - Goldilocks
Track 4 - The Boy Who Was Left Behind
Track 5 - Apollo & Dionysus
Track 6 - Myth and Masonry
Track 7 - The Mythic Structure of the Scottish Rite

Track #1 Truth ≠ Fact

VOICE 1: Cheaters never prosper.
VOICE 2: (Agreeing) That's a fact.
NARRATOR: No, it isn't.

VOICE 2: We had steak for dinner last night.
VOICE 1: We did, that's true.
NARRATOR: No, it's not.

VOICE 1: In what year was the Declaration of Independence signed?
VOICE 2: I believe it was 1776
NARRATOR: Wrong.

VOICE 2: I know today is going to be great!
NARRATOR: No you don't.
VOICE 1: Now wait a minute...

All those statements may well be accurate. And for simple, conversational purposes most of us wouldn't argue with them.. But they reflect a confusion which can cause and has caused great suffering in the world, resulted in literally millions of deaths, divided families, and justified abominable cruelties–the confusion between truth and fact.

Part of the confusion is caused by our use of the term "true-false test." Such tests are almost always designed to test fact, not truth.

We'll talk in a minute about why it makes such a difference, but first let's clarify the terms as we'll be using them here.

A statement of fact is a provable, often measurable, statement of objective reality. If we say "Under normal conditions, water freezes at 32° Fahrenheit," we can get a thermometer and test, or we can go to a recognized objective authority such as a text book or a handbook of physics and look it up.

If we make an assertion of historical fact, for example, "On September 11, 2001, terrorists flew two airplanes into the World Trade Center," we can verify that statement from newspapers, recordings of television shows, history books, and the memories of those still living, Events further back in history can be verified from military reports, the recorded proceedings of governments and organizations, private diaries, public monuments , and other sources

A statement of truth is not testable in the same way. If we say, "Honor and integrity are important qualities in a person," there is no objective thermometer we can use. Instead, we test truth, consciously or not, by a series of questions:

Does it fit with other things I believe to be true?

Does it seem right?

Do others, whom I accept as being mentors or advisors, agree?

Does it seem to call out the best in me rather than the worst in me?

Does it seem that it would lead to happiness for most people?

Does it seem to be fair?

And so on. Obviously these questions and judgements are subjective, nothing at all like the "hard-edged" questions we ask about fact. Also obviously, we use different levels of testing depending on the importance of the truth being expressed. If we are dealing with a statement of religious faith or political position, it is to be hoped that we would insist on very high levels of testing.

But if our friend, Jerry, says, "I had a great time skiing last weekend," we'd probably accept it with no more than the passing thought that, "Yes, Jerry always enjoys skiing."

This is not, in any way, to suggest that fact is superior to truth, or vice versa, any more than an orange is superior to a pear. But they are different, and those differences are significant. We "know" facts. But we "believe" truths. I know that five and five make ten, I believe that lying is wrong.

Society in general tolerates much wider variation in truth than in fact. Most of us are willing to grant others the right to follow the religious truth of their preference, even if it is one we do not believe. We are willing to allow someone to believe that lying is all right, as long as he does not put that belief into action and lie to people—that is seen as doing potential harm to others. In many areas, we're willing to say, "Well, I don't agree, but he's entitled to his opinion."

We are less tolerant about fact, because a person who refuses to accept a fact is regarded is either profoundly ignorant, or not of sound mind, or devious. Thus, you may be a follower of Buddha and I may be an adherent of Christianity, and we will accept the similarities in the ways in which we see the Truth and be tolerant of the differences. But both of us will react, at least with suspicion if not hostility or ridicule to the person who insists that the earth is actually flat and square, or that the Holocaust never took place, or that tomatoes are poisonous, or that a person is a better driver when they have had a few drinks than when they are sober.

Or, as one person said, "If you tell me that two plus two makes five, you had better be introducing a new form of mathematics."

This difference in our reaction to disagreement about a truth and disagreement about a fact explains the statement made earlier that confusion between truth and fact can cause and has caused great suffering in the world, resulting in literally millions of deaths, divided families, and abominable cruelties.

If I think of the tenets of my religion as statements of fact rather than truths, then I am likely to feel suspicion and contempt for anyone who doesn't agree with me. I may think of them as willfully wrong and deliberately obstructionist. I may think that they are either deliberately or unintentionally leading others astray. Once I have demonized a person to that extent, it is only a short step to attack, whether that means shunning, the rack, or the stake. And again and again in our history, it has only been a slightly longer step to war.

Let us be clear, then, that when we are dealing with myth, we are dealing with truths. There may or may not be a sprinkling of fact in the myth. For our purposes, that is unimportant. Our concern is with the truth.

Track #2 Tender Feet and Green Thumbs

During most of the 20th Century, students were taught in school and in college that myths were lies, or, at best, rather pathetic attempts on the part of a pre-scientific culture to explain the world around it. Thus the rainbow myths of the Native Americans were dismissed as an attempt on the part of the poor savages to explain what they could not understand—the Greek myths of Pandora were attempts on the part of the poor Greek savages to explain why there was evil in the world—the stories of King Arthur and the Knights were a mere attempt on the part of the poor English savages to explain human weakness.

Of course, none of the people involved were savages and the myths had nothing to do with rainbows, magic boxes, or the love affairs of a queen and a knight. But American culture in the mid-20th Century went happily along teaching us that myths were lies and deceptions. The word "myth" itself became a synonym for false and dishonest story.

Until Joseph Campbell, probably the 20th Century's greatest teacher of comparative religion and mythology arose and said, "No, a myth is not a lie; a myth is a metaphor."

It's worth a moment to flash back to middle school English Lit. classes. There are two related types of literary image—the simile and the metaphor. A simile uses the words "like" or "as." The easy way to remember is that "simile" is like "similar." Some examples:

He stood like a rock in the storms of life.
She was like a mother to us all.

And, sometimes, a simile can be extended. Here's a familiar example from the poem A Visit from St. Nicholas or The Night Before Christmas.

> As dry leaves that before the wild hurricane fly,
> When they meet with an obstacle, mount to the sky,
> So up to the house-top the coursers they flew,
> With the sleigh full of toys, and St. Nicholas too.

A metaphor does much the same thing, but does not use the words "like" or "as."

John is a rock.

This job's a piece of cake. (But note that "easy as pie" is a simile, not a metaphor)

A mother's love is a lighthouse in a stormy sea.

All the religions of the world have expressed their truths in extended metaphors called myths or parables. Literalists tend to denounce the metaphors as lies because they do not deal with fact (while insisting, of course, that the metaphors of their own faiths are stone cold facts). But even the most denunciative among them still use metaphors all the time. And they use them to describe things which are true, but not factual, just as everyone else does. Look at some common ones.

He has a green thumb.

It is not a *fact* that one of his thumbs is green—it is *true* that he seems to be able to make things grow better than most people. But we do not regard the statement "he has a green thumb," as a lie, because we know it is not intended as a statement of fact.

She is a pillar of the community.

Pillars are generally made of stone, metal or wood, not flesh and blood. No one thinks we mean that the person is a stone caryatid, holding up something called a community. We know that the sentence means she gives a lot of service to the community and makes a difference in the life of the town. The statement is a metaphor, not a fact, but it is true and not a lie.

He is a tenderfoot.

Once that was literal. It referred to a pioneer on the western trek just starting out on a walk of hundreds of miles, before the feet had become callused. Now, we know the statement is not about the pedal extremities, it just means that the person is a beginner.

He's a sly old fox.
   Want to bet he isn't running around on all fours or grooming a bushy tail.

She's a ray of sunshine.
   Not a fact, but not a lie, because it is true she makes us feel like we feel when we see sunshine.

We could go on for hundreds of examples, but the point is clear. Not one of these metaphors is factually correct, but they are not lies, and we use them and others like them almost without thinking because they do express truth.

We also use them because they are efficient. Many of them have become clichés. But a phrase becomes a cliché *because* it communicates effectively. Let's consider that line, "He's a sly old fox." If we were to write out in complete form the thoughts that metaphor conveys, it might read something like this.

He looks at every situation to see what the maximum advantage can be for himself, without regard to others, but is very careful not to appear to be doing so or to get caught in the act.

Five words in the metaphor, thirty-seven words in the explanation. And at that the metaphor has a different emotional tone and impact than does the "full" explanation.

And metaphors can convey meanings it is hard to express precisely.

She is the key to my heart.
I'm caught between a rock and a hard place.
Lady Liberty is the guardian of our country.
His mind is a cesspool
Her life is an open book.

Metaphor plays an important role in our daily communications. Extended metaphor, which we call a myth, forms the deepest level of communication we have on those great questions which concert us at the deepest levels—birth, growing up, marriage, maturity, death and its aftermath are all central foci of great mythic cycles.

One more thought before we leave this specific topic. We've been discussing metaphor and myth expressed in words because that is how it is most commonly done. But it does not have to be in words. The hula, the ballet, and much folk dance is metaphor as well, telling the great stories by movement and gesture. Myth and metaphor transcend limitations of culture and time and means of expression.

Track #3   Goldilocks

If myths are metaphors, if they are parables whose purpose is to tell a story as a means of telling a deeper hidden story which cannot be easily put into words, how does that work? And what is the real story?

The question of how it works is not too difficult, because we are all familiar with the technique, even if we have not thought much about it. Let us consider a myth, story, fable, or parable known to almost everyone. This is based on one of the oldest versions.

>Once upon a time, there was a little girl with beautiful golden hair, so that everyone called her

Goldilocks. She lived with her mother in a cottage in a meadow, in front of a deep woods. Goldilocks liked to play in the meadow, and her mother allowed her to do so, but warned her over and over, "Do not go into the woods to play."

One day Goldilocks tired of playing in the meadow. Looking to be sure her mother was not watching, she slipped into the woods She saw birds and little animals, but when they came near to her, she threw stones at them because she liked to see them run away. After a time, she felt tired and hungry, and wanted to go home, but she soon realized that she was lost and did not know where her home was.

Just then, she came to a strange stone cottage in the woods. A window was open, and so Goldilocks crept up to the window and looked inside.

Now the cottage belonged to three bears, a very large bear, and average size bear, and a very small baby bear. The had gone out for a walk in the evening, leaving the porridge they were having for supper on the table to cool. Goldilocks did not know bears lived in the cottage, but she was hungry, and so she tried the front door. Now the bears were good and honest creatures, thinking no harm of anyone, and so they did not latch the door when they left. So Goldilocks was able to open the door and slip inside.

She went to the table and found a very large bowl of porridge with a large wooden spoon, and so she tasted the porridge. But it was too hot and she threw the spoon on the floor in anger. Then she tried some porridge which was in a middle-sized bowl, but it was too cold, and she threw that spoon down also.

Then she tried the porridge in the smallest bowl and it was just right, and so she eat all of it. She wanted to rest, and so she went to the first of three chairs. It was very high, so high even when she threw the cushion on the floor, she could not sit on it. The second chair was too deep, but the third chair was just right. She sat down in it and rocked back on the back legs of the chair, and it broke in pieces so that she sat with a bump on the floor.

As she got up from the floor, she looked around and saw a twisty stair case in one corner of the room. She went up the stairs and found herself in a bed room. She tried the first bed, which was very large, but it was too hard. The she tried the middle-sized bed, but it was too soft and she sank deeply into the feather-bed on top. The she tried the smallest bed, and it was just right, and she feel asleep.

Soon after, the bears returned from their walk. They noticed that the door was open, although they were sure they had closed it. They went to the table and the big bear saw his spoon thrown on the floor. "Someone has been tasting my porridge," growled the big bear. "Someone has been tasting my porridge as well," said the medium-sized bear. The little bear gave a cry, "Someone has been tasting my porridge, and they have eaten it all up!"

Then the big bear noticed the cushions in his chair. "Someone has been sitting in my chair," he growled. "Why," said the middle-sized bear, "Someone has been sitting in my chair." "Ooh!," sobbed the baby bear, "Someone has been sitting in my chair and they have broken it to pieces."

The bears realized that someone had broken into their home, and that the person might still be there. They searched the first floor and found no one, and then started up the stairs.

The big bear growled, "Look, someone has been sleeping in my bed!" "Someone has been sleeping in my bed, too" said the middle-sized bear. "Someone has been sleeping in my bed," said the baby bear, "and she is still here."

As he said that, Goldilocks awoke and saw the three bears. She gave a scream of fright and jumped out of the window and ran into the woods. She ran and ran, always thinking the bears were right behind her, until she fell exhausted in the woods, and whether she ever found her way home again, none can say.

Seems a straight forward story. But to understand the real story, we have to dig a little deeper. This is essentially the same technique used to understand myths as well as the Degrees of Masonry. Let's see what we can find.

First of all, it belongs to a literary classification known as the "cautionary tale," that is, a story told to teach and to give a warning. In English, the beginning "Once upon a time..." tells us that we are dealing with myth or fable, not fact. A similar beginning in some Native American myths is "In the days of your Grandmother's Grandmother..." and in some Arabic literary traditions a similar beginning is "Let him who would be admonished attend to my words..."

One of the first things which strikes us in the story is the number 3. There are four sets of 3: 3 bears, 3 bowls of porridge, 3 chairs, and 3 beds. So we have two numbers, 3 and 4 X 3 or 12. The threes all relate to the bears, that is they are the possessions of the bears. Goldilocks interacts with them, but they are not hers. Three is traditionally associated with divinity because it is the first "complete number."

One represents unity, the world before creation, the undifferentiated universe. Two represents duality, the division of the world into pairs of opposites–light-darkness, wet-dry, hot-cold, good-evil, and so forth. Three represents reunification, the reconciliation of opposites. That suggests wholeness or completion. For that reason, it is not only the number of divinity, but the number of nature as a reflection or creation of deity. That should not be confused with the physical world, which is symbolized by the number 4. Three is the number of natural processes, uncorrupted nature.

And each set of three also represents balance or reconciliation of opposites. One bowl of porridge is too hot, one is too cold (the opposites) and one is "just right." One chair is too high, one is too deep, and one is just right. One bed is too hard, one is too soft, and one is just right. So not only does the number three suggest the reconciliation of opposites, but the elements which make up each set suggest the same thing.

The number 12 suggests the twelve signs of the zodiac and therefore one year—one complete revolution of the sun about the earth. It also suggests cycle as the year is a cycle. The cycle is associated with lunar consciousness, as opposed to the line, which is associated with solar consciousness. But twelve is also a sacred number of great antiquity. In addition to the twelve signs of the zodiac there are the twelve Tribes of Israel, the twelve Apostles, the twelve labors of Hercules, the twelve gods and goddesses of Mount Olympus, and the twelve gates to the New Jerusalem as visualized in the apocalypse. Twelve thus partakes of the meaning of divinity. It also contains the right triangle—the 3-4-5 right triangle. That reenforces the cyclical symbolism, because the right triangle is a symbol of man, woman, and child, or the cycle of birth and death. And, of course, the cycle of birth and death is one of the symbolic meanings of the zodiac itself

The bear is one of the most powerful, ancient, and complex symbols in the human psyche. There is evidence of bear worship in the painted caves and shrines dedicated to cave bears have been found which date to the last ice age. Bear worship is still practiced on one of the islands of Japan, and the bear holds a very special place in Native American thought. It is the animal most closely associated with mankind as a respected equal. The term Brother Bear is found in the history of many languages. The bear is a symbol of nature.

The bear is a lunar symbol and is associated with lunar consciousness. The probable reasons are that it is largely a nocturnal animal and its deep winter sleep cycle followed by activity in the spring is like the waxing and waning of the moon. It therefore partakes of the lunar symbolism of regeneration.

We associate it with man in nature—it possesses "human" qualities we admire: courage, protection of the young, strength, and intelligence. Even more than intelligence, however, we associate it with wisdom and understanding. It is also a deep symbol of stability, or an anchor to cling to in time of chaos. It is interesting to note that a child in distress will most often cling to a stuffed bear when there is a choice of a teddy bear or other equally soft stuffed animals. This is so true of us (and other cultures as well) that an image of a teddy bear is a recognized symbol of comfort in a hurtful world and some highway patrol officers carry teddy bears to give to children who are involved in the trauma of a car wreck. Of the gifts most often left behind at spontaneous memorials, such as those of the 9-11 bombing, teddy bears lead the list.

For our purposes, then, we can say that a bear represents nature as it should be, order, regeneration, lunar consciousness, wisdom, controlled power, and a linkage to the natural world with overtones of spiritual regeneration and transcendence.

The bears' cottage—the place they live, represents nature and the natural world. It is orderly and beautiful, and is kept so by nature (the bears).

We know little about Goldilocks, other than she is a willful, sneaky, spoiled child with no sense of responsibility or of right behavior. She disobeys her mother and leaves the meadow to enter the forest. She treats small animals cruelly (in one version of the story she has been teasing a kitten in the meadow until the kitten sticks her with its claws and then throws the kitten down and runs into the woods). She breaks into the bear's home, treats their property with disrespect, and then without invitation enters the bedroom and sleeps in their beds—an act forbidden in almost every culture.

We also know that she has golden hair, which tells us she is a solar symbol or a symbol of solar consciousness. But her actions suggest that she has only the negative aspects of solar consciousness. The bears' actions are presented as civilized and generous (they do not pursue her), but her actions are presented as selfish, willful, and crass.

It is worth noting that intelligence is associated with solar consciousness. Consider the words we use to describe someone who is intelligent: bright, incisive, sharp, keen, piercing, and so forth. Wisdom is associated with lunar consciousness. We describe wisdom with words such as reflective, gentle, patient, insightful, deliberate, calm–to name just a few.

The negative aspects of solar consciousness—that is to say the negative aspects of intelligence wrongly applied include such terms as crafty, cunning, deceptive, sneaky, manipulative, cruel, rash, and thoughtless.

Finally, consider the movement of Goldilocks from the meadow to the forest. A meadow is a solar landscape. There are few trees and plenty of sunlight. There are wildflowers. It is possible to see danger approaching long before it can get to you.

Goldilocks is relatively safe in the meadow. In a solar landscape her distorted solar personality is less of a handicap.

But the forest is a lunar landscape. It is dark and shadowed. The raw life force itself is considered lunar, and it is transcendent in the forest.

So bringing all these bits and pieces together, what is the real message of Goldilocks and the Three Bears? It might be stated like this:

The universe exists as a beautiful, complex, complete and harmonious whole. The Greeks gave it the name "cosmos," which literally translates as "embroidery," to suggest its inherent beauty and linkage. There is a sacred or divine component to the universe and to all life. The realization of the component requires that we achieve balance or equilibrium amidst all of the competing forces around us. We are told, Biblically, that we are the masters of creation, but achieving that mastery first requires that we are masters of ourselves. It is a mastery accomplished by fitting into nature, not dominating it.

A person may be of primary solar or lunar consciousness, but both must be present and in some sort of equilibrium for the person to claim his full heritage as a child of God and of nature. The unbalanced solar consciousness has intelligence, but not wisdom, energy, but not judgement. Unbalanced, the negative aspects of the solar consciousness predominate, guile, craft, cunning, thoughtlessness, lack of respect for others, selfishness, and action without reflection of consideration of consequences.

When such a person enters the world of the life force, of lunar consciousness, they are disruptive—they cause a disturbance in the force. They approach the universe with selfish or exploitive intent. As a result, they are blind to the richness of life experience which they would otherwise have had and are seen as an intruder and vandal rather than welcomed as a friend. (Contrast that with the attitude of the individual who, if a hunter, feels a kinship with the hunted and appreciates the gift of life given by the animal so that the hunter's family may live.) It is, essentially, the difference between arrogance and humility.

So any person who wants to live a truly happy and productive life must harmonize himself with nature, viewing it as sacred and as an expression of the divine, of which he is a part and in which he participates. His attitude can neither be selfish nor arrogant. It is very much as St. Francis said, we live with brother sun and sister moon and brother bear and sister brook. We must also be aware of the great cycles of life and death, accepting both as natural and fearing neither. If we cultivate that awareness in ourselves, we will feel the energy of nature and of the universe in our lives. If we do not, we court destruction.

Track #4 The Boy Who Was Left Behind

In the late 1800's and throughout the 1900's, when cultural anthropology was developing as a science, anthropologists noticed that there were certain themes, certain "great ideas" or "archetypal themes" which occur in virtually every culture, no matter how far the cultures are separated in time or geography. Of these ideas, one of the most predominant is that of the quest journey, which is part of the male initiation process. Cultures may or may not have an initiation process for girls. It probably is not necessary, because nature tells a girl in a dramatic and unmistakable way when she becomes a woman—that is when she becomes able to bear children. There is no such dramatic and unmistakable moment for a male.

Yet we have discovered that such a moment of initiation, such a passage from child to adult status is literally necessary if one is to become a truly autonomous adult. Physical changes in the architecture of the brain take place at such a time, and the person literally leaves one state and enters another.

In the Jewish tradition, this is accomplished by the bar mitzvah, but for most contemporary American males the closest thing we have left to a rite of passage is getting a driver's license at the age of 16. The draft once provided such a moment–joining the armed services as a rite of passage indeed. But that is not experienced by the majority of American males. As a result we find young males seeking membership in gangs and other organizations which give them a sense of expanded family and a sense that they have crossed a barrier and become men.

Perhaps the most important contribution Masonry makes to society is that it provides that rite of passage. And it does so using the quest myth, which is probably the oldest human story. Indeed it may be, as the great scholar of mythology, Joseph Campbell, asserted, the *only* story.

It is in the process of the quest that the boy is left behind, and the man emerges.

In general terms, the outline of the quest myth is this. A man, usually young, the hero, becomes aware of a need. It may be a medicine, as in the epic of Gilgamish, it may be food for his people, as in many Native American myths, it may be a spiritual object, as in the grail quest, it may be a weapon to defend his people, as in some Scandinavian myths, it may be a new land in which his people can live, or for the origins–the land from whence his people originally came, or a magic object or spell or other means to defend his family, tribe, or nation as in the *Star Wars* films, or it may be a quest to destroy something, as in *The Lord of the Rings*, or it may be a quest to return home, as in the *Odyssey*. He sets out to find the object of the quest. (In another tradition, he starts the quest by accident, usually by following some animal –which turns out to be magical–into a forest until he is lost an enters into an enchanted realm.)

Along the way he gathers companions who will aid him. He meets an advisor, usually elderly and sometimes not quite human—Merlin is a classic example— who gives him information he must have, and either provides him with something essential to the quest—a magic weapon, a spell, a map, a magical elixir–or tells him how and where to acquire it.

Along the path he meets and overcomes obstacles. Sometimes he loses companions in these conflicts, other times he may gain them. He makes a descent into the underground and/or the ascent of a mountain. A descent into the underground represents a descent into his own self, his ego—the ascent of a mountain usually symbolizes a discovery of his higher nature or a moving out of the earthly realm. Often, he does both.

He may journey through several different realms or kingdoms. These usually represents different stages of human spiritual development or different value systems.

Finally, he approaches the heart of the mystery, the center of the maze, the essence of the quest. Usually he does not have his companions with him at that moment. At the heart of the mystery he experiences revelation and change. He often confronts a figure who represents his father. At that moment, certain parts of his life are validated and he realizes that other parts are no longer true or valid. He leaves the innocence and the values of childhood and becomes autonomous, he becomes a man. Often, he is given a new name. He is now fully responsible for his own actions and free to make his own decisions. He accepts the limitations on those actions and decisions which come with a responsibility to others. He puts away childish things.

In some mythic traditions, he experiences death and rebirth, in others he gains an insight that death is not a significant event. In one way or another he overcomes the fear of death, and with it all fear. In doing so, he enters into a new relationship with the world or with a higher world.

When he rejoins his companions, they are aware of a change in him. Often there is a physical change as well—he may appear older, or his hair may change color, or he may simply seem "different" in some way. He has powers and insights he did not have before. Often he appears to be sadder; becoming an autonomous man means taking upon oneself part of the weight of the world. It is never a story of unmixed joy, because life as an aware adult is not a life of unmixed joy. But he is fulfilling his destiny. The boy has been left behind, and the man has emerged.

Track #5   Apollo and Dionysus

When we were discussing the story of Goldilocks, we talked about solar and lunar consciousness. This division is very important, because it describes two different approaches to life, two different ways of thinking. It is important to realize that each of us participates in both. The question is one of balance and dominance. It is also important not to think of one as "good" and the other as "bad" or one as "positive" and the other as "negative." There are good and bad, positive and negative aspects to each type of consciousness, but the two types themselves are neither good nor bad, they are simply different.

The same, or at least a closely-related pair of differences are referred to as Apollonian and Dionysian, from the Greek gods Apollo and Dionysus. This distinction was first codified by Nietzsche in *The Birth of Tragedy*.

Apollo is associated with the solar consciousness—not surprising, as he was the god of the sun. He is also associated with civilization, order, harmony, the uplifting aspects of music, reason, poetry, sentiment, intellect, control of the passions, and aesthetics.

Dionysus, also known as Bacchus, is associated with lunar consciousness, and is one of the most complex of the gods. He is the god of theatre—the very word "theatre" comes from "theatron" which was the name of his temple. Plays were performed as part of his worship. And the nature of the plays tells us something of the nature of Dionysus. The plays were part of a contest, and all the Greek theatre we have are plays written for the contest. Each playwrite submitted four plays, three tragedies and a satyr play. The tragedies were the beginning of western theatre as we know it and many of you will have encountered productions of them. The most famous, probably is Oedipus Rex, but there are others, including Media, Antigone, and Oedipus at Colonus which are nearly as well know. The tragedies are high works of human art.

The satyr plays, on the other hand, are almost unmixed sexuality, so much so that some have never been translated into English. The Greeks did not find them"dirty" in the sense we would use the word—no one had ever told them that sex was a dirty topic—but they were certainly...... frank. They were a celebration of the basic life force of the universe, and a comment on the very strange things that force can make men and women do.

Dionysus is also the god of wine. More, he is associated with that primal life force, the urge toward life which underlies all of nature. If Apollo is the god of moderation, Dionysus is the god of extremes. His priestess/celebrants, the Bacchai, often fell into a form of madness or delirium, during which they would run screaming and dancing across the countryside, sometimes killing those they encountered. It is possible to think of him as representing the dark forces of nature, as long as we do not think of that as negative. He is "nature, red in tooth and claw." He is life feeding on life, and the necessary death so that new life can come forth. He is the god of ecstasy and enthusiasm (remember that "enthusiasm" comes from *en theos* and literally means to be possessed by the gods.) But he is also the one who sacrifices himself to benefit others. The wine is his blood. If Apollo is the god of creativity, Bacchus/Dionysus is the god of the energy used for creativity.

Obviously, there are positive and negative aspects to both Apollonian and Dionysian consciousness. The Apollonian consciousness is clear, bright, elegant, rational, civilized, and motivated by intellect. But, carried to extremes, it is cold, calculating, indifferent to others, and without emotion or conviction. The Dionysian consciousness is energetic, active, passionate, forceful, dedicated, and filled with life. But carried to extremes it is also demanding, violent, animalistic, rash, impetuous, and hedonistic.

Not surprisingly, it is necessary to strike a balance. In Masonry, the Apollonian consciousness is represented by the compasses and by the sun; the Dionysian consciousness is represented by the square and by the moon. Remember, the ritual does NOT say "I have come to *eliminate* my passions and improve myself, in Masonry." It says, "I have come to *subdue* my passions and improve myself, in Masonry."

The idea is not limited to western thought. You have probably seen the Yin/Yang symbol, which was developed in the Han dynasty of China at about the time of the birth of Jesus of Nazareth. It is drawn as a circle divided in half by a curving line. Half the circle is red (or sometimes white) and half is black. But in the center of the black half there is a dot of red, and in the center of the red half, there is a dot of black. Yang is solar consciousness, male, with all its associations. Yin is lunar consciousness with all its energies. But the symbol shows us that there must always be a balance, Yang cannot function without some of the qualities of Yin---Yin cannot function without some of the qualities of Yang.

Masonry understands, as philosophers have always understood, that both Yang and Yin, both the Apollonian and Dionysian, both solar and lunar consciousness must be present for a person to be a fully-functioning, well-rounded, autonomous and creative individual. But the Dionysian cannot rule, it cannot be supreme in the individual, or he can never become a true man.

Track #6   Myth and Masonry

You can't say you weren't warned. Remember these lines? "Masonry consists of a course of hieroglyphical and moral instruction, taught agreeably to ancient usages by types, emblems and allegorical figures"

Another way of saying the same thing is that Freemasonry presents a series of metaphors, which are related to each other in some ways, and which must be interpreted to understand the "real" story. This is not, as some anti-Masons claim, a matter of "hiding the truth" from the outside world or from our own members until they reach "higher" degrees. It is simply the oldest and most efficient teaching method ever found for teaching truth as opposed to fact.

After giving the important usual warning---that no person speaks officially for Masonry and that each person is entitled to interpret its symbols for himself but it not entitles to insist that his interpretations are right, lets take a look at how this plays out in the Fraternity.

As we have seen, fact is easily learned from a text book. Truth is a matter of developing insight and understanding, and that doesn't come from a textbook exposition—that come when our own individual minds wrestle with something until we come to light. Consider this well-known myth or parable.

"For it is as if a man, going on a journey, summoned his servants and entrusted his property to them; to one he gave five talents, to another two, to another one, to each according to his ability. Then he went away.

The one who had received the five talents went off at once and traded with them, and made five more talents. In the same way, the one who had the two talents made two more talents. But the one who had received the one talent went off and dug a hole in the ground and hid his master's money.

After a long time the master of those servants came and settled accounts with them. Then the one who had received the five talents came forward, bringing five more talents, saying, 'Master, you handed over to me five talents; see, I have made five more talents.' His master said to him, 'Well done, good and trustworthy servant; you have been trustworthy in a few things, I will put you in charge of many things; enter into the joy of your master.'

And the one with the two talents also came forward, saying, 'Master, you handed over to me two talents; see, I have made two more talents.' His master said to him, 'Well done, good and trustworthy servant; you have been trustworthy in a few things, I will put you in charge of many things; enter into the joy of your master.'

Then the one who had received the one talent also came forward, saying, 'Master, I knew that you were a harsh man, reaping where you did not sow, and gathering where you did not scatter seed; so I was afraid, and I went and hid your talent in the ground. Here you have what is yours.'"

As you know, it did not go well for him.

We know we are dealing with truth and myth rather than fact, because of the opening words "it is as if." And the lesson being taught here is not how to calculate compound interest. That would be more effectively taught in a text. What is being taught is a view of the world, a value, a way of looking at life. Men and women have been arguing about the exact meaning of the story for two thousand years. That's how it works. Trying to figure out the meaning is the process of making it real to each individual.

Almost every great system of moral and intellectual development works the same way, and so does Freemasonry.

It's easy to see that the second section of the Master Mason degree uses mythic themes. The story of the murder of Hiram is myth presented in a medieval theatrical form known as a mystery play. (A mystery play by definition is a play based on a minor character or incident in the Bible, consisting of two or more episodes and intended to give moral instruction.) But the Entered Apprentice and Fellowcraft Degrees are based on myth as well.

Remember what we said about the journey of the hero. We can trace the events of the quest journey in the events of the initiation.

- The hero becomes aware of a need. The Candidate becomes aware of a need of some sort, usually for fellowship and also personal growth,
- The hero sets out on the quest. The candidate petitions for the Degrees.
- The hero acquires companions who will help him on the journey and also makes preparation for the journey, both physical and spiritual, gathering supplies and attending a religious service, as in the grail stories, or engaging in other acts of purification and preparation. The candidate meets and is assisted by the senior and junior stewards who help him prepare for the entrance into the Lodge room.

- The hero meets a spiritual guide who tests his worthiness for the quest in some way. In Blue Lodge Masonry, the guide is the Senior Deacon, who begins by "propounding the usual interrogatories."
- The hero meets with someone who gives him something necessary for the journey. The candidate attends prayer and God's grace is asked for him.
- The hero makes a journey during which he meets and overcomes obstacles. The candidate makes one or more circumambulations of the room, during which he symbolically meets with three closed and guarded doors through which he must pass.
- The hero encounters a figure, human or not, who represents wisdom and insight, or, alternately, represents his greatest fear, and in either case often represents his own father as well, and also has the power to grant his goal or show him the final path to that goal. The candidate encounters the Worshipful Master of the Lodge, who has the power to grant his goal, and who shows him the final path by directing the Senior Deacon to teach him to approach the East to receive Masonic Light.
- The hero enters into the heart of the mystery. The candidate approaches the altar.
- The hero enters into some sort of new relationship with the world or into a relationship with a higher world. The candidate takes the obligation which makes him a Mason.
- The hero achieves the goal, even though it may be a different goal than he first understood. The candidate receives Masonic Light. In doing so, a process of change has started which, in most cases, will make him a different person in some ways than he was before.

Track #7   The Mythic Quest of the Scottish Rite: An Overview

The mythic quest of the Scottish Rite is a large enough topic to require a CD of its own, but a brief overview may be useful here, just to give an idea of the way in which the Rite uses myth and metaphor to teach.

Again, the usual warning applies.

The Scottish Rite is divided into four bodies: The Lodge of Perfection, the Chapter of Rose Croix, the Council of Kadosh, and the Consistory. There is a quest associated with each body, and, together, they form a complete mythic cycle of initiation.

The Lodge of Perfection consists on the 4th through the 14th Degrees of the Scottish Rite, and one can include the three Degrees of the Blue Lodge. Here the quest is for Light, which is a symbol of the awakening of the person's spirituality and the opening of the pathway to inspiration.

The Chapter of Rose Croix consists of the 15th through the 18th Degrees. The purpose of the quest here is to strengthen the spark of the divine, the connectedness to the universe discovered in the Lodge of Perfection, and to learn to make it the guiding force in the person's life.

The Council of Kadosh is the 19th through the 30th Degrees. The goal here is to understand the ways in which various religions and philosophies have understood that divine spark, that connectedness and to find ways to express it in the affairs of the world.

The Consistory is the 31st and 32nd Degrees. The quest goal here is self-examination and understanding and self-empowerment. That completes the process.

The Scottish Rite, then, uses the great mythic theme of the quest to start with the candidate, a person is has a vague awareness that he is not complete, that there is something more to both the world and himself than he understands and aid in his transformation into an autonomous, self-aware, self-motivated human being, aware of his spiritual nature, in control of his passions, and dedicated to the welfare of humanity. He has walked the footpath which leads within himself and discovered his heritage.

Written as an audio CD to accompany study materials for the College of the Consistory of the Guthrie Scottish Rite Temple

The Most Radical Era
19th Century Values

CD Script for

The College of the Consistory

Track 01 - Overview

Track 02 - Progress: "Every Day in Every Way"

Track 03 - Duty: "Stern Daughter of the Voice of God"

Track 04 - Honor: "Without it, all is dross"

Track 05 - Sentiment: Emotion+Intellect
Track 06 - Idealism: "We live, Mr. Worthing, in an Age of Ideals"
Track 07 - Law and the Individual: "The law, Sir, is an ass."
Track 08 - Spirituality: "He hath within him a spiritual nature"
Track 09 - Rationality: "But sir, is it reasonable?"
Track 10 - Social Consciousness: "Let each find some good work to do"
Track 11 - Reform: "To set free the Captives of power"
Track 12 - Nature: "My heart leaps up"
Track 13 - Eloquence: "Word strung to word like a strand of pearls"
Track 14 - Breeding: "With men or horses, sir, bloodline will tell"
Track 15 - Cultural Chauvinism: "The White Man's Burden"
Track 16 - Summary: Mr. Ingersoll's Oration

Track 01 ~ Overview

We think, today, of the 19th Century as a time of great conservatism— rather stuffy and repressed. Nothing could be further from the truth. More things changed during that century, more long-held views of man and God and nature were turned upside down, than in any period before or since. The Victorians, far from being stiff and unthinking, made and welcomed changes in science, philosophy, social conditions, family life, economics, education, technology, health, transportation, international relations, spirituality, the legal system, and much more. They invented both childhood and Christmas. They laid the foundation of the world in which we live.

In many ways, the values of the 19th Century were codified in the Ancient and Accepted Scottish Rite of Freemasonry. They form its ethical, philosophical and moral base. And they have given it its strength and endurance.

For the most part, the values of the 19th Century have not disappeared— useful answers to continuing problems seldom do. In many cases we have gone beyond the ideas and solutions provided by those values, but we have done so by building on them, not rejecting them.

On this CD, we'll look at some of the major values of the Victorians, illustrating them with quotations from the literature of the times. In some cases, those comments will be in the form of satire; the Victorians enjoyed poking fun at themselves; and in some cases we'll take examples from the arts. Then we'll look at a few of the ways those values appear in the Scottish Rite. Finally, we'll consider how the values appear at the beginning of the 21st Century.

Track 02 ~ Progress - "Every Day in Every Way"

The most fundamental value of the 19th Century, the one on which almost all the others were built, was a belief in progress. That seems a strange value to us—we take it for granted. Prior to the 19th Century, however, very few people believed in progress as a condition of the world and society. For thousands of years, people had believed the world was deteriorating, not progressing. There had been, long in the past, an Age of Gold. That was a time when everything was perfect. Man, nature and God lived in perfect happiness and harmony. Christians equated the Golden Age with the Garden of Eden. But as time passed, the balance was interrupted, like a top beginning to wobble as it spun down. The Age of Gold was followed by the Age of Silver, and then the Age of Brass, and then the Age of Iron. The more time passed, the further we moved from the Age of Gold, the worse things got. And they would continue to get worse. The best man could do was to try to hold things together, to make sure things got worse as slowly as possible. But tomorrow would be worse than today, and today was worse than yesterday.

That idea began to change during the Enlightenment, when Leibniz postulated the theory which would later come to be known as "Optimism," but it was the Victorians who rejected it completely in favor of a belief in Progress.

Progress meant that things were getting better, not worse. The task of man was not to hold back the tide of chaos, but to create a future which was brighter than today. "Every day in every way," they said, "things are getting better and better."

Almost literally, there was an engine driving this belief in Progress, and it was the steam engine—a development which had as profound an effect on the 19th Century as the computer has had on ours. Steam engines literally transformed the face of Europe and America. Steam locomotives made railroads possible, and railroads provided fast and cheap transportation of both goods and people. Steam engines made it possible to build mills and factories where there was no falling water to turn the water wheels which had powered the machinery before. Steam powered farm equipment meant larger plots of land could be worked and harvested and the trains could deliver that produce to markets much further away.

In 1851, the great Crystal Palace Exposition was held in London—essentially the first World's Fair. Technically, it was called "The Great Exhibition of the Works of Industry of all Nations." The Crystal Palace was built in Hyde Park to house the event. It was a daring feat of engineering and architecture, breaking new ground at every step. The building was made almost entirely of sheets of glass connected by cast iron rods. It was a wonder of the world, 408 feet by 1,848 feet in size, with a floor area of 989,884 square feet. And while it was called the "Crystal Palace," it was also called the "Palace of Progress."

It celebrated innovations in chemistry (the first artificial dye was introduced there) agriculture, mechanization, and inventions in every possible field. The exhibition was celebrated in song, in poetry, in painting and in plays. Millions of people visited it. If anyone had doubted that the world was progressing, rather than retrogressing, all he had to do was look around.

It's hard to overestimate the importance of the value of Progress. It gave rise to social reform, to a belief in the importance of education, and of the idea of planning for the future. It was understood that Progress applied to society and to the human condition as much as to machinery and economics.

Pike captured the essence of Progress in human life in a passage on page 691 in *Morals and Dogma*.

> *The normal condition of man is that of progress. Philosophy is a kind of journey, ever learning, yet never arriving at the ideal perfection of truth. A Mason should, like the wise Socrates, assume the modest title of a "lover of wisdom;" for he must ever long after something more excellent than he possesses, something still beyond his reach, which he desires to make eternally his own.*

Perhaps not surprisingly, the value of Progress, as well as reaction against it, showed clearly in religion, and continues to this day. This was especially true in America. It was not the ideal of Progress which motivated the great American poet, James Lowell, to write "Once to Every Man and Nation" in 1845, but the ideal of progress clearly appears. The poem was quickly set to the hymn tune "Ebenezer" By Thomas Williams. It still appears in the hymnals of many denominations. Listen to the words of the first and third verses.

> *Once to every man and nation, comes the moment to decide,*
> *In the strife of truth with falsehood, for the good or evil side;*
> *Some great cause, some great decision, offering each the bloom or blight,*
> *And the choice goes by forever, 'twixt that darkness and that light.*

> *By the light of burning martyrs, Christ, Thy bleeding feet we track,*
> *Toiling up new Calv'ries ever, with the cross that turns not back;*
> *New occasions teach new duties, time makes ancient good uncouth,*
> *They must upward still, and onward, who would keep abreast of Truth.*

New occasions teach new duties——ancient good becoming uncouth. That is the essence of Progress, and, predictably in the United States, it gave rise to a powerful counter movement in the fundamentalist religious community.

We do not know who wrote the words and music to "'Tis the old time religion." It was first published in the later 1800's by Charles Tillman and became very popular in some areas of the country. Almost at once the title was changed to "Give Me the Old Time Religion." Since it was only necessary to change one word to create a new verse, many were. It was especially popular at camp meetings and revivals, and remains a favorite of some denominations today, It doesn't take many verses to figure out that the speaker isn't interested in Progress, at least as it applies to religion.

> Give me that old time religion,
> Give me that old time religion,
> Give me that old time religion,
> It's good enough for me.
>
> It was good enough for Mother
> It was good enough for Mother
> It was good enough for Mother, and

It's good enough for me.

It was good enough for Father,
It was good enough for Father,
It was good enough for Father, and
It's good enough for me.

We're told, in subsequent verses, that is was good enough for Moses, Daniel, David, and many others.

Even those who believed in and longed for the Progress of humanity knew it was going to take a long time. Pike wrote:

> *The progress of the human race towards truth of any kind is slow and painful. It travels toward it in circles. At times, it retrogrades, and then again it makes progress forward. But the day will be long in coming when the masses of men will not need guides and rulers, or when they will no more need priests and kings.*
>
> *But the world does move, and we must not despair, though little come of our labors in our own time. Surely the Earth will at last become God's true Temple, the habitation of Truth and Love, when all men will constitute one people, living as the children of a common Father should, in obedience to His eternal laws of Equity and Charity.*

The value of Progress is central to our world, of course. We expect science and medicine to make our lives better, longer, richer, and more rewarding. We anticipate that our children will live in a world even better than ours. The Scottish Rite teaches that value in many of the Degrees, pointing out that we have an obligation to labor for the advancement of all humanity.

Track 03 ~ Duty - "Stern Daughter of the Voice of God"

> "Stern Daughter of the Voice of God!
> O Duty! If that name thou love . . .
> Thou, who art victory and law
> When empty terrors overawe,
> From vain temptations dost set free,
> And calm'st the weary strife of frail humanity."

Stern Daughter of the Voice of God. That is a powerful metaphor for Duty. And Duty was a powerful force for the Victorians. To do one's duty was an absolute incumbent upon every Victorian, man woman and child. It is clearly codified in another Victorian institution, the Boy Scouts.

> *"On my honor, I will do my best to do my duty to God and my country and to obey the Scout law; to help other people at all times; to keep myself physically strong, mentally awake, and morally straight."*

It was a given of the 19th Century that the highest pleasure was a sense of duty well performed. Men had a duty to protect the nation and the family, to insist on justice, to speak truthfully, and to act with integrity at all times. They also had a legal duty to guide the members of their family. Being the head of the household was a legal as well as cultural position. The law of the time made a man's wife subservient to him, but placed upon him the duty of seeing her well-treated and cared for.

Duty was the theme of thousands of sermons and of many novels and popular stories. Young women had a special duty, and that was to exert a civilizing influence upon men. Ultimately, as many novels told them, their highest calling was to find a man who was headed down the wrong path, and by the influence of their friendship and example, to reform him.

Consider this exchange between Miss Lucie Manette and Sydney Carton in Charles Dickens' *A Tale of Two Cities*. It occurs in Chapter 19, at one of the emotional high points of the novel. Carton has just confessed a misspent life (mild, by our standards) to Miss Manette, admitting that he had hoped she could love him, but knowing that she cannot.

> *But without it, can I not save you, Mr. Carton? Can I not recall you—forgive me—to a better course? ...*
>
> *No, Miss Manette. If you will hear me through a very little more, all you can ever do for me is done. I wish you to know you have been the last dream of my soul. In my degradation I have not been so degraded but that the sight of you with your father, and of this home made such a home by you, has stirred old shadows that I thought had died out of me. ...*
>
> *Since it is my misfortune, Mr. Carton, to have made you more unhappy than you were before you knew me—*
>
> *Don't say that, Miss Manette, for you would have reclaimed me, if anything could, you will not be the cause of my becoming worse."*
>
> *Since the state of your mind that you describe, is, at all events, attributable to some influence of mine—this is what I mean, if I can make myself plain—can I use no influence to serve you? Have I no power for good with you, at all?*

Not surprisingly, Duty also attracted satire. Brothers Gilbert and Sullivan had a major romp with the idea in their operetta, *The Pirates of Penzance*, subtitled *A Slave of Duty*. Our hero, young Frederick, was apprenticed to a pirate crew by accident as a young boy (His nursemaid was told to apprentice him to a pilot, and misunderstood the word). He has now reached his 21st birthday, and so is no longer an apprentice. He therefore tells the pirates, all of whom are his friends, that he now considers it his duty to lead the police against them, even though it saddens him to do so. First, however, he intends to find a maiden who will marry and reform him. He finds a bevy of young ladies (all daughters of the Major General) and, in a song, asks if one of them will take him on as a project.

> *"Oh, is there not one maiden breast,*
> *Which does not feel the moral beauty*
> *Of making worldly interest*
> *Subordinate to sense of duty?*
> *Who would not give up willingly*
> *All matrimonial ambition,*
> *To rescue such an one as I*
> *From his unfortunate position?"*

A young lady named Mabel accepts the challenge, but then Frederic learns that, while he has lived 21 years, he was born in leap year on February 29, and so he is still indentured as a pirate, and will be for another 63 years. It is his duty, therefore, to return to the pirates and help them defeat the police. Ultimately, of course, it all works out.

But while they may have poked a little fun at it, the 19th Century held duty literally as sacred. The entire society placed personal desire and pleasure far below duty in importance. Doing what you wanted to do was seen as self-indulgent and weak. Only duty mattered.

In one way or another, virtually every Degree of the Rite stresses the importance of duty. It is first driven home in the fourth Degree, when a voice from off stage tells the candidate:

> *"Duty is with us always, inflexible as Fate. In health or sickness, in prosperity or adversity, Duty is with us always, exacting as necessity. It rises with us in the morning, and watches by our pillow at night. Duty is with us always, imperative as Destiny."*

Albert Pike, writing in *Morals and Dogma* says on page 350

> *"On the volume of Masonic life one bright word is written, from which on every side blazes an ineffable splendor. That word is* DUTY.*"*

And again on page 219, he writes

> *"To make honor and duty the steady beacon lights that shall guide your life-vessel over the stormy seas of time; to do that which is right to do, not because it will insure your success, or bring with it a reward, or gain the applause of men, or be "the best policy," more prudent or more advisable; but because it is right, and therefore ought to be done...are some of the duties of a Mason."*

The virtue of Duty is still real. It has weakened in our time—resulting in the fact that the armed services now have to spend a great deal of time and effort explaining the concept. But a little reflection will tell you that a society operating purely upon self-interest, with no one doing what is right just because it is right, can't last very long. We still admire as heroes those men and women who find a duty to perform and do so, even at the cost of their lives. The teachings of the Scottish Rite about duty are as important now as when they were first penned.

Track 04 ~ Honor - "Without it, all is dross"

Honor is another essential and central value of the 19th Century. To do the honorable thing was imperative, and to have forfeited your honor was so serious a thing that the only honorable thing such a person could do was to commit suicide. If a man were deemed to have lost his honor, he simply would have no friends. Men and women turned their backs on him in the public street. If he entered a restaurant to eat, those sitting at tables near him would leave. If he went to someone's home, the door would probably be shut in his face. His name would not be spoken aloud.

It was possible to redeem lost honor, but it was not easy. Some major sacrifice was required, such as going to fight in an honorable war in a foreign land. Stories of the French Foreign Legion come to mind. In the majority of cases, however, such an individual usually moved to another country and started life over again under an assumed name.

Our own time is, in some ways, less judgmental than the 19th century, for good or ill, but even now we are not comfortable in the presence of a man or woman who has done some dishonorable act, and such a person usually ends up in a much lower rung of society.

The phrase "death before dishonor" was taken very literally. Death was not seen as a bad thing—dishonor was.

The honor of a woman was especially precious, and men were expected to make any sacrifice to protect it. Until fairly recently in this country, death was a common punishment for rape, because it was accepted that the rapist had forced upon the woman, literally, a "fate worse than death."

The virtue of honor appears in many of the Scottish Rite Degrees. A man was not only the guardian of his own honor, and the honor of any women in his household, each man was also the individual guardian of the honor of his country.

Pike reflects on honor in this passage from *Morals and Dogma*.

> *"Honor and Duty are the pole-stars of a Mason, by never losing sight of which he may avoid disastrous shipwreck. Thus Palinurus watched, until, overcome by sleep; and the vessel, no longer guided truly, he fell into and was swallowed up by the insatiable sea. So the Mason who loses sight of these, and is no longer governed by their beneficent and potential forces, is lost; and, sinking out of sight, will disappear unhonored and unwept."*

As we would expect, the Degrees in the Council of Kadosh which deal with knighthood feature honor very strongly. It is well to do so, For while we speak less of it today than in years past, honor is still important to us. Rare is the man who will not become angry if wrongly accused of being a liar. And it is still a high compliment to say that a man does what he says he will do, and that he acts honorably.

Track 05 ~ Sentiment = Emotion + Intellect

Sentiment is a difficult value for most of us to understand today, because in many ways our own time is a reaction against sentiment. We've kept the word in our vocabulary primarily in the form of "sentimental," and we tend to equate that with weakness or folly.

The Victorians saw it differently. Both sentiment and reason needed to be present, and needed to be balanced. Sentiment might be defined as the emotional context of a situation. Again, since we have come to regard emotions as somewhat weak and "frilly," it's well to remember that being emotional is not limited to getting choked up at the sight of a rose. Pride is an emotion, as are anger, determination, fear, patriotism, triumph, joy, protectiveness, love, and many other very powerful states of mind. The American poet, James Russell Lowell, wrote that "Sentiment is intellectualized emotion precipitated, as it were, in pretty crystals by the fancy."

The amazing thing is that sentiment is another example, like duty, of a culture deciding how a person's mental and emotional structures should react, and then making that real. It was real, and it cut across all sorts and conditions of men and women in both England and America.

The most obvious example is the Victorian melodrama. When these are performed today, we usually find them extremely comic, if they are played with deadly seriousness. The Victorians did not. Such plays as "East Lynn," or "The Drunkard" moved the emotions of the audience powerfully. They wept for the heroine in distress, they cheered the hero, they hissed and booed (and sometimes shot) the villain. We know from newspaper accounts at the time that this was as real in the mining towns of Colorado and California as anywhere else. Strong, rough men were moved to tears and wept openly.

Many of the popular songs of the day also moved to strong emotions. "The Curfew Shall Not Ring Tonight" told the story of a young woman, whose father had been wrongly convicted of murder and who was scheduled to be hanged that night when the curfew bell rang. She ties herself to the clapper of the bell, knowing that she will be killed, so that when the bell is rung there is no sound. There were hundreds of such songs, and the audience wept through them all. Perhaps the most famous example:

Father, dear Father, come home with me now,
The clock in the steeple strikes one
You promised you would hurry right home from the shop
As soon as your day's work was done.

The fire has gone out, the house is all dark,
And mother's been watching since tea
With poor Brother Billy so sick in her arms
And no one to help her but me.

In the following stanzas, the child comes again and again to the saloon, trying to convince her father to come home. He does not, and the infant dies.

Predictably, some people took sentiment to extremes and the Aesthetic Craze was born in the later 1800's, in which a few people did nothing but sit around feeling the depth and beauty of their own feelings. Some males took to carrying a lily with them, so they could contemplate its beauty at a moment's notice. This, as you can imagine, was meat and drink to Gilbert and Sullivan, who wrote "Patience, or Bunthorn's Bride" to satirize the movement.

Two aesthetic poets are surrounded by a bevy of beautiful young things whose minds have the collective depth of a teacup. They are talking with Patience, a milkmaid, who is the heroine of the work.

> [Young Thing}: *Ah! Patience, if you have never loved (sigh) you have never known true happiness.*
>
> [Patience]: *But the truly happy always seem to have so much on their mind. The truly happy never seem to be quite well.*
>
> [Young Thing]: *There is a trancendentality of delirium—acute accentuation of supremest ecstasy—which the earthy might easily mistake for indigestion. But it is not indigestion—it is aesthetic transfiguration!*

Aesthetic craze aside, the basic value of sentiment—the idea that a mind should be balanced between reason and feeling makes very good sense and is regarded now as essential for mental health.

Pike regarded sentiment or feeling as equally important with reason. It is the feeling which impels to action, and reason which tells us the action to be taken. This passage from Pike's book, *The Meaning of Masonry*, page 10, illustrates the point.

> *A Mason's contentedness must by no means be a mere contented selfishness; like his, who, comfortable himself, is indifferent to the discomfort of others. There will always be in this world wrongs to forgive, sufferings to alleviate, sorrows asking for sympathy, necessities and destitution to relieve, and ample occasion for the exercise of active charity and beneficence. And he who sits unconcerned amidst it all, perhaps enjoying his own comforts and luxuries the more, by contrasting them with the hungry and ragged misery and shivering wretchedness of his fellows, is not contented, but only unfeeling and brutal.*

Track 06 ~ Idealism - "We live, Mr. Worthing, in an age of Ideals"

> *"We live, as I hope you know, Mr. Worthing, in an age of ideals, The fact is constantly mentioned in the more expensive monthly magazines, and has reached the provincial pulpits, I am told, and my ideal has always been to love someone by the name of Earnest. ... From the moment my brother told me that he had a friend called Earnest, I knew I was destined to love you."*
> *"You really love me, Gwendolen?*
> *"Passionately."*

Brother Oscar Wilde was writing satire when he wrote the play, "The Importance of Being Earnest," and most ideals were slightly more sophisticated than that of Gwendolen, but she spoke the truth when she said the 19th Century was an Age of Ideals.

That is important for our understanding. We normally name eras of time after they are over. The Age of Enlightenment did not speak or particularly think of itself as championing Enlightenment—that was a judgement of history. The same was true of the Renaissance. But the Victorians were very aware of living in an age of ideals, an age in which the task of the entire society was to conceive of perfection and then strive to make it real. Some have since come to refer to this as "Victorian hypocrisy" because the practice always fell short of the ideal. But that is to confuse the 19th Century's concept of an ideal. It was supposed to be unreachable. The Victorians practiced ideals much as a weight-lifter practices weight lifting. The goal is always to lift more than you can. The Victorian equivalent was to strive for a better set of ideals than you could manage to live. The poet Robert Browning expressed it well with the line "A man's reach should exceed his grasp, or what's a heaven for?"

There have been only a few eras in history when a society has defined a purpose for itself as the Victorians in both England and America defined a goal of discovering and living Ideals. The years following the American Revolution was such a period, when almost all the members of the society saw themselves as building a new and idealized nation. Another such era occurred when America was united in a war to "make the world safe for democracy." The years of the presidency of Ronald Reagan is another, when much of the society saw itself as participating in a rebirth of the American spirit.

Idealism is important to the Scottish Rite, because it teaches at its most fundamental level that a life is something to be consciously built—not something which just happens. On page 192 in *Morals and Dogma*, Pike wrote:

"Man is no bubble upon the sea of his fortunes, helpless and irresponsible about the tide of events. Out of the same circumstances, different men bring totally different results. The same difficulty, distress, poverty, or misfortune, that breaks down one man builds up another and makes him strong. It is the very attribute and glory of a man, that he can bend the circumstances of his condition to the intellectual and moral purposes of his nature, and it is the power and mastery of his will that chiefly distinguishes him from the brute."

Track 07 ~ The Law and the Individual - "The Law, sir, is an ass."

It can come as a surprise to learn that Victorians, in America and especially in England, had considerable disdain for the Law. As Dickens has a character say in *Oliver Twist*, "The law, sir, is an ass." With the important exception of lawyers who handled the wills and financial affairs of families, and who were looked upon as family friends and confidants, lawyers are almost always portrayed as remarkably stupid, grasping, or evil. Consider this from Brothers Gilbert and Sullivan's 1875 hit comic opera, "Trial by Jury."

The Judge has a song in which he tells how he became a Judge. He has told us that, tired of having no cases as a young lawyer, he "fell in love with a rich attorney's elderly, ugly daughter." The rich attorney sent many cases to the young attorney, until, finally:

"At length I became as rich as the Gurneys,
an incubus then I thought her,
So I threw over that rich attorney's
Elderly, ugly daughter:
The rich attorney my character high
Tried vainly to disparage—-
And now if you please, I'm ready to try
This Breach of Promise of Marriage.

For now I'm a judge, and a good judge, too.
Thought all my law be fudge
Yet I'll never, never budge,
But I'll live and die a Judge
And a good judge, too."

There was a great class distinction when it came to the law—there were virtually two sets of laws, one for the lower sort of commoner and one for the upper classes. Gentlemen and Ladies, for example, were generally tried in special courts. If a member of the aristocracy were convicted of murder (and a member of the House of Lords could be tried only in the House of Lords) he was hanged with a velvet rope.

Criminal law simply did not enter into the thinking of most middle and upper class Victorians. They were supposed to be guided by the virtues, not by laws—and it was understood that the virtues required a much higher code of conduct than did the laws. At the same time, if one became convinced that something forbidden by law was, nevertheless, the right thing to do, it was considered morally right to break the law.

The 19th Century believed firmly in the morals of Republican Rome—and some of those morals seem very harsh by our standards. They were fond of reproductions of the painting by Jacques-Louis David—usually called "The Lictors Bring to Brutus the Bodies of his Sons." The painting alludes to a moment in Roman history when the only two sons of Brutus are convicted of plotting to help restore the monarchy to Rome. Brutus is the judge, and, without flinching, he condemns both his sons to death. The general Victorian attitude was that he did exactly the right thing.

In the same way, it was considered unfortunate, but appropriate, for a Victorian father to disown a daughter who had disobeyed—especially if she had allowed herself to become pregnant.

A part of this attitude came because the Victorians believed strongly in individualism. They placed much more importance upon the individual than on society. Individuals, pursuing their highest goals and virtues, would naturally improve society. There were very few laws which applied to individuals anyhow—we have multiplied the number of laws a thousand-fold. No drugs or substances were illegal, for example. It was up to the individual to make careful and restrained use of such substances if he chose to use them.

But the disdain for the law was limited to criminal law; the laws of God, of nature, and of science were held in high regard, and considered far more important than mere human enactments.

Many of these attitudes are clearly reflected in the Scottish Rite. The Degrees condemn those who take all the law allows them to take, even when to do so is not right, equitable, generous, or fair. They also make clear that our obligations to our fellow humans go far beyond merely that which is required by law.

But, more than most Victorians, Pike believed that the law really did apply to everyone. On page 156 in *Morals and Dogma*, for example, he writes:

> *"It conduces, and in no small measure, to the beauty and glory of one's country, that justice should always be administered there to all alike,. And neither denied, sold, nor delayed to any one; and that the interests of the poor be should be looked to, and none starve or be houseless, or clamor in vain for work."*

And while he clearly believed in law, Pike did not believe in being judgmental. He warns against that attitude in Degree after Degree, and reminds us that when we look at someone who is in trouble with the law, we should remember that we do not truly know what his motives were. And he further tells us—

> *"Remember that, tempted like him you might have fallen like him, and perhaps with even less resistance."*

Track 08 ~ Spirituality - "He hath within him a spiritual nature"

Spirituality was of great importance to the 19th Century. Each man and woman had a spiritual aspect to their natures, and it was the duty of each to find and nourish that spiritual nature. Indeed, it was to triumph over the animal nature in humanity. Sermons were very popular in the 19th Century, and literally hundreds of books of sermons were published, given as gifts, and, apparently, actually read. Great pulpit men had a status we reserve for rock stars today.

The spiritual pervaded all aspects of the popular culture. You have probably seen at least one color print of a Victorian painting showing children being protected by an angel. The typical Victorian believed absolutely in angels, and that belief melded into a common belief in many sorts of spiritual beings. A photograph of fairies in a garden (confessed to have been a fake some 50 years after the fact by the two little girls who faked it) simply confirmed the common belief. But while the less reasoned aspects of spirituality led eventually to spiritualism and a flourishing of false mediums, seances, and Ouji boards, a belief in the spiritual nature of man was regarded simply as acknowledging an obvious fact. Ralph Waldo Emerson, in a Phi Beta Kappa address in 1867, said:

> *"Great men are they who see that spiritual is stronger than any material force; that thoughts rule the world."*

Freemasonry, of course, had long taught that man has a spiritual component to his nature and that the spiritual must take power over the animal. It is symbolized in the Blue Lodge Degrees by the movement of the compasses (symbol of the spiritual nature) from under to over the square (symbol of the material). Albert Pike saw that as the central and most important lesson of the Scottish Rite in particular and of Masonry in general. *Morals and Dogma*, page 854.

> *"Freemasonry is the subjugation of the Human that is in man by the Divine' the Conquest of the Appetites and Passions by the Moral Sense and the Reason; a continual effort, struggle, and warfare of the Spiritual against the Material and Sensual."*

And he becomes more specific on the following page.

> *". . .the Mason must first attain a solid conviction, founded upon reason, that he hath within him a spiritual nature, a soul that is not to die when the body is dissolved, but is to continue to exist and to advance toward perfection through all the ages of eternity, and to see more and more clearly, as it draws nearer unto God, the Light of the Divine Presence. This the Philosophy of the Ancient and Accepted Rite teaches him; and it encourages him to persevere by helping him to believe that his free will is entirely consistent with God's Omnipotence and Omniscience; that God is not only infinite in power, and of infinite wisdom, but of infinite mercy, and an infinitely tender pity and love for the frail and imperfect creatures that He has made."*

Track 09 ~ Rationality   "But sir, is it reasonable?"

It is worth repeating the opening of that last quotation— "the Mason must first attain a solid conviction, founded upon reason, that he hath within him a spiritual nature" because it serves as an introduction to the next great 19th Century value; Reason.

It may seem strange than an age which highly valued spirituality, sentiment, and such concepts as honor and duty, should also place a high value upon the virtue of rationality, but there is no question that they did so. For one thing, the Victorians loved learning things. Lectures, usually illustrated with magic lantern slides—the 19th Century equivalent of power point, were extremely popular.

Societies were formed to bring popular lecturers to town. Speakers who performed experiments in the physical sciences during the presentation were especially enjoyed as well as those showing photographic images of foreign lands. Most of the world's great museums were establishing during the 1800's. The Victorians used a term we have largely dropped out of our language, at least in their usage. It was a high compliment to a man or woman to say that they "had a good understanding." It meant that they were reasonable and rational, and could be expected to be thoughtful in their responses and reactions.

Reason and rationality are very important to the Scottish Rite. References to reason fill more than a page in the index to *Morals and Dogma*. And Pike summed up the position clearly with one line in the 33°

"True religion consists in the equilibrium of God's two greatest gifts to man—Faith and Reason."

And he hit upon another aspect in that chilling line from the 32°

"You are here to think, if you can think; and to learn, if you can learn."

Track 10 ~ Social Consciousness - "Let each find some good work to do"

"God has ordained that life shall be a social state. We are members of a civil community. The life of that community depends upon its moral condition. Public spirit, intelligence, uprightness, temperance, kindness, domestic purity, will make it a happy community, and give it prosperity and continuance. Wide-spread selfishness, dishonesty, intemperance, libertinism, corruption, and crime, will make it miserable, and bring about dissolution and speedy ruin. A whole people lives one life; one mighty heart heaves in its bosom; it is one great pulse of existence that throbs there. One stream of life flows there, with ten thousand intermingling branches and channels, through all the homes of human love."

So wrote Albert Pike on page 197 of *Morals and Dogma*, and he was expressing one of the great 19th Century values. It was considered very important to find something to do which benefitted others. You will recall the opening scene of *A Christmas Carol*, when the two gentlemen call upon Scrooge for a contribution to help provide some Christmas cheer to the poor and homeless. He turns them away, of course, but they were typical of most Victorians, trying to do something to improve the lot of the less fortunate. And, in that context, remember the encounter between Scrooge and the ghost of Jacob Marley.

"It is required of every man that the spirit within him should walk abroad among his fellow-men, and travel far and wide, and if that spirit goes not forth in

life, it is condemned to do so after death. It is doomed to wander through the world and witness what it cannot share, but might have shard on earth, and turned to happiness.

"Oh captive, bound and double-ironed! Not to know that no space of regret can make amends for one life's opportunities misused! Yet such was I! Oh! Such was I!

"But you were always a good man of business, Jacob.

"Business! Mankind was my business. The common welfare was my business; charity, mercy, forbearance, and benevolence, were, all, my business. The dealings of my trade were but a drop of water in the comprehensive ocean of my business."

This sense of social consciousness was new in the world. In every western society of which we have record prior to the 19th Century, responsibility in the sense of providing time and resources had been limited to a person's family, extended family, or tribe. Occasionally, it had included one's immediate neighbors or "affinity group" such as other members of a religious group or work group such as the guild, or, almost uniquely, other Freemasons. The 19th Century vastly expanded this sense of social responsibility.

And Albert Pike, through the Degrees of the Scottish Rite, expanded the social responsibility of Freemasonry. The Blue Lodge Degrees taught, and still teach, a responsibility limited to members of the Craft and their families. Pike extended that sense of responsibility to the entire world.

"Good Masons do the good thing which comes in their way, and because it comes in their way; for a love of duty, and not merely because a law, enacted by man or God, commands their will to do it. Not in vain does the poor or the oppressed look up to them. They are kind fathers, generous citizens, unimpeachable in their business, beautiful in their daily lives. You see their Masonry in their work and in their play. It appears in all the forms of their activity, individual, domestic, social, ecclesiastical, or political. True Masonry within must be morality without. The true Mason loves not only his kindred and his country, but all mankind; not only the good, but also the evil, along his brethren. He has more goodness than the channels of his daily life will hold. It runs over the banks, to water and to feed a thousand thirsty plants. He has a salient longing to do good, to spread his truth, his justice, his generosity, his Masonry over all the world. His daily life is a profession of his Masonry, published in perpetual good-will to men."

Track 11 ~ Reform - To Set Free the Captives of Power

A natural consequence both of the belief in Progress and the value of social consciousness was Reform. Especially in England and America, the world changed forever in the 19th Century. It became, on the whole, a much more humane place. Charles Dickens was one of the most indomitable reformers, and he brought about reform by writing novels showing things the way they were. Profound changes in orphanages, the courts, and economic protection for the middle class came out of his novels. Outbreaks of disease and several years of really bad smells motivated parliament to revamp the sewage system of London, making it a model of the time. Public hospitals were built in both countries. Charitable institutions flourished. The general attitude was "if we can make it better, we must make it better," and there was very little the Victorians did not believe they could make better. Schools were reformed and new systems of education were tried. The worst of the insane asylums were closed and new means to treating the mentally ill were introduced.

Prison reform was a topic of great public debate. It was agreed that the prisons as they existed were a national disgrace, but there was little agreement on how to improve them. New styles of prison architecture were tried. Some were designed to completely isolate each prisoner, some were designed for communal living, some were built around classrooms and some around workshops. The Victorians were certain that if they looked long and hard enough, they would find an answer.

We are still looking.

Pike was very aware of the importance of reform, and expressed it many different ways. In one passage in the *Offices of Adoption* he wrote:

> "Not the head but the heart must elevate the poor; must remove the causes of poverty by the charity that alleviates and the justice that cures; must heal the drunkard of his fiery thirst; must reform the criminal, instead of hanging him to save trouble; must cut down the gallows, and turn the prison into a school for the improvement of the heart, instead of leaving it as it is, the den of vengeance and of rage, that

> turns what were once little children into wild beasts, an institution for hardening the heart and utterly depraving the soul, in which the fiend would be the only fitting principal instructor."

He brings together both social consciousness and reform in these powerful words from the book *Words Spoken from the Heart*, page 10.

> *[Freemasonry] has at heart the welfare in this life of the people among whom it exists,--in this life for its own sake, and not merely as a term of probation, and of preparation for another. This field of labor and exertion is large enough for it. To set free the captives of power, and deliver those who are imprisoned in the houses of bondage of craft, to make the life of the poor less a burden to them and some human hearts happier, to teach men their rights and enlighten those whom Ignorance and Error hold in fetters, is the work that it requires of its Initiates.*
>
> *"And it thinks that every man that works to benefit others, earns the right to have, and is worthy of, honour and reward, It holds that no creed is of value, except as it bears fruit in action; that what those learn that sit at its feet and listen to its teachings is chiefly valuable because it enables them to enlighten others. It is the Advocate and Defender all the world over, of free government and Liberty of Conscience; its Mission the Apostolate of Truth, Justice and Toleration.*
>
> *"It constitutes a great Brotherhood, of men of many tongues and races, cherishing for each other a warm affection, cultivating the sympathies that make the hearts of thousands beat in unison,*

> thrilling with the same emotions, inspired by the same impassioned aspirations, the leaves upon the one great tree of the Scottish Free Masonry."

The idea of Reform does not seem as compelling to us today, perhaps because it seems the most pressing have already been made. But we are still faced with the problems. Unwanted pregnancy, especially among teenagers, remains a very serious issue. There are great ethical questions raised by medical advances. What is death? Should a person be required to continue living when it is nothing but a burden. Human cloning raises other questions. Is your clone human? Does He own himself, or do you own him? Suppose you have a clone and you are left an inheritance. Do you get all the money, does He share in it?

And the problem of prisons is still with us. Are prisons effective? Is it right to continue punishing someone after they have served a sentence? If not, what about the laws requiring sex offenders to register? If, as the Rite teaches, our task is to continue to improve society—maybe the topic of Reform isn't a dead letter.

Track 12 ~ Nature - "My heart leaps up"

> *My heart leaps up when I behold*
> *A rainbow in the sky:*
> *So was it when my life began;*
> *So is it now I am a man;*
> *So be it when I shall grow old,*
> *Or let me die!*
> *The child is father of the man;*

*And I could wish my days to be
Bound each to each by natural piety.*

That phrase "natural piety" is quite literal—In Wordsworth's poem "My Heart Leaps Up" he is expressing one of the major values of the 19th Century, a love of nature and a belief that nature is the handwork of God and reveals God. Not much had been written about nature in the popular culture before the Victorians. A society has to have a certain amount of leisure time and a certain amount of wealth before nature is seen as anything but an obstacle. Most people do not revel in the beauty of a swift river if they are worried about how to ford it. We praise the beauty of a mountain range only when we are not afraid of dying in the attempt to cross it. We delight in the crystal magic of a snowfall when we are watching it from inside by the fire, or at least know that we can be inside in a matter of minutes.

But the 19th Century had transportation and resources, and enjoying nature became an important part of Victorian social and emotional life. They invented the idea of the picnic and enjoyed taking nature tours. It was a firmly held value and belief that God could be more easily understood through His work in nature than in almost any other way. Wordsworth's poem is an example, but there are many others. As we have seen a good indication that an idea is important to a culture is when it shows up in the form of hymnody, and several popular hymns celebrated God's revelation in nature. One of the best-known was written by Maltbia Babcock, and is still commonly sung today:

*This is my Father's world, and to my listening ear
All nature sings and round me rings The music of the
    spheres
This is my Father's world; I rest me in the thought*

Of rocks and trees, of skies and seas;
His hand the wonders wrought.

This belief in nature as revealing God's handiwork and telling us something of His thought continues in our own era. Most of us feel something spiritual in nature, a beautiful landscape or sunset touches at more than the intellectual level.

The image of God revealed in nature is found throughout the Scottish Rite.

Pike devotes some of his most beautiful language to the topic, which he obviously felt deeply. This passage is in *Morals and Dogma*, page 215

"The humblest object beneath our eye as completely defies our scrutiny as the economy of the most distant star. Every leaf and blade of grass holds within itself secrets which no human penetration will ever fathom...Wherever we place our hand we lay it on the locked bosom of mystery. Step where we will, we tread upon wonders.. The sea side, the clods of the field, the water worn pebbles on the hills, the rude masses of rock, are traced over and over, in every direction, with a hand-writing older and more significant and sublime than all the ancient ruins and all the overthrown and buried cities that past generations have left upon the earth, for it is the handwriting of the Almighty."

And earlier, on page 64, he writes:

"Nature is the great teacher of man, for it is the Revelation of God. It neither dogmatizes nor attempts to tyrannize by compelling to a particular creed or special interpretation. It presents its symbols to us,

and adds nothing by way of explanation. It is the text without the commentary and gloss that lead to error and heresy and persecution."

The Scottish Rite teaches the importance of nature as a source of spiritual "grounding." Whether a degree begins at dawn amidst the ruins of the Temple, or in the gloaming on the shores of the dead sea, or in the forest as a full moon appears above the horizon—part of the lesson is that we need to return to nature from time to time; not just to recharge our "spiritual batteries," but to regain a perspective and sense of proportion. As our time becomes more and more hectic in its pace we need, more than ever, to spend a few quite moments with nature. "Don't forget to smell the roses," is good advice.

Track 13 ~ Eloquence - "Word strung to word, like a strand of richest pearls"

Yet another Victorian value which can be hard for us to understand is the value placed on eloquence. Our age has defined communication as the transmission of information, and we have tended to associate information with data. The Victorians had a much broader definition of communication, because it dealt with both the hard information, the data, and the intellectual and emotional context. The way something was said was at least as important as what was said. Men and women studied rhetoric, and valued the well-turned phrase, the thoughtful utterance, very highly. Thought was to be clothed in carefully-chosen speech. They would have found the text of a typical e-mail today to be largely incomprehensible, and highly insulting. It was, in fact, a deliberate insult to speak to an equal in as few words as possible. That was how one spoke to a servant. It was a social skill to speak well.

The dialogue we read in Victorian plays often seems to us to be artificial—we doubt that anyone ever spoke that way in real life. But, in fact, they did. They realized the inherent richness of the English language—which is truly one of the most flexible and nuanced on earth.

Victorians loved words for their own sake. Crossword puzzles developed during this time as did the game of anagrams. Word games were the most popular from of family entertainment and were played around kitchen tables and the parlors of large country homes.

The value of eloquence meant that ideas could be given force and beauty, just by the way they were phrased. It did not necessarily mean long and involved sentences, only that the utterances were carefully considered.

One writer has referred to today's typical communications as "cook book writing." That is to say the most information is given in the shortest possible form. That works well for cook books, in which the writer is not trying to communicate a feeling or a context. But it lacks the richness of a communication which enjoys the words themselves, their sounds and "taste upon the tongue," to communicate something more than hard fact. Consider this passage in modern speak.

"Late at night one December, I was sitting up reading some old books, just about to go to sleep. The fire in the room was dying out. I was startled to hear a noise."

Compare that with:
> *"Once upon a midnight dreary, while I pondered, weak and weary, over many a quaint and curious volume of forgotten lore; while I nodded, nearly napping, suddenly*

there came a tapping, as of someone gently rapping, rapping on my chamber door. "'Tis some visitor," I muttered, "tapping at my chamber door—Only this, and nothing more. Ah, distinctly I remember it was in the bleak December, and each separate dying ember wrought its ghost upon the floor."

The second example, of course, is from Edgar Allen Poe's poem The Raven. The data content of the two passages is roughly the same. But the Poe passage tells us much more, because we know something of the state of mind of the speaker, more about the setting, and we also have a general feeling of mood or tone. It is simply richer.

Consider these example from the work of Pike. The first is a paraphrase—the second is Pike's language.

Low class men are more likely to put you down than higher class men.

"If you seek for high and strained carriages, you shall, for the most part, meet with them in low men. Arrogance is a weed that ever grows on a dunghill."

It is wrong to be greedy.

"It is only man who continues to accumulate after he has more than enough; and yet he fancies that God made him after His own image."

Incidentally Pike, who was one of the greatest orators of the 19th Century, who was in constant demand as a speaker, and whose orations were published in volumes of Southern literature, knew that eloquence could be a danger in the wrong hands. He warns against that in *Morals and Dogma*, on page 91.

> *"If you have eloquence, it is a mighty force. See that you use it for good purposes—to teach, exhort, ennoble the people, and not to mislead and corrupt them. Corrupt and venal orators are the assassins of the public liberties, and of public morals."*

The question of eloquence is important because it gives an important hint as to how you should watch the Degrees. Strive to take in the totality, not just the literal meanings of the words, but the rhythm, sounds and feelings of the words. Just as the symbols have to be understood by thought and reflection, and not just as themselves but in context, so it is with the words of the Degrees. There are some important ideas you just can't write in a cook book.

Track 14 ~ Breeding - "With men or horses, sir, bloodline will tell"

The Victorians meant two things by "breeding," both of which can be a little shocking to us. One is manners or deportment. Good breeding showed in the way a person dressed, the way they carried their bodies (posture was very important to the Victorians), and the way they spoke.

The other meaning was quite literal. Most members of the Victorian upper classes derived their income from land, and English farmers and landowners had been carefully breeding livestock for hundreds of years. Long before the laws of genetics were known, people had been breeding for desirable characteristics in livestock and other animals. By the time of Darwin, the common pigeon had been bred into more than 200 recognized varieties. Cattle were bred to produce more milk or more beef. Horses were bred up in size and endurance or streamlined for speed. It was obviously possible to improve the general breed by the careful selection of pairs to be mated.

Victorians in both England and America saw no reason why the same standards should not be applied to people. It was the duty of a Victorian father to inquire into the family history of a man who wanted to marry his daughter; especially to look for cases of insanity or other evidence of "bad blood." Many Victorian mothers kept lists of eligible bachelors (informally called "stud books" after the books on an estate which recorded the breeding lines of prize animals).

And there were ideal standards in the breeding and appearance of cows, hogs, horses, dogs, and almost every other animal. Why not people, and, especially, why not women? Beauty pageants are a Victorian invention.

We've kept many indicators in our popular language. We speak of a person as "coming from good stock"—or bad stock. We speak of a person being well-bred. We describe manners or habits of which our society disapproved as been "ill-bred." We may describe a person as being "high-spirited," or "sulky," or "brooding," or "quirky;" all terms which originally applied to prize livestock. In our recent slang, we have referred to young, good-looking women as "fillies," and to virile men as "studs."

The concept of breeding, or being of good breeding or bad breeding—the same thing as good blood and bad blood—was simply part of the real world for the 19th Century. It forms the theme of Mark Twain's book *Puddinhead Wilson* and Oscar Wilde's play "The Importance of Being Earnest," as well as countless Victorian dime novels and three-volume romances. It was the constant topic of conversation for ladies over a cup of tea in the afternoon.

The value of breeding shows up in the Scottish Rite in an interesting way. Pike almost certainly believed that only men of good breeding would join Masonry and the Rite. So the Degrees make the point, over and over again, that they are not the only ones who matter. Pike points out the moral excellence of the working man and of work itself. He warns often against arrogance.

> *"There are men who boast that neither they nor their children work nor have to work. Neither do swine."*

He points out that not all of a man's wealth, indeed not all of the wealth of the world, gathered together and tripled, is of as much value as the soul of a beggar in rags, if that beggar is a true man.

Track 15 ~ Cultural Chauvinism - "The White Man's Burden"

> *"Take up the White Man's burden—*
> *The savage wars of peace—*
> *Fill full the mouth of famine*
> *And bid the sickness cease:*
> *And when your goal is nearest*
> *The end for others sought,*
> *Watch sloth and heathen Folly*
> *Bring all your hopes to nought."*
>   Rudyard Kipling

Cultural chauvinism is a difficult value to discuss, because it is so loaded with emotional baggage; but it is essential in understanding the 19th Century. There simply was no doubt in the mind of the typical Englishman or American that their culture was the best on earth, albeit the Englishman and American would argue bitterly over which was better.

It's easy to understand. Both nations were experiencing an explosion of progress in human rights, science, medicine, agriculture, education, reduction of poverty. There were institutions for the care of orphans, the elderly, and the infirm. Every day was filled with new promise. There was a natural desire to extend these benefits to the rest of the world. Add to that the fact that, in America, there had been an awakened interest in religious evangelism. It seemed only reasonable to send both missionaries and technicians to convert and improve the life of the others.

It must be admitted that a very great deal was accomplished. Hospitals were built in parts of the world which had no scientific health care at all. (Except for those foolish native healers—many of whose herbs form the basis of modern pharmacology.) Railroads and dams were built, steam power and then electricity were brought to many parts of the world. Admittedly, there was no cultural sensitivity shown—our way was so obviously best that foreigners who resisted or did not want to adopt our ways were clearly only being stubborn.

It was not without its comic consequences. In the late 1800's one of the largest Protestant denominations in America was sending many missionaries to China. It was reported back that the Chinese women wore pants! This was so obviously a hindrance to the work of the church that the denomination formed ladies sewing circles to make proper dresses to be sent to the missionaries. The rallying cry of these circles (I'm perfectly serious) was "Let's take the pants off the women in China."

And Brother Mark Twain remarked"

> *"We have sent many missionaries to the peoples of the Sandwich Islands. Thus far, the peoples of the Sandwich Islands have been too gracious to send missionaries to us."*

Of course we were exploiting their resources at the same time we were extending them benefits, but we knew that was only a fair trade. Both England and America thought nothing of uniting, subdividing and forming nations where none had been before. After all, you have to have a nation. The nations in the middle-east today are essentially those created by the British in the early 1900's. In America, all through the 1800's we waged what amounted to a war of genocide against Native Americans, rewarding army officers for wiping out Native American men, women and children. It was very nearly government policy that "the only good Indian was a dead Indian." And through most of the 1900's government agencies actively tried to destroy Native American culture and cultural practices so the people would "be like us."

Internationally, most of this came to a screeching halt after the Second World War, of course, when we saw the horrors that can be created when one nation or nationality decides that it is inherently superior to all others. Hitler is as object lesson not easily forgotten.

And yet, while we do not speak of the White Man's burden now save in derision, in fact the attitude of Cultural and religious chauvinism is still with us. In the war in Vietnam we tried to force the idea of nationhood on people whose concept of government was tribal. We still insist that democracy is the best form of government, even for people who live happily under different forms of government. We believe that the role of women in every country should be what it is in the United States. There is still great intolerance for other religions and other cultural practices. What toleration there is, is usually grudging.

The Scottish Rite is one of the very few institutions which teaches—insists upon—the ideal of toleration. It appears as a virtue in many of the Degrees and in the obligations of the Rite. In *Morals and Dogma*, Pike explores many religious faiths and, generally, does so with compassion and understanding.

And that is well. For, if we no longer speak of the White Man's burden, we still seem to have a powerful urge to make the world over in our own image. Pike reminds us that the world is a reflection of God. Just perhaps He knew what He was doing.

Track 16 ~ Summary, Mr. Ingersoll's Oration

Looking for a way to sum up the values of the 19th Century in its own words, I decided upon a speech by Robert Ingersoll. Ingersoll is one of the most important figures in 19th Century American thought. He was a vastly popular orator of the day. He was also highly controversial. Known as "the great agnostic," he lectured on the abuses of organized religion in the 1800's.

Those abuses were considerable. In many parts of America, religion had become a means not of freeing its followers but of enslaving them. Many popular fundamentalist "preachers" used fiery oratory to build large followings whom they exploited for their own financial gain. Instead of following the teachings of Jesus of Nazareth to show people that they had no need to live in fear, they used those teachings to portray a God who was hostile to them and to humanity, and who was just waiting for a chance to condemn them to the fire for eternity. Ingersoll took them on in public debate and in speeches. He was not an atheist as sometimes charged. He was an agnostic saying, in essence, I do not claim my limited human mind can comprehend God, but I do claim that this powerful, bitten, vindictive old man you describe can't be the right image.

In 1879 Ebon Clark Ingersoll, Robert Ingersoll's younger brother, died at the age of 47. He had been a Congressman and had chaired several important committees, including the Committee on the District of Columbia, the Committee on roads and canals, and the Committee on railroads. He was a widely loved man, and had a reputation for absolute integrity.

Robert Ingersoll had asked Ebon to make the remarks at Robert's funeral. Now, through a twist of fate, it is Robert who is delivering an "Oration at his Brother's Grave." Listen carefully, and you will hear nearly all the values we have discussed.

> *My friends — I am going to do that which the dead oft promised He would do for me.*
>
> *The loved and loving brother, husband, father, friend, died where manhood's morning almost touches noon, and while the shadows still were falling toward the west.*
>
> *He had not passed on life's highway the stone that marks the highest point, but, being weary for a moment, lay down by the wayside, and, using his burden for a pillow, fell into that dreamless sleep that kisses down his*

eyelids still. While yet in love with life and raptured with the world, He passed to silence and pathetic dust.

Yet, after all, it may be best, just in the happiest, sunniest hour of all the voyage, while eager winds are kissing every sail, to dash against the unseen rock, and in an instant hear the billows roar above a sunken ship. For, whether in mid-sea of 'mong the breakers of the further shore, a wreck at last must mark the end of each and all. And every life, no matter if its every hour is rich with love and every moment jeweled with a joy, will, at its close, become a tragedy as sad and deep and dark as can be woven of the warp and woof of mystery and death.

This brave and tender man in every storm of life was oak and rock, but in the sunshine He was vine and flower. He was the friend of all heroic souls. He climbed the heights and left all superstitions far below, while on his forehead fell the golden dawning of the grander day. He loved the beautiful, and was the color, form, and music touched to tears. He sided with the weak, and with a willing hand gave alms; with loyal heart and with purest hands He faithfully discharged all public trusts. He was a worshiper of liberty, a friend of the oppressed. A thousand times I have heard him quote these words: "For justice all place a temple, and all seasons, summer," He believed that happiness was the only good, reason the only torch, justice the only worship, humanity the only religion, and love the only priest. He added to the sum of human joy; and were everyone to whom He did some loving service to bring a blossom to his grave, He would sleep tonight beneath a wilderness of flowers.

Life is a narrow vale between the cold and barren peaks of two eternities. We strive in vain to look beyond the heights. We cry aloud—and the only answer is the echo of our wailing cry. From the voiceless lips of the unreplying dead there comes no word; but in the night of death hope sees a star, and listening love can hear the rustle of a wing.

He who sleeps here, when dying, mistaking the approach of death for the return of health, whispered with his last breath: "I am better now." Let us believe, in spite of doubts and dogmas and tears and fears, that these dear words are true of all the countless dead. And now to you who have been chosen from among the many men He loved, to do the last sad office for the dead, we give his sacred dust. Speech cannot contain our love. There was, there is, no greater, stronger, manlier man.

Written as an audio CD to accompany study materials for the College of the Consistory of the Guthrie Scottish Rite Temple

The Guild Lodge of

St. Canice

A reconstruction of a meeting of a Scots Operative Lodge in the early 1500's

by

Jim T. Tresner

for the 100th Anniversary Celebration of
Welcome Lodge № 54
Churchs Ferry, North Dakota
1999

Cast List

The Guild Master
The Warden of the Lodge
Euin, a Fellow of the Craft
   (the Senior Steward)
Harol, a Fellow of the Craft
   (the Junior Steward)
Jeffery, an Entered Apprentice
Dongal,   "   "
Griswold,   "   "
1 or more additional Entered Apprentices
Colin, the Candidate
Terence, a Fellow of the Craft
   (the Tyler)
Master Philip
Master Lukus
   (the oldest Master present)
Master Denni
Doran the musician, a Fellow of the Craft
   (musician optional)
Mikel, a Fellow of the Craft and a Piper
   (Piper optional)

NOTE: For obvious reasons, the Apprentices should be played by Brethren who are as young as possible. It is very important that Colin, the candidate, be played by a young man.

Setting

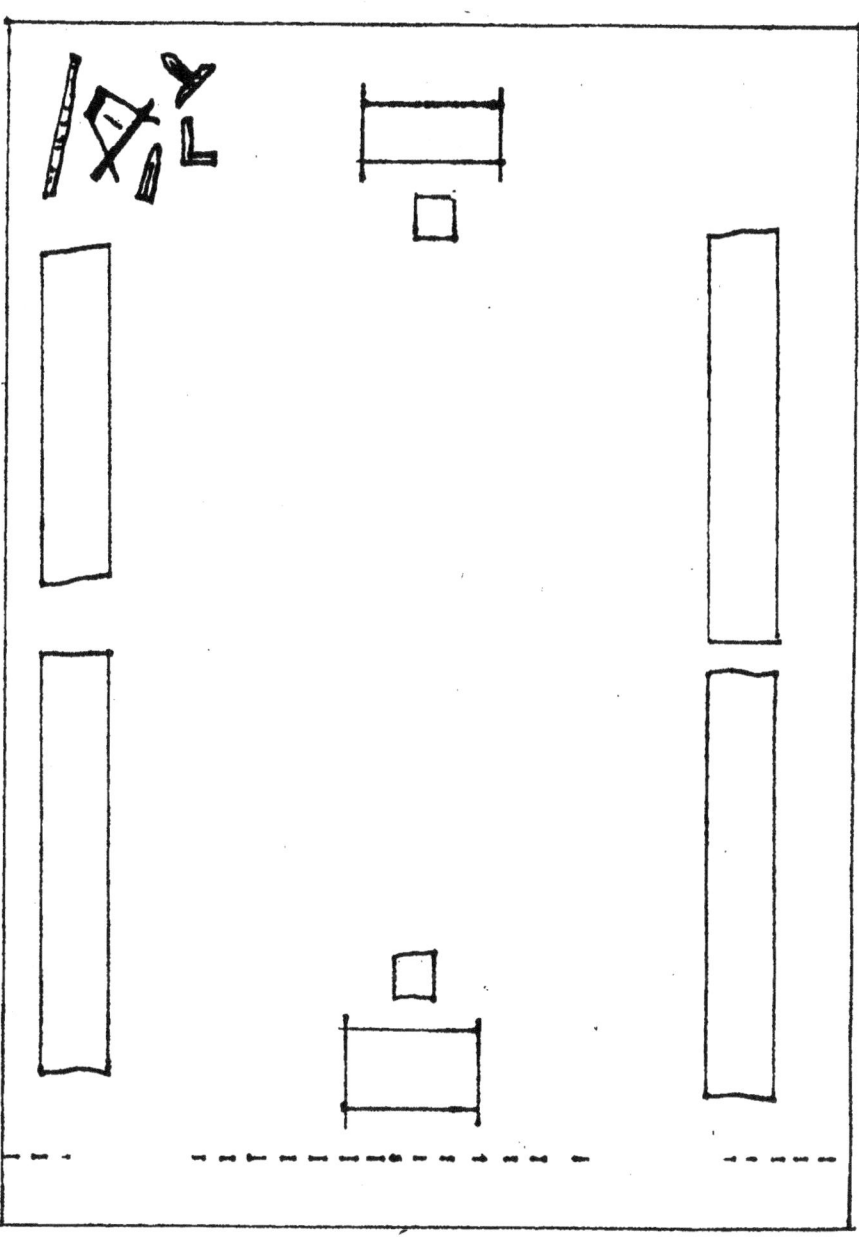

Prologue

Used if there is no Brother present who would prefer to explain the play ad lib. *Done by a Brother in modern dress.*

Brethren and friends,

Tonight, we journey to Scotland, in the first decade of the 1500's, when Masonry was beginning its transition from the operative guild—a collection of workers in stone—to speculative Masonry, an organization more concerned with thought and philosophy.

What you will see is, in part, speculation. Certain parts of the script are based on the Regius Poem, the earliest known Masonic document, dating from about the year 1390. Other parts come from the earliest preserved Scots Masonic catechisms. Our purpose is to show how some parts of our ritual and practices may have evolved.

A lodge, at the time, was usually a large lean-to, built against the side of the cathedral or castle on which the masons were working. Many masons lived in the lodge, especially those whose families lived in distant towns. In the winter months, when building was impossible, the masons worked in the lodge, carving the stone which would later be added to the interior of the building. It was a combination meeting room, work room, administrative office and dormitory.

Those familiar with Lodge rooms today will notice certain differences. There is no altar, it has not yet evolved from a simple table, placed in front of the Master for his convenience. There is no Volume of Scared Law. The printing press had been invented about sixty years before the time of our lodge meeting, and the first press in England was set up some 20 years later, but very few printed books were available in Scotland at the time, and the hand-written copies of the Gospels were so very expensive that it is unlikely a Lodge would have had one. The prayers and ceremonies of the lodge are still based largely on Catholicism. Not for another 200 years would Masons open their Lodges to Brothers of all faiths.

Aprons were work garments and probably were not worn in lodge, unless a Brother were actually working at carving stone. Since coming into the lodge was, literally, a matter of coming home in the evening, it is reasonable to assume that they became as comfortable as possible. The apron may have started to take on a symbolic meaning—it seems to have done so early in the history of Masonry—but that symbolism probably did not yet extend to the wearing of aprons in Lodge.

Throughout its history, symbols have entered and left the Masonic system. Some have become more rich and complex over time, others have simplified. We have made suggestions of symbols in various stages of development.

Our purpose here is less to recreate history than to recreate an attitude, the feeling of these early Brothers who while trying to earn their daily bread and live a good life, were laying the foundations of the greatest fraternity the world has seen.

The Guild Lodge of St. Canice

When lights come up (if on stage or indoors) or when it is time to start (if staged outside) the Stewards enter, carrying platters of food and flagons of "wine" [see props notes].

They place them on the banker (bench) in the SE corner. Some Entered Apprentices drift in with them. There should be somewhere between 5 and 10 Entered Apprentices, although a smaller or larger number can be used depending of size of playing area, available cast, and available costumes.

The Warden enters, looks about and sees that preparations are going forward. He has a few words with one or both of the Stewards, then gets the attention of the Entered Apprentices.

WARDEN: Here, now, lads, there be time a-fore the Guild Master comes, and it's time we should be well using. *Pointing to the bankers in the N.E. corner.* Sit ye down on the banker here. Jeffery, Dongal, bring me the slate and trestle. Griswold, bring me the compasses, the square, the plumb, the level and the rod.

Jeffery and Dongal, two Apprentices, bring in a trestle and slate from the far N.E. corner [see props notes] and place them where the audience can see them There is a rag with the slate, which they also bring with them. Griswold goes to the corner and brings in the tools. Jeffery and Dongal X to their seats on the bench.

GRISWOLD: *handing them to the Warden* Be these what ye be wanting, Master?

WARDEN: Aye, lad, but handle them with respect! A Mason's nay more good than his tools.

GRISWOLD: *X to his seat* Aye, Master.

[At this point, members of the Guild start drifting in, one or two at a time. A total of five or six enter over the next three minutes. Some are carrying tools which they add to those in the NE corner. One had a chisel and sharpening stone, and sits on a banker (bench) on the South side to put an edge on the chisel. The Warden nods to some of them if they catch his eye, but he continues without interrupting his speech]

WARDEN: *holding up the rod* Now first of all, who remembers the name of this rod?

SEVERAL APPRENTICES TOGETHER: It's called an Ell, Master. It's a Ell-rod, Master. *(One Apprentice)* It's a Virga. Master.

WARDEN: And who was it who said it was a Virga?

AN APPRENTICE: I did, Master.

WARDEN: Lad, lad. ye must learn the names. This be an Ell or, as some do call it, an Ell-rod. The Virga Geometralis be nearly twice as long.

SAME APPRENTICE: I'll not forget, Master.

WARDEN: Now, pay close attention, lads, for this be one of the most important things for ye to learn. A Mason who canna' make his own tools, nor test them for trueness, is no Mason. Ye've been told that there are secrets known only to the Craft—and this do be one of the most important. Ye are not to reveal this to others, on your oaths. Do ye swear?

APPRENTICES: I swear. Aye, I swear, (etc.)

WARDEN: Then look ye. I mark a point. *marks point in center of slate with chalk (Drawing A)* And around that point, I scribe a circle. *Sets one point of compasses on dot, and scribes a circle with the "chalk leg" of the compasses (Drawing B)* Then, against one side, I draw a line. *draws line on right side of circle, using rod and chalk (Drawing C)* And I draw a parallel line on the other side. *draws line on left side (Drawing D)*

Now, here's the trick to remember the figure. *points to dot* "God is the center of all things." *points to circle* "Light to all about He brings." *swings finger around circle on the word "about," then indicates line on left side* "St. John Baptizer came before" *indicates line of right side* "The Evangelist did Christ adore." Now, say it together.

APPRENTICES: *as the Warden makes the same gestures as before*
"God is the center of all things
Light to all about He brings:
St. John Baptizer came before,
The Evangelist did Christ adore."

WARDEN: 'Tis good. Once again.

APPRENTICES: *a little faster*
"God is the center of all things
Light to all about He brings:
St. John Baptizer came before,
The Evangelist did Christ adore."

WARDEN: Good, good. Now watch ye again.

"The Evangelist shines with God's own glow" *(as he says these words, the Warden lines the rod up with the straight line on the right of the drawing. He then moves the rod to the center of the figure, so that the edge passes through to top, bottom, and point in the circle, and draws another line. With a rag, he erases the original right-hand line [Drawing E])*

"The Baptist, facing God, bows low" *(as he says these words, he draws one line from the point at which the Baptist's line intersects the circle to the top of the semicircle and another line from the point of intersection to the bottom of the semicircle and erases the original line. (Drawing F) SEE DRAWINGS IN NOTES AT END OF PLAY)*

Now, look ye here. *indicates the 90° angle thus formed* This be yer square, and this be how ye try a square. Whereso ye place a point on the half-circle and connect it with the ends, ye form a square. *He puts a point on the circumference and connects it with the top and bottom to illustrate* When ye need to make a square to test the work, mark it thus on the ground, and line the arms thus ere ye fasten them.

This is a secret of the guild, and nay to be shared without it, for the making of the tools is the proper knowing of the craftsman.

And there be more. Extend this line thus *uses the rod to draw a chalk line extension (see Drawing G)* and ye can make the level. *picks up wooden level and lays it on the line to illustrate* and the plumb *picks up wooden plumb and places it in the angle, so that the base rests on one line and the side rests on the other.*

And it be profit to ye to remember this. Build yer life as ye build yer tools. Act uprightly, be respectful to yer superiors, be patient and generous to them that work subordinate to ye. *tapping the dot in the circle* And remember that God do be in the center of all things.

Now, come hither and apply the tools and study the drawing.

The apprentices, chattering, pick up the tools, apply them, comment, etc. The Warden moves off to talk with the men who arrived earlier.

OPTION #1 - If a Piper is available

In the distance, we hear the sound of the Pipes, playing a medieval melody and approaching.

WARDEN: *Getting the attention of the Apprentices and men.* The Guild Master's coming, and the pipes are calling the Brothers to the meeting. *To the apprentices.* Take ye the tools, the trestle and slate back to the corner, and wipe the slate to make it ready.

They do so. The Brother who was sharpening the chisel stops his work, removes his apron, and places it, the chisel and the sharpening stone in the corner as well. Then all stand near the door to welcome the Guild Master.

OPTION #2 - If no Piper is available

Terence enters X to Warden, and says:

TERENCE: Brother Warden, his worship the Guild Master is coming.

WARDEN: *Getting the attention of the Apprentices and men.* The Guild Master's coming. *To the apprentices.* Take ye the tools, the trestle and slate back to the corner, and wipe the slate to make it ready.

They do so. The Brother who was sharpening the chisel stops his work, removes his apron, and places it, the chisel and the sharpening stone in the corner as well. Then all stand near the door to welcome the Guild Master.

The Guild Master enters (preceded by the Piper, if one is used) accompanied by Master Philip and Master Lukus. They go around the group greeting and speaking. As the Guild Master first greets each man they shake hands, each pressing the hollow between the thumb and first finger twice and then once as they do so, and covering the clasped hands with the left hand so that the process cannot be seen. When the Guild Master greets the apprentices, they do not shake hands. Instead, the apprentices stand as he approaches and each bows his head and then looks up as the Guild Master speaks to him.

At last the Guild Master goes to his seat in the East, and the Warden to his seat in the West. Terence takes a sword and retires to the post of the Tyler.

The Guild Master takes the small setting maul from the table in front of him and raps two or three times on the table for attention.

GUILD MASTER: Welcome Masters. Brother Warden, we shall allow the apprentices to remain. Be all others in this Lodge here as of right?

WARDEN: They be, your Worship.

GUILD MASTER: 'Tis well. Brother Lukus, ye be the eldest here. Invoke a blessing upon us. Let all be upstanding.

All rise

LUKUS: Holy Mary, Mother of God, be with us and ask yer Holy Son to bless our work. Holy St. Michael the Archangel be with us, guard us against all enemies, and give us victory in our struggles. In the Name of the Father, the Son and the Holy Ghost, Amen.

All cross themselves on "Father, Son and Holy Ghost"

ALL: So mote it be!

All sit

GUILD MASTER: {*if production is being done outdoors* - A pleasure 'tis, my Masters and Fellows, that the clement weather do allow us to meet thus out of doors. The Lodge do be a little hot this time of year.} First, I'd tell ye that the new stone for the carvings in the chancel be on its way to us. Next week should see it here, so, Master Philip, ye and yer 'prentices can make ready for the fine work.

PHILIP: Thank ye, yer Worship.

GUILD MASTER: And then, praise be, the corn, oil and wine for the quarter beginning on Lammas has already arrived. 'Tis rare that it be ahead of its time!

(Laughter and amusement on the part of all there, for such supplies were usually late)

Last, I spoke this morrow with Brother Langinus, the Disposer of the Work from the Cathedral. He be pleased with the rate of the building, and hath assured me we'll have adequate supply of straw when 'tis time to pack the cathedral walls for the winter. He's ordered extra, for they fear a winter as harsh as the last. And he's promised us extra wood for the fires in the Lodge.

(Murmuring about how cold it was last winter and expressions of approval of the extra straw and wood.)

GUILD MASTER: Brother Warden, hath any made complaint against another to ye that we should consider?

WARDEN: Nay, yer Worship. I've heard naught of discord at all.

GUILD MASTER: And I have heard none from the Cathedral. Do ye have the monies to pay the Masters and workmen when we leave?

WARDEN: Aye, Guild Master, and I have the accounting ready when it shall please ye to hear it.

(Meanwhile, Master Denni and his apprentice, Colin, have been approaching. They reach the door about this point. Master Denni speaks to Terence. If there is a door, Terence

knocks loudly on it four or five times, and Harol (the Junior Steward) comes to the door and opens it, sees who it is, and retires to his place. If there is no door convenient, Terence leads them into the playing area.)

GUILD MASTER: God give ye good den, Master Denni. Be this the young man of whom ye spoke to me?

DENNI: Good den to ye, yer Worship. Aye, this be Colin, who thinks he would become a Mason.

GUILD MASTER: Good den to ye, Colin.

Colin, awestruck, bows his head but does not answer.

GUILD MASTER: Methinks he be a likely lad. Master Denni, as ye ken, if that the guild ratify him as 'prentice, both ye and he must certain assurances give. Do ye wish that I proceed?

MASTER DENNI: I do, Guild Master.

GUILD MASTER: I invite ye, then, to join me here. Colin, stand ye there by the Warden.

(Colin moves to stand by the Warden. He is obviously very nervous. Master Denni X to in front of Guild Master. Be sure to stand open--face the audience and only turn slightly toward the Guild Master.)

GUILD MASTER: Brother Philip, will ye propound the interrogatories?

MASTER PHILIP: Aye, yer Worship. *He moves to the East also, so that he and Denni are standing fairly close to each other. Both are facing the audience so the audience can see. Philip picks up the crucifix from the table in front of the Guild Master and holds it out to Denni. Denni places his hand upon it.*

MASTER PHILIP: Master Denni, do ye certify to us that Colin be a free man, neither a bondsman nor a serf, so that he may legally become yer apprentice of his own free will?

MASTER DENNI: Aye, I do.

MASTER PHILIP: Do ye certify that, so long as this Colin be an apprentice and not a fellow, ye shall pay him from yer own purse, and not pass those charges to the Lodge nor yet to the Cathedral?

MASTER DENNI: I do.

MASTER PHILIP: Hath Colin a mind retentive, so that he be able to remember that which ye teach him?

MASTER DENNI: Aye, He hath.

MASTER PHILIP: That being so, do ye certify to us that ye will teach him fairly and fully, so that, when he do leave ye, he may fairly earn a good wage to his credit and to the craft's?

MASTER DENNI: I do.

MASTER PHILIP: Finally, and to that end, do ye certify that ye will take special care that he be fully instructed in Geometry, for that be a sacred science, and much needful to the Mason?

MASTER DENNI: I do so certify to this and all.

Denni kisses the crucifix and replaces it on the table, then he and Philip X to the sides of the room. The Guild Master addresses Colin, who looks up at him.

GUILD MASTER: Colin, ye have heard the assurances of Master Denni. Now, ye must by tested yerself. Brother Warden, ascertain if Colin be acceptable as an apprentice.

WARDEN: Aye, yer Worship. Colin, the oldest rule of Masons be that no man may be made an apprentice without he be strong and sound of body. For the work of a Mason be hard, it requireth the quarrying, carving, carrying, and setting of stone. That all here may be assured that ye be sound and whole of body, remove yer tunic and footgear, and, clad in yer clouth *[pronounced "clout"]* walk ye slowly about the craft and return here to me.

Colin removes his tunic and footgear—see costume notes—and walks slowly once about the room. His arms are by his sides, but held a little away from the body so that it can be seen that his arms are strong and not withered or deformed. As he passes the Guild Master, the Guild Master stops him.

GUILD MASTER: Colin, carry this cross with ye to the Warden.

The Guild Master gives the crucifix to Colin, who continues his circumambulation. In the West, he gives the crucifix to the Warden who holds it out to him. Colin places his hand upon it.

WARDEN: *To the group* Do any here question that Colin is strong and able to do the work of a Mason? *none answer* Now Colin, listen well and answer what I ask ye. Do ye swear to live in the house of Master Denni for 7 years, serving him faithfully and learning from him duly?

COLIN: *very softly* I do, Master.

WARDEN: *not unkindly* Speak louder, Colin, for all must hear ye.

COLIN: I do, Master.

WARDEN: Do ye also swear to us that ye be a free man, and under obligation to none?

COLIN: I do, Master.

WARDEN: Do ye swear that ye be not a thief?

COLIN: Aye, Master.

WARDEN: That ye have killed no man?

COLIN: I do, Master.

WARDEN: That ye have a good name, and have done naught to bring shame upon yerself or yer family?

COLIN: I do, Master.

WARDEN: Do ye love God and the Holy Church?

COLIN: I do, Master, with all my heart. *He kisses the crucifix, the Warden places it on the table in front of him.*

WARDEN: *to Guild Master* Yer Worship, ye and the Brothers have heard. Be ye satisfied?

GUILD MASTER: Masters and Fellows, ye have heard what Colin hath deposed. If any have further question or be not satisfied, speak now.

He looks around the room. Members are nodding in agreement, etc. The apprentices are being very careful not to move or appear to be trying to express an opinion.

GUILD MASTER: Masters, attend me.

The Warden, Master Philip, Master Lukus and Master Denni X to the East and confer briefly with the Guild Master. They then return to their positions.

GUILD MASTER: Colin, the Masters be content that ye be entered as an apprentice among us. Reclothe yerself, then go with Master Lukus and Master Denni to the preparation room, and learn what they teach ye, then come ye back to us.

MASTER LUKUS: Jeffery and Griswold, bring me the slate and trestle.

Lukus, Denni and Colin move to the space representing the preparation room where Colin puts on his tunic and footwear. Depending on the circumstances, this may be an area to the NW of the Warden, but it should be an area in which they can clearly be seen and heard. Jeffery and Griswold bring the slate and easel, chalk and rag to them, and then return to assist in the lodge room itself. While the following dialogue takes place in the "preparation room," the fellow crafts and apprentices prepare the lodge for a banquet. The table will be set in the middle of the room, running "East," and "West." Two saw-horse type trestles are set up, then planks are set on them to make a table about 3 feet wide and eight feet long. A white table cloth is spread over the planks and the bankers are brought forward to serve as seats at the table. The Guild Master's chair is placed at the East end and the Warden's chair is placed at the West end. Flagons are set on the table at each place. A large punch bowl is set on the table near the Warden's end. The Stewards, who have supervision of the process, pour the ingredients of a punch into the bowl and mix it. Platters containing slabs of cheese and baskets containing loaves of unsliced french bread are also placed on the table. Baskets or bowls of nuts are also provided. When all is ready, the Stewards, using ladles, place some punch in each flagon. All this will need to happen quickly and quietly. It will take a lot of rehearsal to make this go well. Meanwhile, the following takes place in the "preparation room."

LUKUS: Colin, listen well. *To Denni* Be ye a mason?

DENNI: Aye.

LUKUS: How shall I know that?

DENNI: By signs, tokens, and points of my entry.

LUKUS: What be the first point?

DENNI: Ye tell the first point, I'll tell ye the second.

LUKUS: The first do be to heill and conceal that which should be known only to masons.

DENNI: The second be the sign of my obligation.

LUKUS: Where be it ye was entered?

DENNI: At the honorable lodge.

LUKUS: What makes a true and perfect lodge?

DENNI: Seven masters, five entered apprentices, a day's journey from a burroughs town, withouten bark of dog or crow of cock.

LUKUS: Do nay fewer make a true and perfect lodge?

DENNI: Five masons and three entered apprentices.

LUKUS: Do nay fewer?

DENNI: The more the merrier, the fewer the better cheer.

LUKUS: What be the name of yer lodge?

DENNI: The Guild Lodge of St. Canice.

LUKUS: Who were St. Canice?

DENNI: The holy saint did come to Scotland in the year of Grace 565, where he did spread the word of God, and built kirks and monasteries at Inchkenneth and St. Andrews; wherefore that he be a great builder, Scots masons do hold him in high repute.

LUKUS: How stands your lodge?

DENNI: East and west as the temple of Jerusalem.

LUKUS: Where were the first lodge?

DENNI: In the porch of Solomon's Temple.

LUKUS: Be there any lights in yer lodge?

DENNI: Aye, three. Ane in the north-east, ane in the south west, and ane in the eastern passage. The first do denote the master, the second do denote the warden, and the third do denote the craft.

LUKUS: What be the key to your lodge?

DENNI: A well-hinged tongue.

LUKUS: Where lies that key?

DENNI: *tapping his teeth* In a bone box.

LUKUS: Now Colin, ye must get these questions and answers by heart, for if ye do visit another lodge, it is thus they will ask to find if ye be truly entered as an apprentice.

DENNI: I'll help ye to learn.

LUKUS: Colin, ye know that in the kirk there be the pictures in the colored glass, which tell the stories of the saints and the life of Christ. And ye know that we carve those into the stone, and other pictures as well. Those images or symbols be for the teaching of those who enter the church. But there do be some as have a special use for masons, and even some we carve into the stone to decorate the work, though their special meanings be known to us alone.

(If it happens that Denni draws better than Lukus, Denni can do the actual drawing. If neither draw well, but one of the apprentices does, Lukus can call out to him and have him come to do the drawing. Note that if more space on the slate is needed, Lukus can erase earlier drawings with the rag, but some should be left for Colin to erase at the end.)

LUKUS: *(drawing a checkered pavement about three or four squares by three or four squares—Drawing S-1)* Ye've seen the checkered floor of the nave of the church here, and ye'll see it in many churches. But we're told it first was used on the ground floor of the Temple built by Solomon. It will teach ye many things. Look ye, to walk across this pave is like unto walking through yer life. For certain 'tis ye will find joy and sorrow, and mayhap good and evil. But the good St. Augustine hath told us that be but illusion, and that just like the pave be all of a piece, so be yer life.

(drawing a pot of burning incense, Drawing S-2) And this be a thurible [THUR-a-bell], like that incense burner the priest does use to incense the altar. Ye know the sweet scent of the smoke and that it is pleasing to God. But think ye, Colin. There do be two elements which be represented here. For, as ye know, the thurible contains charcoal which burns with a fierce heat, and the thurifer [THUR-e-fur] casts incense upon the charcoal, so that it burns and sends aloft the smoke. Ye must have both, for without the charcoal, the incense cannot burn, and without the incense, the charcoal hath nay the smoke. The charcoal should teach ye that in all things ye should be as determined and hot as the charcoal, and it will need that, if ye are to learn all ye must as an apprentice. And the incense should teach ye that everything ye do is seen by God and is an offering to God. See that ye offer Him only yer best!

(holding up the piece of chalk he is using—or taking it from the person drawing if Lukus himself is not doing so, and then returning it) And think ye about the chalk itself. See how easily it makes a mark. Be ye that willing to make yer mark upon the world and the lives of others, for ye know not what good ye may do in the world. So leave no chance to be of service untaken.

(drawing a scallop shell, Drawing S-3) This be a sea shell, of the kind called a skal-LOP. It's the special symbol of one who has gone on pilgrimage to the Holy Land, and ye've seen it carven often into the columns of

the church. Let it remind ye that yer life is a pilgrimage as well.

Now this be a special symbol I'm about to show ye, Colin. I've nay doubt ye've heard the old gaffers and gammers, telling tales by the fireside. And ye've heard, of how, in times long past, the villagers did kill a man, when 'twas time to harvest the grain, and hang him in the field, so that his death would bring new life to the earth. Have ye heard the stories?

COLIN: Aye, Master Lukus.

LUKUS: And then, when the word of God was preached among them, they did change the custom, so that they took the first sheaf of whatever corn they grew there, and did tie and twist the sheaf to represent the figure of a man, *(does drawing S-4 as he talks)* and did suspend that same figure by a leg from a tree or pole in the field, and so it is in our villages to this day. Had ye heard that, Colin?

COLIN: Aye, master.

LUKUS: Now in different places, Colin, they do grow different corns. The corn grown in these parts is mostly oats. I dare swear ye et a porridge of oats when ye broke yer fast this morning.

COLIN: I did, Master Lukus.

LUKUS: The oats be important, Colin. The grain keeps us fed, and ye know that, every winter, we stack the oat straw deep against the sides of the walls newly built, so that the mortar will not freeze too hard and weaken.

So the corn do bring us life and strength. And the figure made of the corn *(taps drawing)* and thus suspended, be a symbol of that life and strength, but held in suspension, outside of time, ye might say, waiting to change and grow—just like the seed grain in the field must spend a time in waiting ere it grows into a new plant.

Ye be like that, Colin, for ye are leaving yer nonage and preparing to enter life as a true man. Do ye understand?

COLIN: I'm——I'm not sure, Master Lukus.

LUKUS: *laughing good naturedly* Well, there be time to learn and understand, Colin. And faith, not everybody does. Take the cloth and clean the slate *Colin does so*. As I've said, ye must learn these as best ye can, but Master Denni and I both will be glad to teach ye. Return we now to the Guild Master.

They return to the lodge room. Walking around the table, the Warden and Denni go with Colin to the West. The Guild Master stands as they approach. He hands an apron to Colin.

GUILD MASTER: Colin, take from me this leather apron, the symbol of yer apprenticeship. In the course of yer work, this apron, in protecting ye, will take stains upon itself. See that ye keep yer own life free of stain, and protect the guild as the apron does protect ye.

One thing more ye now must learn, and that be the word of an apprentice, with which ye can prove to others that ye be entered upon the rolls of the guild as of right. Lean here, that I may give it to ye.

Colin and the Guild Master embrace. The Guild Master seems to whisper in Colin's ear, and then Colin whispers back in the Guild Master's ear.

GUILD MASTER: 'tis well! Come and join us at the festive board, Colin, and learn from us all. *All move to the table to sit, the apprentices, with Colin, sit in the northwest.*

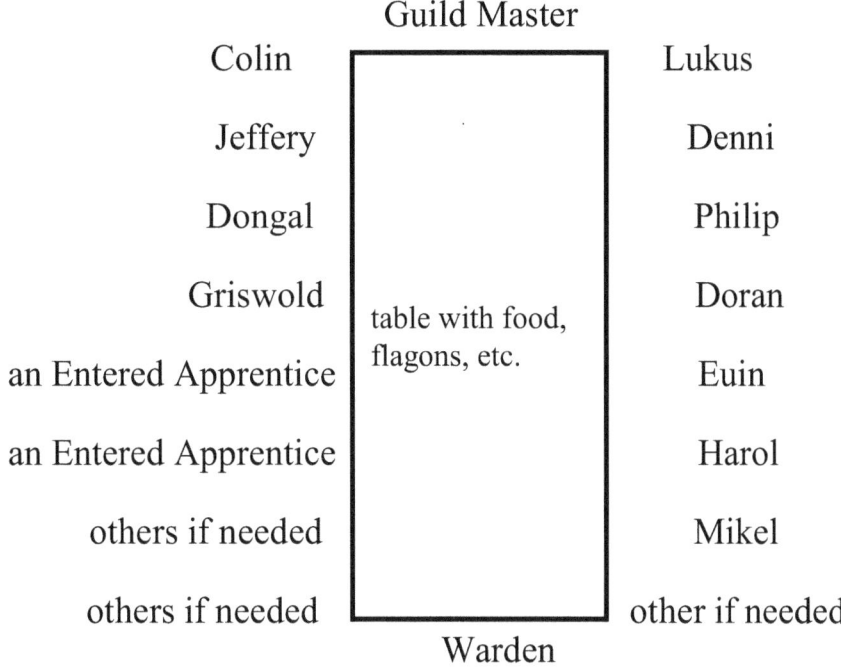

GUILD MASTER: Brother Doran *(or, if the musician is played by a Brother who already has another character name, use that name)* give us a song to lighten the heart.

Brother Doran, who plays the guitar (assuming that no Brother can be found who plays a lute) plays the following. NOTE: that if someone who has a speaking part if also the musician, the Guild Master uses that character name rather than saying "Brother Dorian." He plays and sings the first stanza solo, and then the Cast joins in singing, or the soloist can sing the whole thing by himself. Note that if a guitarist cannot be found but a piper can, it can be played on the pipes. If desired, the lyrics can be printed and handed out to the audience so they can join in singing.

The 7 Laws of Masonry

The first true law that Masons hold, it be the law of One:
To crave the blessings of the Lord, e're any task's begun.
E're any task's begun, my Brothers, and faithful may we be.
    Praise Father, Son and Holy Ghost to all eternity.

The next true law that Masons hold, it be the law of Two:
To come we at the Master's call when there be work to do.
When there be work to do, my Brothers, and faithful may we be.
    Praise Father, Son and Holy Ghost to all eternity.

The next true law that Masons hold, it be the law of Three:
To aid a Brother and his clan with love and charity.
With love and charity, my Brothers, and faithful may we be.
    Praise Father, Son and Holy Ghost to all eternity.

The next true law that Masons hold, it be the law of Four
The secrets of our craft to keep within the lodge's door.
Within the lodge's door, my Brothers, and faithful may we be.
    Praise Father, Son and Holy Ghost to all eternity.

The next true law that Masons hold, it be the law of Five:
To cheat nay brother nor nay lodge, if we would hope to thrive.
If we would hope to thrive, my Brothers, and faithful may we be.
    Praise Father, Son and Holy Ghost to all eternity.

The next true law that Masons hold, it be the law of Six:
A Brother warn if danger come through man or Satan's tricks.
Through man or Satan's tricks, my Brothers, and faithful may we be.
    Praise Father, Son and Holy Ghost to all eternity.

The last true law that Masons hold, it be the law of Sev'n: To keep a tongue of good report before both earth and heav'n.
Before both earth and heav'n, my Brothers, and faithful may we be
    Praise Father, Son and Holy Ghost to all eternity.

GUILD MASTER: 'Tis of good cheer, Brother Doran. Now Colin, the custom be that I will ask questions, and the brothers here will answer them. This be done for thy instruction, so attend well.

The Guild Master will ask the questions, starting with Brother Lukus and going around the table. The tradition was that each Brother arose when addressed and remained standing as he answered the question. If a Brother did not know the answer, he would arise, bow to the Master, and sit down again.

GUILD MASTER: Master Lukus, *(Lukus arises)* as Masons, we be charged by our tenure to certain things. What be the first of these?

LUKUS: We be charged to obey the Moral Law, Guild Master, to be true Children of the Church, to be good men and true, and of honor and integrity. *(sits)*

GUILD MASTER: Well said, Master Lukus. Master Denni *(Denni arises)* How stands a Mason in regard to the Prince?

DENNI: Guild Master, A Mason be a peaceable subject to the crown, wheresoever he be, and be never concerned in plots and conspiracies against the king's peace. *(sits)*

GUILD MASTER: 'Tis true, Master Denni. Master Philip *(Philip arises)* Ye had heard Master Denni. If, then, a Mason is to be a peaceable citizen, what do we do if a Mason be a rebel?

Master Philip starts to speak, then looks uncertain, bows to the Guild Master, and sits.

GUILD MASTER: Brother Doran?

DORAN: *(arises and bows to Guild Master)* Guild Master, His rebellion itself is not to be countenanced, and the Lodge hath no part in it. But the Brother, if he be convinced of no other crime, is to be pitied as an unhappy man and the Brethren cannot expel him from the Lodge, for his relationship to the Lodge remains indefeasible, which is to say that his relationship to the Lodge cannot be voided, terminated, nor undone. *(sits)*

GUILD MASTER: Ye say truly, Brother Doran. Brother Warden, lead us in a toast to Brotherhood.

all rise

WARDEN: Brother Stewards, supply any who be in want. *The Stewards ladle punch into any empty flagons* Brothers, I give ye Brotherhood—stronger than iron, more lasting than stone.

ALL: Brotherhood—stronger than iron, more lasting than stone!

they drink and are seated

GUILD MASTER: Brother Euin *(Euin arises)* How stands a Mason in regard to his Lodge?

EUIN: Nay man may be 'prenticed, Guild Master, without he be a good man and true, of discreet age, nor yet a bondsman, nor an immoral or scandalous man, but of good report. No Master nor Fellow may be absent from Lodge, especially when warned to appear, withouten good reason which he shall disclose to the Warden or Guild Master. *(sits)*

GUILD MASTER: Ye say well, Brother Euin. Brother Harol *(Harol arises and bows to Guild Master)* How do the Guild Master be selected?

HAROL: All preferment among Masons is grounded upon real worth and personal merit only, Guild Master, so that the Lords may be well served, the Brethren not put to shame, nor the Royal Craft despised. Therefore, nay Guild Master nor nay Warden be chosen by seniority, but for his merit. It was thus we chose ye, Guild Master.

Vocal agreements from the Masters and Fellows at the table. Harol sits.

GUILD MASTER: Thank ye, Brethren. Brother Mikel *(Mikel arises)* Tell Colin some of the laws and customs under which we labor.

MIKEL: All Masons shall work honestly on working days, Guild Master, that they may live creditably on Holy Days. Craftsmen are to avoid all ill language and call each other by no disobliging name, but to call each other "Brother" or "Fellow" and act courteously within and without the Lodge. *(he sits)*

GUILD MASTER: True do ye speak, Brother Mikel. Brother Warden, propose a toast to the Craft.

WARDEN: Brother Stewards, see that no one is in want. *All stand. The Stewards ladle punch as needed. Then the Warden says:*

WARDEN: Brothers, I give ye the Craft—builders in stone, brothers in blood.

ALL: The Craft—builders in stone, brothers in blood. *all drink and sit*

GUILD MASTER: Brother Philip, *(Philip arises)* How be Masons to act in Lodge?

PHILIP: We may enjoy ourselves with innocent mirth, Guild Master, but we do be charged to avoid all excesses. We be forbid to force any Brother to eat or drink beyond his inclination, or to say aught offensive, or that may forbid an easy and free conversation, for that would blast our harmony and defeat our useful purpose. And especially are we forbid to bring private piques or quarrels within the door of the Lodge. Nor may we hinder a Brother from going when his occasions call him. *(sits)*

GUILD MASTER: Aye, Master Philip, and that last is a good remembrancer. Masters, fellows and apprentices, the hour grows late and morn will come early enough. We should give some thought to rest. Brother Doran, give us a song to end upon.

As before, Doran or the actor playing the music either sings the following himself or leads the cast or cast and audience in singing.

DORAN:

And Therefore Be Merry

We've met in our counsels to learn and to build,
From first-stone to spire by the craft of our guild.
We've feasted and fested and shared in good cheer,
And brotherhood glows in the hearts of those here.
    And therefore be merry, set sorrow aside,
    For Masons be brothers, what ever betide.

As this stanza begins, the cast starts to leave, leaving Doran alone on stage. Doran repeats the chorus, if necessary, to give time for them to exit.

Now Masters and Fellows, Apprentices, too;
The walls want a-building, there's work we must do.
With trowel and with mortar, with rod and with plumb
Build we to God's glory 'till all hath been done.
    And therefore be merry, set sorrow aside;
    For Masons be brothers, what ever betide.

As journey ye forth to yer home or yer cot,
Keep ye in yer heart that which here ye have got.
Ye best here can work who can best here agree,
Go forth with the blessings of brothers on ye.

And therefore be merry, set sorrow aside;
For Masons be brothers, what ever betide.

If an actual stage is being used, Doran should finish in a spot light on an otherwise dark stage. If not, he should be alone by the end. He bows to the audience, and exits. In the (no doubt) thunderous applause which follows, the cast come very quickly on stage (or into the room, etc., drop a group bow, and then exit.

FINIS

THE END

THAT'S ALL WE WROTE

SCORES
DRAWINGS
PROP NOTES
COSTUME NOTES
PRODUCTION NOTES

The 7 Laws that Masons Hold

[Musical notation with lyrics: "The first true law that Masons hold, it be the law of One to crave the blessings of the Lord e're any task's begun. E're any task's begun my Brothers and faithful may we be. Praise Father, Son and Holy Ghost to all eternity."]

The first true law that Masons hold, it be the law of One:
To crave the blessings of the Lord, e're any task's begun.
E're any task's begun, my Brothers, and faithful may we be.
    Praise Father, Son and Holy Ghost to all eternity.

The next true law that Masons hold, it be the law of Two:
To come we at the Master's call when there be work to do.
When there be work to do, my Brothers, and faithful may we be.
    Praise Father, Son and Holy Ghost to all eternity.

The next true law that Masons hold, it be the law of Three:
To aid a Brother and his clan with love and charity.
With love and charity, my Brothers, and faithful may we be.
    Praise Father, Son and Holy Ghost to all eternity.

The next true law that Masons hold, it be the law of Four
The secrets of our craft to keep within the lodge's door.
Within the lodge's door, my Brothers, and faithful may we be.
    Praise Father, Son and Holy Ghost to all eternity.

The next true law that Masons hold, it be the law of Five:
To cheat nay brother nor nay lodge, if we would hope to thrive.
If we would hope to thrive, my Brothers, and faithful may we be.
    Praise Father, Son and Holy Ghost to all eternity.

The next true law that Masons hold, it be the law of Six:
A Brother warn if danger come through man or Satan's tricks.
Through man or Satan's tricks, my Brothers, and faithful may we be.
    Praise Father, Son and Holy Ghost to all eternity.

The last true law that Masons hold, it be the law of Sev'n:
To keep a tongue of good report before both earth and heav'n.
Before both earth and heav'n, my Brothers, and faithful may we be
    Praise Father, Son and Holy Ghost to all eternity.

And Therefore be Merry

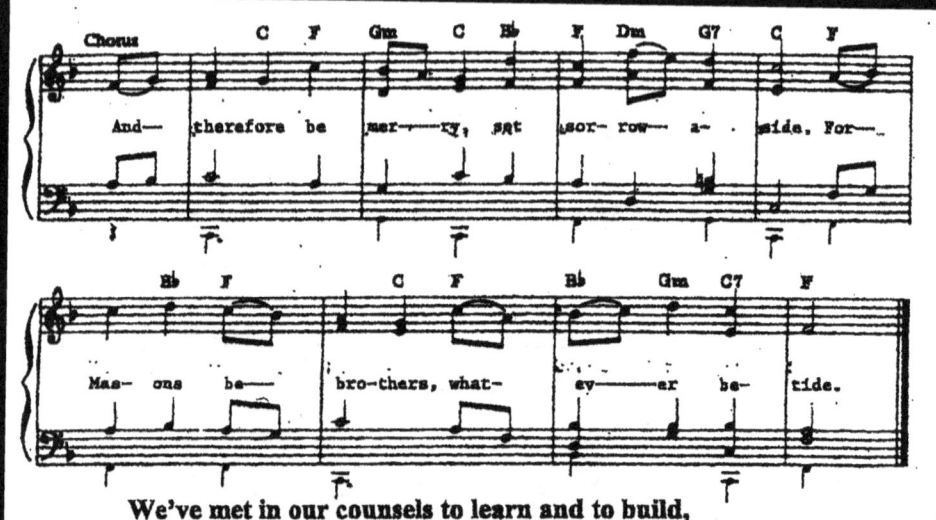

We've met in our counsels to learn and to build,
From first-stone to spire by the craft of our guild.
We've feasted and fested and shared in good cheer,
And brotherhood glows in the hearts of those here.
    And therefore be merry, set sorrow aside,
    For Masons be brothers, what ever betide.

Now Masters and Fellows, Apprentices, too;
The walls want a-building, there's work we must do.
With trowel and with mortar, with rod and with plumb
Build we to God's glory 'till all hath been done.
    And therefore be merry, set sorrow aside;
    For Masons be brothers, what ever may betide.

As journey ye forth to yer home or yer cot,
Keep ye in yer heart that which here ye have got.
Ye best here can work who can best here agree,
Go forth with the blessings of brothers on ye.
    And therefore be merry, set sorrow aside;
    For Masons be brothers, what ever may betide.

HAND PROPS LIST

Platter(s) with slabs of cheese
Baskets with loaves of french bread (unsliced)
1 flagon or tankard per cast member (see notes)
1 dagger for each cast member
Bowls or baskets of nuts
Large punch bowl (see notes)
Ladle for punch bowl
Bottles or jugs of "ale" or "wine"
Platters to carry food, bottles, etc. (see notes)
Slate (see notes)
Trestle to hold slate (see notes)
Chalk (see notes)
Rag
Compasses (see notes)
Square (see notes)
Plumb (see notes)
Level (see notes)
Ell-rod (see notes)
Chisel
Hand-held sharpening stone
Apron, leather, stained with work
Apron, leather, new
Crucifix (see notes)
Small setting maul type gavel
Sword for Tyler
White table cloth
Guitar or Lute (optional) (see notes)

SET PROPS LIST

Bankers (benches - see notes)
Table trestles (see notes)
Planks to form table top (see notes)
Chair for Guild Master (see notes)
Chair for Warden (see notes)
Small tables (2) one in front of Guild Master and one in front of   Warden
Torches (optional - see notes)

PRODUCTION NOTES
Drawings
Progression of the lines & circle

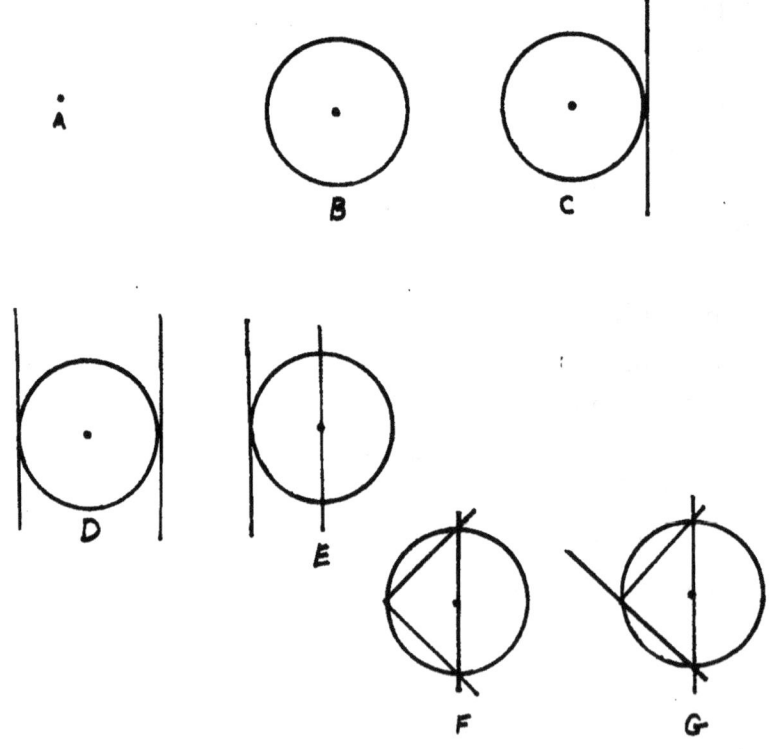

Symbols

S-1

S-2

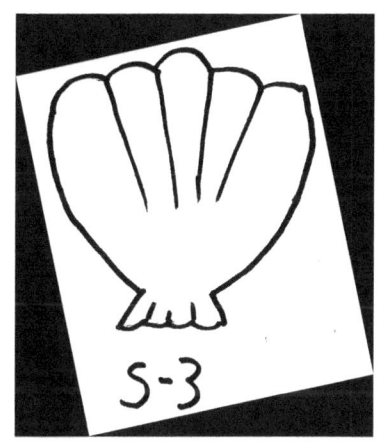

S-3

S-4

Where All This Came From

This whole thing started because M∴W∴ Jim Savaloja, PGM of North Dakota, asked for it. Those who think it should never have happened are invited to blame him.

Although no claim is made for historicity (it's a play, not a lecture) it is not impossible that lodges, in the transition from operative to speculative, might have been something like this.

The questions and responses in the preparation room were adapted from the Edinburgh Manuscript, while the "Ancient Charges" formed the basis for the questions at the table. Material from the Regius Poem is scattered throughout.

For a good description of the clothing and other matters relevant to the play, see "Our Predecessors: The Mediæval Masons of The Regius Manuscript," Inaugural Address by Bro. A.C.F. Jackson in Volume 89 of the *Transactions of Quator Coronati Lodge*.

The tune used for The Seven Laws That Masons Hold is the medieval carol "The Seven Joys of Mary." The song And Therefore be Merry is sung to a carol tune by the same name but with different words.

Birdseed

I'm writing this in my favorite place on earth. More than 70 years ago, my Grandfather bought some land on the side of a mountain in Chipita Park, Colorado, not far from Pike's Peak, and had a cottage built here. A few years later, an itinerant artist was in the park, sketching the cottages, and Grandad bought this sketch from him. I have been here nearly every summer since I was born, and many of my richest and most prized memories center on this place.

Today, I've spent a large portion of a beautiful morning watching the birds and squirrels at an old steel pie plate, nailed to a post at the corner of the porch and filled with mixed birdseed. I've also been putting out some dried corn for the chipmunks, and a few minutes ago one climbed up on the bench on which I am sitting and sat for a while on one of my hands, while eating out of the other. There is something deeply humbling and strangely spiritual in that. Something so small and frail trusting something hundreds of times his size. I forgave his ancestors for stealing my baby bottle when I was a toddler (as I was assured by my mother and grandmother when it disappeared).

The birds are an endless source of fascination. The most numerous are the Steller's Jays, large blue and grey and black and white raucous birds which try to drive the others off, without success. They have loud, demanding voices like people who are always looking for something about which to be offended. Often, when they are not looking, a very small mountain wren pops into the pie pan and eats some of the smaller seeds. And every now and again we are visited by a magpie, a large beautiful black and white bird which is magnificent in flight, but whose landings could benefit from a little practice. It heads at the pan and drops into it like a brick (when it doesn't miss it completely). There are others, but those form the majority.

I have been thinking about yesterday.

Yesterday was one of those remarkable days which come along too seldom in a lifetime. I was sitting on the porch with some of my favorite people, and some I have only recently come to know. There was Jimmy Dean Hartzell. He's been a good friend for decades, is powerfully spiritually intuitive, and delivers the best winding stair or middle chamber lecture I have ever heard. Something literally magical happens in the Lodge when he does it. There were Brothers Clay Comer and Tim Driskell, two of the most genuinely good men I know. Jimmy, Clay and Tim had come with me from Oklahoma. There was Brother Kevin Barlow, good friend of many years and, like Jimmy, an electrician by trade. (Thinking about it, I seem to have an inordinate number of electricians as good friends—one wonders if that means anything.)

Then, from Colorado, there were Brother Cliff Porter, who wrote the Foreword to this book, and who, having kindly read and proofed it, suggested the need for a final retrospective, which is why this is being written. He is one of the most important voices in tomorrow's leadership of Freemasonry, one of the creators of thesanctumsanctorum.com the fastest-growing Masonic website, and also therelevantmason.blogspot.com where he

But J Digress...

posts his own edgy and exciting material. He had brought with him a bottle of remarkably good hand-crafted whiskey. There was Brother Timothy Hogan, the only practicing alchemist I know, who gives remarkable lecture-demonstrations of the art and whose books I hope you have read. And Brother Walt Stewart, who as a very young artist had been the friend and illustrator for the author Manly P. Hall, and who has painted some remarkable trestleboards for Cliff's Lodge.

It was an amazing gathering of ideas and talent. Missing in person, but with us in spirit, was Brother Robert G. Davis (Grand Cross, General Secretary of the Guthrie Scottish Rite Bodies, and a man who has done a vast amount of good for the Scottish Rite, not just in Oklahoma but in the United States). And I spent the day, discussing Freemasonry, with a well-drawing pipe, a most agreeable drink, the birds and chipmunks, and as a special treat, a brief afternoon thunderstorm with the thunder echoing between the mountains. Surely I am unlikely ever again to have so rich, rewarding and complete an experience.

A digression: there is a story of a young married couple who had invited both families to their home for Easter Sunday dinner. It amounted to a good-sized group, and the young couple were, like most, fairly impecunious. And thus it was that the young wife decided to make a ham loaf rather than purchasing and baking a ham large enough to feed the group. But she was determined to make a good impression. She researched recipes, found one which seemed the best, and worked for days to make a ham loaf so good that everyone would enjoy it. Shortly before dinner, the husband came into the kitchen to find his wife in tears. Doing his best to calm her, he asked what the problem was. Sobbing on his shoulder she said, "I've worked so hard, and I wanted it to be so good, and I just tasted it. I made Spam!"

I empathize. When Cliff suggested that I should write a kind of summary of what I think Freemasonry is, I realized that after nearly fifty years of thinking about Masonry, talking about Masonry, and writing about Masonry, I've probably made spam. But for better or worse, here we go. You might try adding a little horseradish sauce.

Which brings me back to the birdseed.

I'm convinced that, like the mixed birdseed, Freemasonry is not one thing, but rather many different things. The jays wanted one kind of seed, the wren another, the magpie a third, and the chipmunks wanted dry corn. And they all found it. And I have known Brethren like those birds. Some, like the jays, try to boss the whole thing, proclaiming loudly that they are both in the right and in command. Some are like the wrens, quietly coming in and enjoying the seed they want, and trying not to start any fights. And some are like the magpies, plopping their capacious bottoms in the pan (when they don't miss) and scattering seed on the ground, getting what they want, even if it means other birds have to work harder or even go without.

What is Freemasonry? If you know how to look, it is whatever you want to find (see what I mean about a spam-like cliché?).

For some Brothers, it is a way to structure some time; a place for farmers, retirees, and others without a clock-determined schedule to gather in the mornings, drink coffee, eat day-old doughnuts, play dominoes, and complain about the weather. That is what they want, and that is what they find, and that meets their needs. And power to them. For the most part, they are the ones who pay dues year after year, find the extra money when the Lodge needs repairs, and often teach the lectures to new members. Without them, there would have been no Lodge to join when it was time for me to receive the Degrees. Their ancestors are the ones who quietly kept the Fraternity alive during the anti-Masonic movement. I am honored to count some of them among my Masonic friends.

For some Brothers, Masonry is all about the ritual. They truly love it, some for the beauty of the language, some for the truths it conveys, and some because of a pride in the ability to memorize it and repeat it accurately. Without them, the ritual would have been lost long ago. And yes, it has been known to get a little out of balance. Some have been known to insist that there is nothing in Freemasonry except the ritual, confusing the path with the destination. Some are so focused on saying the right words that they literally do not know the meanings of some of the words they are saying. (My friend, Tim Heaton, spent months trying to find out what a "cladsteen" Mason was, after promising he would not hold Masonic conversation with one. It was only when he heard the Degree in another Lodge that he found the word was "clandestine.") But there are many—Jimmy Dean is an example—who understand that the ritual is a powerful tool of transformation. That it can somehow cut across time and space, and directly and permanently change men. I've seem him do it, and I have talked to Masons who have told me that their lives changed when they took the Degrees. I've had wives tell me that Masonry changed their husbands and made them better men. And I agree with my friend Richard Fletcher, P∴G∴M∴ of Vermont and Executive Director of the Masonic Service Association of North America, who says that no man ever arose from a Masonic altar the same man he was when he knelt there.

For some men, Freemasonry is a civic club—not surprising when you remember that almost all the civic clubs were started by Freemasons. They value it because of the good it can do in the community. They are deeply involved in the Masonic charities. It is hard to argue with them, considering all the needs in society. Various Masonic organizations help children with orthopaedic problems, screen school children to identify vision problems and prevent blindness, help children with learning disabilities to learn and teach children with dyslexia how to read, fund research into diseases, and provide help for individuals, along with much, much more. And even those of us who believe that charity is an *expression* of Masonry, rather than the *purpose* of Masonry, cannot help but applaud what they accomplish.

Some, admittedly, join because they think it will help them get ahead in business or in social life. They are the only ones who will not find what they seek.

But some join because they feel it will help "knock off some of the rough edges" and help them be more at ease and skillful in various social situations. I have known men who joined for that reason, and since their real purpose was self-improvement, they have found what they sought.

Some Brothers join Masonry because they want to be closer to their fathers and grandfathers, even if those men are dead. They are seeking a connection with their past, and generally they find it.

Some join because they want to make friends with men they respect. They want to make friends with men who believe in standards. They understand that friendships take time to build and that there is a profound difference between friends and acquaintances.

Some join because they know they are a "work in progress" rather than a finished piece. That is becoming rare in the world. So many people feel like they are already everything they are going to be, and that what they are is the "fault" of fate, or environment or genetics, or the position of the stars, or powerful others of some sort. The real Mason takes responsibility for his life, and realizes that he is not yet everything he could or should be. He sees growth and development as a life-long process, not something that stopped when he graduated from high school, or college, or married, or joined the military. He seeks to grow morally, ethically, and spiritually, and he sees that Freemasonry can facilitate that growth. And he has another important characteristic, which he counts of Freemasonry to strengthen. He has a certain humility of attitude. Oliver Cromwell is far from my favorite person in history, but he delivered one line which is of paramount importance: "I beseech you by the bowels of Christ, think it possible that you may be mistaken." At the time it was believed that all emotions, especially mercy and compassion, resided in the bowels (we still speak of a "gut reaction"). (I digress again.) So he is saying, "I beg you by the mercy and compassion of Christ, don't forget that you may be wrong." Pike warns against the same thing, when he urges us not to be "wise in our own conceit." This kind of Mason never forgets that, no matter how strongly he holds some belief, he may be wrong and others may be right. That is a great leap in personal maturity.

And some join because they are on a quest, even if they do not recognize it as such, to find spiritual growth and fulfillment. Not religious growth; that is the function of religion, not fraternity. But there is in some men a sense of something lost, some tie broken, some path forgotten, some connection to the deep peace and wisdom of the past which they sense they once had, and with which they need to reconnect. And if they seek with sincerity and insight, they will find it.

Let me quote again that astonishing line from the monitorial section of the Middle Chamber lecture:

> *You have this evening, my Brother, pressed beneath your feet, transmounted and transcended all the powers and passions, the senses and sciences of man. Now remember, that while many have made the ascent of that flight of winding stairs, not one, by Masonic consent, has ever passed downward.*

I take that sentence seriously. To me, there is something in Freemasonry, some key or path, which allows a person to go above and beyond everything we can learn, everything we can sense. It leads us to gnosis, to intuition, to inspiration. I might even go so far as to claim that Freemasonry is a sort of fly-paper, cleverly designed to trap those with a Mystery-shaped hole in their spirit, and say "seek here."

I know, of course, that Masonry is not a direct descendent of the ancient Mysteries, but it is their spiritual god-child (no pun intended). From what little we know, Freemasonry appears to use techniques and structures not unlike some employed in the Mysteries, and arguably the goal is the same—to lead to a breakthrough, a moment of gnosis, enlightenment, understanding, a shattering of the world and its reassembly into something else.

The problem is that when I write about this, it can seem so wacky, so (as a friend puts it) "oooga-booga." And it isn't that at all. It's natural, not "super-natural," and in one form or another, it is within the common experience.

Consider this. "There is a process, mysterious, unknown, and so far, at least, unknowable, in which an individual, by inducing in him/herself the proper state of mind, can through the manipulation of symbols bring something into being which was not there before, without regard to either space or time." Sounds like the Twilight-Zone. But it is just a description of creativity (manipulating symbols is how we think); and if you have ever written a poem or a story, or the words of a song, or created a new recipe, made a drawing, or figured out a way to fix a car without a manual, you've done it.

And if you have ever been touched to tears by the beauty of a piece of music, or been moved by the laughter of children, or looked deeply into the eyes of your dog and seen the trust there, or flashed back to memories of Christmas in childhood at the smell of vanilla, then you have felt it. There is nothing oooga or booga about that.

Almost every culture has sensed that there is some sort of spiritual energy or current or thread which runs through everything and connects everything. Some religious sub-groups or political sub-groups have denied its existence, others have predicated parts of their theology or social structure upon it. What you believe is entirely up to you, of course, but it can hardly be thought of as "strange" or "wacky."

Essentially, we are taking about self-transcendence—that moment when you become more than you are. We are talking about moving to another level of consciousness. Again, there is nothing oooga-booga or "new age" about that, either. You have probably had an experience like one of these:

You are walking down a noisy street in a city. It is hot and loud and uncomfortable. You see a church and go in for a few moments. It is cool, quiet—almost silent, the light streams in through the colored glass. And all the frustration, the tension, just goes away. And your mind feels a refreshment that is deep and satisfying.

Or it has been a rough day at work. All day long you have had to deal with problems caused because other people are incompetent or will not make a decision. You've been chewed on and chewed up. You resent it, and every muscle in your body is tight. And you come home, and your young son or daughter runs up to you and says "I'm glad you're home, Daddy!" And your mood, your thinking, everything, changes instantly.

Or you go to your special place—perhaps a place where you fish or hunt, or a special shady corner of the back yard where you just like to sit, wherever it is. You go there because you know it will be good for you, calming to the spirit. It is.

Those are instances of changes in levels of consciousness. And we feel them, we know they are real.

But isn't this self-transcendence, this learning how to change levels of consciousness the function of religion rather than a Fraternity? It depends, I suppose, on the religion.

It is not the function of most denominations of Christianity. Understandably, the emphasis there is on salvation, not self-awareness. In fact, some denominations have already defined the nature of man as utterly depraved, and the only self-awareness they support is the individual's awareness of his own abominableness. But others encourage the person to "look within," and rejoice in his/her relationship to the divine.

It is not the function of some understandings of Judaism, and it is of others.

It is important in Hinduism, Buddhism, and other religions, although some of them classify transcendence as a natural human condition and not a product of religious faith.

So is self-transcendence a function of religion? Yes, no, maybe. It really does not make any difference. It could be said that charity is a function of religion, but that doesn't mean that only religions should concern themselves with charity. There are few places in our world in which a man can focus on himself, his ethical and spiritual nature, and work on developing his spiritual talents and awareness. Those few are not in competition, unless they truly enjoy self-mutilation.

For me, there are three settings, three situations, which are more likely to lead to moments of transcendence than any other: the church service of Evensong, a well-performed Degree in a spiritually-aware Lodge, and sitting on the porch in the Colorado Rockies, watching the birds and chipmunks.

All of this proceeds from the essential question any man must ask if he hopes to attain wisdom as well as knowledge: "Who am I, really?"

And just possibly, the answer or a key to it may be found in the birdseed.

Jim Tresner

Index

23 Lives of Albert Pike, The. 240

A

Abalard. 140
Abe Lincoln's Axe. 135
Academic Community, discovery
    of Freemasonry. 272
Adoptive Masonry, Pike's Ritual. 254
Aesthetic Craze. 345
Aesthetics School of Masonic Thought.75
Albert Pike and the Question of Race.245
Alchemy. 101, 194
Aldebaran, traditional associations. 40, 41
All is Vanity - Allen Gilbert. 158
Analysis of Members Joining
    in Classes. 27
Annoying Prospect of Living, The. . . . 270
Antediluvian Herb Tea. 140
Anthropological School of
    Masonic Thought. 74
Antimasons. 97
Apollo, characteristics. 175
Apollo & Dionysus. 319
Apollonian Consciousness. . . . .
          102, 126, 174, 176, 197, 319
Arcturus. 44
    traditional associations. 45
*Art and Architecture of
    Freemasonry, The*. 272
Artifact, The ,W. Michael Gear. 273
Astrological Symbolism. 289
    Aldebaran. 40, 41
    Arcturus. 44
    Arcturus-Master Mason. 45
    Bootes. 44
    Fomalhaut. 40
    lodge ceiling. 38, 42
    Orion. 44
    Polaris. 46
    Regulus. 39, 45
    Sirius. 46
    Spica. 45
    Virgo. 45
Astronomy. 38
Attribute, defined. 56
Audience goals. 65
Authentic School of Masonic Thought. 73

B

Balance of solar and lunar
    consciousness. 321
Barber shop. 9
Before the Flood. 138
Believers & Belongers. 29
Birdseed. 415
Boaz. 196
Boobydom. 252
Bootes. 44
Boy Who was Left Behind, The. 316
*Breeding: "With Men or Horses, Sir,
    Bloodline Will Tell"*. 364
Brethren
    Abd-el-Kader. 52
    Barlow, Kevin. 417
    Bolivar, Simon 52
    Carroll, Lewis. 149
    Comer, Clay. 416
    Davis, Robert G.. 5, 7, 49, 233, 416
    deHoyos, Art. 7
    Devereaux, Damon. 233
    Dexter, Kris. 164
    Driskell, Tim. 416
    Dunant, Jean. 53
    Fletcher, Richard, P∴G∴M∴
        . . . . 233, 266, 421
    Fox, Claude. 9
    Haggard, The Rev. Forrest. . . . 126
    Hartzell, Jimmy Dean. 233, 416, 421
    Heaton, Tim. 421
    Hodapp, Christopher. 273
    Hogan, Timothy. 35, 192, 417
    Jennings, Jr., Joseph, ... 233
    Kipling, Rudyard. 366
    Leazer, Dr. Gary. 267
    MacNulty, Kirk. 192
    Manning, Joe R., P∴G∴M∴. . . . 51
    Marsengill, Jerry. 8
    Morris, Dr. S. Brent. 35, 273

Pike, Albert. 240
Porter, Cliff. Foreword, 4, 35, 61, 421
Pound, Roscoe. 7
Robinson, John. 269
Scott, Sir Walter. 158
Shipe, Robert T., P∴G∴M∴. . . . 27
Stewart, Walt. 417
Twain, Mark. 270, 368
Wilde, Oscar. 346
Worrel, Thomas D.. 192
Brotherhood. 11, 76, 83, 89
   I didn't take him to raise. 12
Brotherhood: Do We Really Mean It?. . 9
Brown, Walter Lee, cited. 246
Browning, Robert, cited. 349
Buber, Martin. 237
Bullock, Steven, *Revolutionary*
   Brotherhood. 272

C

Campbell. Joseph. 124, 318
Candidate(s). 33
   attitude in a Degree. 34
   focus on. 28
   preparation room. 95
Carroll, Lewis, cited. 59
Ceres. 45
Change. 24
Character. 219, 235
Charity. 343
Chartres Cathedral, *Portail Royal*. . . 200
Christmas Carol, A, cited. 354
Class conferrals. 26
   subsequent participation. 27
Communication Theory. 62, 228
   guaranteed failure. 71
   physical condition of Lodge. . . . 69
   status. 63
   video communications. 68
   written communications. 67
Community
   factors leading to happiness and
      welfare. 353
   factors leading to ruin. 353
Compasses. 14
Compasses Above: The Spiritual
   Aspect of Masonry. 13

Compassion. 48
Complete Idiot's Guide to
   Freemasonry. 273
Connectedness. 122
Consciousness
   balance of solar and lunar. . . . 322
   level of. 245
   lunar. 320
   Masonic representation of. . . . 320
   social. 355
   solar. 320
Convivio, cited. 201
Crux Flamant. 150
Cultural and Personal Symbols
   Scott, Sir Walter. 158
Cultural chauvinism: "The White
   Man's Burden". 366
Curl, James Stevens, *Art and*
   Architecture of Freemasonry. . 272

D

Dante. 201, 208
Death. 127
   as approaching friend. 128
   attitudes toward. 128
   dread of. 129
   ritual references. 128, 129
   symbolism. 290
Desk Lamps and Candles. 24
Dexter, Kris, design for double eagle. 164
Dickens, Charles
   Christmas, Carol, A. 354
   Tale of Two Cities, A. 338
Dionysian Consciousness
    . . . . 102, 126, 174, 177, 197, 320
Dionysus, characteristics. 175
Double Eagle. 179
Dragons. 7
Duty. 110, 222, 254, 336, 338,
               340, 342, 352, 357
Duty: "Stern Daughter of the
   Voice of God". 335
Dweller on the Threshold. 196

E

Ego. 238

*Eloquence: "Word strung to
   Word Like a Strand of Pearls"*... 361
Emblem, defined.................. 56
Enlightenment, The............... 267
Ensign, defined................... 56
Equality......................... 222
Eulogy to Mother, cited........... 195
External spirituality.............. 30

F

Fabulous Beast, The............... 7
Fact - Truth, differentiation........ 300
Faded Plastic Flowers............. 127
Failure in Communications......... 71
Faith............................ 29
   Believers/Belongers........... 31
   child-like..................... 141
   doubt and question essential... 140
   fundamentalism.......... 30, 265
   relationship to Spirituality..... 31
   social changes in............. 29
Family...................... 83, 130
   dysfunctional................. 132
Fan My Brow and Call Me Moses..... 91
Fellowcraft Degree... 143, 178, 191, 425
Fomalhaut, traditional associations... 40
Footpath Within, The.............. 299
Four Royal Stars, The.............. 39
   positive and negative aspects.... 43
Fraternal School of Masonic Thought.. 76
Freedom......................... 357
Freemasonry (see Masonry)
Freemasons for Dummies.......... 273
Fundamentalism................... 30
   always to be opposed......... 266
   authoritarian nature.......... 268
   Bigotry, Intolerance, Racism, etc.266
   expressions of.............. 265
   Masonic..................... 266
Fundamentalism is not Faith...... 265
Future of Masonry................. 18

G

Gabriel.......................... 40
Gate of Souls, The................ 290
Gilbert & Sullivan,
   Patience, or Bunthorn's Bride... 345
   Pirates of Penzance, The...... 339
   Trial by Jury................. 349
God revealed in nature............ 360
Goldilocks....................... 307
   interpretation................ 310
   story........................ 309
Good Masons.................... 356
Great Aunt Effie and Moses........ 77
Guild Lodge of St. Canice......... 376

H

Haggard, The Rev. Forrest, 33°, G.C..125
Hermit, The...................... 44
Hero, tragic..................... 118
Hero's Journey.............. 124, 318
Hildegard of Bingen.............. 100
Hiram.......................... 119
Historic School of Masonic Thought
   see Authentic School......... 73
Hodapp, Christopher, *Freemasons for
   Dummies*.................. 273
Hogan, Timothy................. 192
Holsinger, Bruce, cited........... 100
Honor: "Without it All is Dross"..... 339
Honor merited by serving others.... 357
Hunting of the Snark, The.......... 59

I

I Had it Good................... 130
Icon, defined.................... 56
Iconography.................... 56
*Idealism: "We Live, Mr. Worthing,
   in an Age of Ideals"*.......... 344
*Importance of Being
   Earnest, The*, cited.......... 346
Imposition of Ashes, The......... 141
Individualism................... 350
Ingersoll, Robert, *Oration at His
   Brother's Grave*............. 369
Initiation....................... 317
   Masonic and Hero's Journey
      compared................ 325
Insigne, defined................. 57
Intellectual stimulation........... 123
Intolerance (see also Toleration). . 52, 60
Isis............................ 45

J

Jachin......................... 196

Jacob, Margaret, cited. 272
Justice (see also Themis). 357

K

Kabbalah. 194, 202
Karg, Barb. 273
Koch, Rudolf, cited. 167
Korzybski, Alfred. 146

L

Large Compassion, A. 48
*Law & the Individual: "The Law, Sir,
   is an Ass"*. 346
Leadership. 87
Leazer, Dr. Gary, cited. 267
Leo. 40
Lesser lights. 101, 178
Life not merely a period of probation. 357
Little Sand in the Gears, A. 87
Living the Enlightenment, cited. 272
Lodge Ceiling. 38, 42
Logo, defined. 57
Longfellow, cited. 220
Lowell, James, *Once to Every Man
   and Nation*. 334

M

MacNulty, Kirk. 192
Masonic
   products. 75
   character. 234
   communication. 62
   elitism. 49
   expertise. 7
   language. 91
   secrecy. 210
   representation of solar and lunar
      consciousness. 320
Masonic "Schools of Thought". 72
   Aesthetics School. 75
   Anthropological School. 74
   Authentic School. 73
   Fraternal School. 76
   Mystical School. 75
   Rhapsodial School. 76
   Textual Criticism School. 73

*Masonic Art of Pedal Vulneration or
   How to Shoot Yourself*. 228
Masonic Information Center. 270
Masonic Renewal. 226
Masonic Symbols Don't Mean. 145
Masonry
   advocate and defender of free
      government. 357
   international, multi-racial
      Brotherhood. 357
   tasks of in this world. 357
   and Ancient Mysteries. 74
   benefits of. 121
   changes in. 136, 137, 216, 295
   compassion. 48
   contributions to History. 104
   discovery by Academic
      community. 272
   effect on Individual. 8
   evolutions in. 293
   future of. 18
   goal of. 144
   individual interpretation. 7, 420
   one can start over. 143
   popular culture. 273
   relevance today. 105
   spiritual aspects. 13, 32
   survival and growth. 271
Master Mason Degree. 116
   Lessons in. 120
Memories of a Barber shop. 10
Mensa. 23
Metaphor. 305
   in Masonry. 322
Michael. 40, 41
Milton, John. 14
Mirror Mirror on the Wall. 18
Morals and Dogma, cited. . . 14, 17, 49
   52, 60, 110, 111, 129, 144, 248
   264, 334, 334
Morning After, The. 33
Morris, Dr. S. Brent, *Complete Idiot's
   Guide to Freemasonry*. . . 273
Moss-backs. 88

Most Radical Era: 19th Century
    Values................... 327
Mother Goddess.................. 45
Multiplex Masonry................ 72
Murrah Building Bombing.......... 51
Mystic ladder.................. 202
Mysteries of Eleusis.............. 45
Mystery Play................ 118, 119
Mystical School of Masonic Thought. . 75
Myth
    control of your own........... 124
    source of information about man. 74
Myth and Masonry............... 322
Myth & Science................. 304
Mythic Structure of the Scottish
    Rite, The.................. 326

N

Nature: "My Heart Leaps Up"....... 358
Nietzsche, *The Birth of Tragedy*..... 320

O

O'Neal, Robert 208
Obstacles and Outside Influences:
    Willie Wonka and the Lodge.... 215
Octothorn....................... 150
Offices of Adoption, cited........ 357
Ogden & Richards............... 146
Oklahoma Survey of Young
    Master Masons.............. 275
Old Dog Barks Backward, The....... 80
Ophiuchus...................... 44
Oration at his Brother's Grave, Ingersoll 170
Orion, Lodge ceiling............... 43
Our Really Rather Radical Brother
    Albert Pike................. 108
Overstreet, Bonaro, cited........... 47

P

Patience, or Bunthorn's Bride, cited. . 345
Pedal Vulneration................ 225
Penalties...................... 193
Pentagram..................... 151
Pigeons in the Rocket............ 102
Pike, Albert.................... 240
    equality of Women........... 254
    faith and reason............. 140
    future of race relations........ 262
    Indians..................... 257
    labor relations.............. 108
    non-physical forces........... 16
    philosopher................. 244
    radical..................... 108
    religion.................... 267
    slavery..................... 250
    subjugation of the Human....... 17
    symbolism of Lodge Ceiling..... 38
    toleration................... 52
    woman's sexuality........... 256
    work...................... 110
Pike, Albert, The Meaning
    of Masonry 346
Pike, Albert, *Offices of Adoption*..... 358
Pike, Albert, *Words Spoken from the*
    Heart..................... 359
Pirates of Pensance, cited......... 339
Piscis Australes................. 40
Plane of the Ecliptic.............. 197
Poe, Edgar Allen................ 241
    Raven, The, cited........... 364
Polaris
    Location on Lodge Ceiling...... 46
    Traditional associations........ 46
Portal................. 194, 202, 292
    Guardians.................. 196
Preparation room................. 95
Prepared..................... 94
Privacy, Peace, & Harmony........ 210
Progress: Every Day in Every Way... 330
Psychopompos.................. 125

Q

Quadrivium..................... 200
Quest...................... 31, 32
Quest myth.................... 318

R

Race
    definition of................ 246
    perception of in 1800's........ 246

Rationality: "But, Sir, Is it Reasonable?". 351
Rebirth. 293
Referent, defined. 57
Reform: "To Set Free the Captives of Power". 355
Regionalisms. 91
Regius Poem. 210
Regulus
    Raphael. 39
    traditional associations. 40
Relevance of Masonry. 105
Religion. 140
    Faith and Reason. 140
    Freemasonry friend and asset of. 32
    Freemasonry not a. 31
    Fundamentalism. 265, 266
    Trinities. 60
Reunions. 52
Revolutionary Brotherhood. 272
Rhapsodial School of Masonic Thought. 76
Rites of passage. 318
Ritual. 92, 289
    cited. 92, 217
    condenses experience. 114
    delivery of. 78
    framework. 112
    hard-wired response to. 112
    importance of. 78, 80, 111
    in daily life. 112
    life-changing effect of. 79
    Middle Chamber. 424
    morning routine. 112
    not "how to" manuel. 92
    relationships, in. 113
    Rhapsodial School. 76
    sense of Identity. 114
    sets mood for events. 114
    teaching tool. 113
    Textual Criticism School. 74
Ritual: Who Needs It?. 111

S

Sacred Geometry. 44
Scientific School of Masonic Thought see Authentic School. 73
Secrecy. 210
Sefirot. 202
Self-development. 75
Self-transcendence. 424, 428
Semiotics/semiology, defined. 57
Sentiment: Emotion + Intellect. . . . 340
Sex
    ancient associations. 99
    as metaphor for power of life. . . 97
    four symbolisms of. 99
    manifestation of divine energy. . 99
    metaphor for power of Life. . . . 98
    Pike's Attitude toward. 256
    Pike's view of women's. 256
    representation of universal energy. 99
Sex as Symbol. 97
Sheaf of grain. 45
Shibboleth. 45
Shipe, Robert T., cited. 27
Short Ramble Through Freemasonry and Communication Theory, A. . 62
Signal, defined. 58
Signet, defined. 58
Sirius, Traditional associations. 46
Skulls. 157
Slack. 85
Slavery. 250
Smith, Douglas, *Working the Rough Stone*. 272
Social Consciousness: "Let Each Find Some Good Work to Do". . 353
Something Fishy in the Lodge. 289
Speculation. 124
Spica. 45
Spirituality
    external. 30
    forces. 16
    meanings of. 15
    over time. 29

quest for young Masons....... 278
reflected in Masonry.......... 74
Spirituality: "He Hath Within Him a
  Spiritual Nature"............. 349
Spirituality essential part of Masonry. . 14
Starry Canopy, The. 38
State of the Craft, Analysis of Those
  Joining in Classes............. 27
Status......................... 63
Swastika....................... 150
Symbol, defined............ 57, 146
Symbolism (see also Symbols). . 56, 145
  Aldebaran.................. 41
  Androgen................. 101
  Apollonian Consciousness..... 102
  astrological................. 38
  circle..................... 291
  Compasses = Faith........... 14
  death and rebirth............ 44
  defined.................... 57
  Dionysian Consciousness..... 102
  fish....................... 292
  Fomalhaut.................. 40
  Hanged man................ 208
  how does it work........... 169
  hunt, the................... 44
  Lesser Lights.............. 101
  Mystic ladder.............. 202
  portal..................... 194
  Regulus.................... 39
  solar..................... 289
  starting over.............. 143
  three..................... 59
  Tree of Life............... 197
  Twelve Fellowcrafts........... 38
  vesica piscis.............. 194
  winding Stairs............. 199
  words..................... 66
  X........................ 197
Symbolism of the Fellowcraft
  Degree, The............... 191
Symbology. defined.............. 58
Symbols (see also Symbolism)..... 145
  1 - 2 - 3.................. 312

Apollo..................... 175
associated meanings......... 172
bear...................... 313
burning cross.............. 150
categories of.............. 147
crux flamant............... 150
cultural and personal....... 158
defined................... 147
double eagles.............. 164
five-pointed star, history....... 152
flaming cross.......... 149, 150
intellectual and emotional
  responses............... 155
man as symbol-using critter.... 146
manipulation of............. 166
meta-meanings............. 161
numeral 5................. 153
octothorn................. 150
pentagram............. 151, 152
skull..................... 157
study of.................. 145
swastika.................. 150
Themis.................... 164
trigger chain for word "white".... 173

T

Tarus..................... 40, 41
Temple Shook with Hate, The........ 51
Tender Feet and Green Thumbs. ... 303
Textual Criticism School of
  Masonic thought............. 73
The Everything Freemasons Book... 273
Themis.................... 164
Third Thought, On................ 58
Thompson, Effie (Aunt)............ 77
Three...................... 59
Toleration. 51, 55, 61, 266, 280, 357, 378
Tragedy, Rule of................ 118
Tragedy of the Third Degree, The. ... 116
Tramp Abroad, A, quoted.......... 270
Transcendence..... 291, 299, 300, 301,
  322, 434-436
Transformation
  Aldebaran................ 40, 41
  Sirius..................... 46

Tree of Life. 126, 197, 202
Tresner, Jack N., Sr. 87, 131, 134
Trial by Jury, cited. 349
Trivium. 200
Trophy, defined. 58
Truth. 357
Truth ≠ Fact. 299
Truth - Fact, differentiation. 301
Twelve Fellowcrafts. 38
Type, defined. 58

U

Unconditional trust. 85
Using Masonry. 121

V

Vesica Piscis. 99, 194, 291
Victorian values
    breeding. 366
    character. 219
    cultural chauvinism. 359
    duty. 337
    eloquence. 363
    equality. 222
    honor. 341
    idealism. 346
    law and the individual. 348
    nature. 360
    progress. 332
    rationality. 354
    reform. 357
    sentiment. 343
    social consciousness. 355
    spirituality. 352
Virgo. 45

W

Watcher of the East. 40, 41
Watcher of the North. 39
Watcher of the South. 40
When is a Symbol an Emblem?. . . . 56
Wilde, Oscar, *Importance of Being
       Earnest, The*, cited. 346
Willie Wonka. 216
Winding Stairs. 199

Work, Henry Clay, *Come Home, Father*,
       cited. 344
Words as symbols. 66
Work in Progress, A. 233
Words Spoken from the Heart, cited. 359
Working the Rough Stone. 272
World, work to be done in. 343
Worrel, Thomas D.. 192
Worshipful Master, Powers of. 213

X

X. 197

Y

Young Masons. 81
    Nature of. 21, 297
Young, John. 273

About the Author

Jim Tresner is the Grand Orator of the Grand Lodge of the State of Oklahoma and holds Ph.D. in communications.

He is a perpetual member of Garfield Lodge #501 in Enid, Oklahoma, Past Master and perpetual member of Albert Pike Lodge #162 in Guthrie, Oklahoma, a member of the Oklahoma Lodge of Research, a member of Oklahoma College, Masonic *Societas Rosicruciana in Civitatibus Foederalis* and Past Sovereign Master of Father Murrow Chapter, Allied Masonic Degrees.

He was awarded the Medal of Honor by the Grand Lodge of Oklahoma, has served as the Grand Lodge Official Spokesman on matters of Freemasonry and Religion since 1993, and has served on numerous Grand Lodge Committees. He is the Publications Editor for the Grand Lodge of Oklahoma and the editor of the state Masonic magazine. He is an honorary Past Grand Master of the Grand Lodge of Arkansas and was awarded the Grand Master's Medal of Honor by the Grand Lodge of Kansas.

In the Scottish Rite, Brother Tresner holds the 33°, the Supreme Council Certificate of Honor, and the Grand Cross of the Court of Honor. He is Director of the Work for the Guthrie Scottish Rite Temple, and the book review editor for the *Scottish Rite Journal*.

A perpetual member of the York Rite, he was made a Knight Commander of the Temple by the Grand Encampment.

He was the 1995 Anson Jones Lecturer for the Texas Lodge of Research, the 1995 Pires Lecturer for the Dallas

Scottish Rite Bodies, and the 1996 Lecturer for the Iowa Lodge of Research. In 1997 he delivered the Jack Ball Lecture for Albert Pike Lodge #1169, San Antonio. In 1999 he was elected to membership in the Society of Blue Friars, an international organization of Masonic writers and researchers. In 2001 he was awarded the Mackey Medal for Excellence in Masonic Research by the Scottish Rite Research Society.

In 2005, he received the Duane E. Anderson Medal for Excellence in Masonic Education from the Grand Lodge of Minnesota.

He serves on the Steering Committee and the Task Force of the Masonic Information Center in Silver Spring, Maryland.

His books include *Vested in Glory: The Regalia of the Scottish Rite; Albert Pike: The Man Beyond the Monument; From Sacrifice to Symbol: The Story of Cornerstones and Stability Rites; The Craft's Noyse: Composers who were Freemasons; Further Light: Helpful Information for New Master Masons;* and, with Robert G. Davis, *A Shared Spirit.*

www.ingramcontent.com/pod-product-compliance
Lightning Source LLC
Chambersburg PA
CBHW070733170426
43200CB00007B/510